DATE DUE

IDENTITY THEFT AND HOW TO PROTECT YOURSELF

Second Edition

by
Margaret C. Jasper

Oceana's Legal Almanac Series:
Law for the Layperson

Oceana Publications

You may order this or any Oceana publication by visiting Oceana's website at http://www.oceanalaw.com

Library of Congress Control Number: 2006922576

ISBN 0-19-532155-3
ISBN 978-0-19-532155-5

Oceana's Legal Almanac Series: Law for the Layperson
ISSN 1075-7376

©2006 Oxford University Press, Inc.

To My Husband Chris

Your love and support

are my motivation and inspiration

-and-

In memory of my son, Jimmy

Table of Contents

CHAPTER 6:
IDENTITY THEFT LEGISLATION

CHAPTER 7:
MINIMIZING YOUR RISKS

CHAPTER 8:
RESOLVING YOUR IDENTITY THEFT PROBLEMS

CHAPTER 9:
IDENTITY THEFT RISKS FOR BUSINESSES

APPENDICES

ABOUT THE AUTHOR

MARGARET C. JASPER is an attorney engaged in the general practice of law in South Salem, New York, concentrating in the areas of personal injury and entertainment law. Ms. Jasper holds a Juris Doctor degree from Pace University School of Law, White Plains, New York, is a member of the New York and Connecticut bars, and is certified to practice before the United States District Courts for the Southern and Eastern Districts of New York, the United States Court of Appeals for the Second Circuit, and the United States Supreme Court.

Ms. Jasper has been appointed to the law guardian panel for the Family Court of the State of New York, is a member of a number of professional organizations and associations, and is a New York State licensed real estate broker operating as Jasper Real Estate, in South Salem, New York.

In 2004, Ms. Jasper successfully argued a case before the New York Court of Appeals which gives mothers of babies who are stillborn due to medical negligence the right to bring a legal action and recover emotional distress damages. This successful appeal overturned a 26-year old New York case precedent, which previously prevented mothers of stillborn babies from suing their negligent medical providers.

Margaret Jasper maintains a website at http://www.JasperLawOffice.com.

Ms. Jasper is the author and general editor of the following legal almanacs:

AIDS Law
The Americans with Disabilities Act
Animal Rights Law
Auto Leasing
Bankruptcy Law for the Individual Debtor
Banks and their Customers
Becoming a Citizen

Buying and Selling Your Home
Commercial Law
Consumer Rights Law
Co-ops and Condominiums: Your Rights and Obligations As Owner
Copyright Law
Credit Cards and the Law
Custodial Rights
Dictionary of Selected Legal Terms
Drunk Driving Law
DWI, DUI and the Law
Education Law
Elder Law
Employee Rights in the Workplace
Employment Discrimination Under Title VII
Environmental Law
Estate Planning
Everyday Legal Forms
Executors and Personal Representatives: Rights and Responsibilities
Harassment in the Workplace
Health Care and Your Rights
Hiring Household Help and Contractors: Your Rights and Obligations Under the Law
Home Mortgage Law Primer
Hospital Liability Law
How To Change Your Name
How To Protect Your Challenged Child
How To Start Your Own Business
Identity Theft and How To Protect Yourself
Individual Bankruptcy and Restructuring
Injured on the Job: Employee Rights, Worker's Compensation and Disability Insurance Law
International Adoption
Juvenile Justice and Children's Law
Labor Law
Landlord-Tenant Law
Law for the Small Business Owner
The Law of Attachment and Garnishment
The Law of Buying and Selling
The Law of Capital Punishment
The Law of Child Custody
The Law of Contracts
The Law of Debt Collection
The Law of Dispute Resolution
The Law of Immigration

The Law of Libel and Slander
The Law of Medical Malpractice
The Law of No-Fault Insurance
The Law of Obscenity and Pornography
The Law of Personal Injury
The Law of Premises Liability
The Law of Product Liability
The Law of Speech and the First Amendment
The Law of Violence Against Women
Lemon Laws
Living Together: Practical Legal Issues
Marriage and Divorce
Missing and Exploited Children: How to Protect Your Child
Motor Vehicle Law
Nursing Home Negligence
Patent Law
Prescription Drugs
Privacy and the Internet: Your Rights and Expectations Under the Law
Probate Law
Real Estate Law for the Homeowner and Broker
Religion and the Law
Retirement Planning
The Right to Die
Rights of Single Parents
Small Claims Court
Social Security Law
Special Education Law
Teenagers and Substance Abuse
Trademark Law
Victim's Rights Law
Welfare: Your Rights and the Law
What if It Happened to You: Violent Crimes and Victims' Rights
What if the Product Doesn't Work: Warranties & Guarantees
Workers' Compensation Law
Your Child's Legal Rights: An Overview
Your Rights in a Class Action Suit
Your Rights Under the Family and Medical Leave Act
You've Been Fired: Your Rights and Remedies

INTRODUCTION

Last year, almost 9 million Americans had their personal information stolen, and the stolen information was used to incur credit card debt, access bank accounts, and cause numerous personal and financial problems for the victim. Most of these victims have no idea how their personal information was obtained and what they should do to unravel the damage that has been done to their credit rating.

This legal almanac explores the law of identity theft. Identity theft is the illegal use of another's personal identifying information, such as the individual's name and social security number, without their knowledge or consent, to commit some type of financial fraud. This almanac also discusses the trends associated with the serious problem of identity theft, the various ways in which identity theft is accomplished, the guidelines to minimize the chances of becoming a victim of identity theft, and the recourse one has if they fall victim to this serious crime.

The interrelationship between identity theft and the individual's right to privacy is also explored. State and federal legislation that has been passed in order to combat identity theft, as well as pertinent case law involving identity theft, is also examined.

The Appendix provides sample documents, applicable statutes, and other pertinent information and data. The Glossary contains definitions of many of the terms used throughout the almanac.

CHAPTER 1:
OVERVIEW OF IDENTITY THEFT

IN GENERAL

Identity theft is a crime that occurs when someone wrongfully obtains and uses another individual's personal information in some way that involves fraud or deception, typically for financial gain. One may first become aware that they are the victim of identity theft when they notice that they are being billed for items they never purchased, or a credit account they never opened appears on their credit report.

Recent surveys estimate that nearly 10 million consumers are victimized by some form of identity theft each year. Many identity theft victims have reported that unauthorized persons have cleaned out their bank accounts, obtained credit in their name and, in some cases, have completely taken over their identities.

Victims of identity theft are not only victimized by the criminal who misappropriated their identity, but are further victimized by the system when their credit rating is ruined through no fault of their own as they try to undo the damage caused by unauthorized procurement of credit in their name.

Fortunately, the individual whose identity is stolen is often protected from financial loss by insurance or loss limits and reimbursement provisions. They nevertheless bear the tremendous emotional burden that identity theft causes, including loss to reputation, damage to their credit rating, and the time, nuisance, and out-of-pocket expenses of trying to clear their name.

Thus, although the primary victim of identity theft is the individual whose personal information has been misused, the financial burden is often carried by the other "victims" of identity theft, such as the retail merchants, banks, utility companies and other credit grantors. In addition, taxpayers also indirectly bear some of this financial burden when social services are fraudulently obtained or when refunds are sent to individuals who file fraudulent tax returns.

HOW IDENTITY THIEVES OBTAIN YOUR PERSONAL INFORMATION

You may think that you diligently protect your personal information and, therefore, you are not a likely victim of identity theft. Unfortunately, intercepting your personal information is easier than you think. For example, identity thieves prey upon unsuspecting consumers while they are making their everyday transactions, such as banking and grocery shopping.

Virtually every day-to-day transaction made requires the consumer to share some type of personal information, such as their name, address, phone number, bank account number, social security number, or credit card number, etc. Following are some of the ways identity thieves intercept an individual's personal information:

1. They steal wallets and purses containing identification, credit cards, and bank ATM cards.

2. In public places, they target ATM users by watching the victim use the card, sometimes using high powered binoculars, and obtaining the card number and personal identification number (PIN). This is known as "shoulder surfing." The identity thief subsequently either steals the card from the victim, or makes a counterfeit card, and goes back to the ATM to steal the victim's money. Consumers are advised to be aware of any persons who are loitering around or near the ATM machine. They are also advised to carefully scrutinize their bank statements for any unauthorized ATM withdrawals.

3. They steal mail, including bank and credit card statements, pre-approved credit offers, telephone calling cards and tax information.

4. They complete a "change of address form" to divert the victim's mail to another location.

5. They rummage through trash for personal data. This is known as "dumpster diving." They retrieve copies of the victim's checks, credit card or bank statements, or other records that typically bear identifying information and make it easier to get control over accounts in the victim's name and assume their identity.

6. They fraudulently obtain the victim's credit report by posing as a landlord, employer or someone else who may have a legitimate need for—and a legal right to—the information.

7. They obtain the victim's business or personnel records at their place of business.

8. They obtain personal information from the victim's home.

9. They intercept personal information that is shared over the Internet.

10. They buy the victim's personal information from "inside" sources. For example, an identity thief may pay a store employee for information about a customer that appears on an application for goods, services or credit.

11. They illegally obtain tax information by claiming to have a legal right of access to these records.

12. They pose as a telemarketers or someone taking a survey, and trick the victim into divulging personal information. Obtaining personal information under false pretenses is an illegal tactic known as "pretexting." The pretexter then sells the personal information to third parties who often use this information for illegal purposes.

13. They send e-mail messages to the victim, purportedly from the victim's Internet service provider, stating that the victim's "account information needs to be updated" or that the victim's "credit card is invalid or expired and the information needs to be reentered to keep the account active." If confronted with this message, the consumer is advised to contact their Internet service provider directly and not to divulge any personal information.

IDENTITY THEFT CRIMES

There are many schemes that identity thieves engage in once they obtain the victim's personal information. For example:

1. They call the victim's credit card issuer and, pretending to be the victim, ask to change the mailing address on the credit card account. The imposter then runs up charges on the account. Because the bills are being sent to the new address, it may take some time before the victim realizes there's a problem.

2. They open a new credit card account using the victim's name, date of birth and social security number. When they use the credit card and don't pay the bills, the delinquent account is reported on the victim's credit report.

3. They establish phone or wireless service in the victim's name.

4. They open a bank account in the victim's name and write bad checks on that account.

5. They file for bankruptcy under the victim's name to avoid paying debts they've incurred, or to avoid eviction.

6. They counterfeit checks or debit cards, and drain the victim's bank account.

7. They buy cars by taking out auto loans in the victim's name.

8. They steal checks from the victim's home, office or mailbox and forge the victim's signature on the check. Stolen checks do not have to be blank. Perpetrators often remove the ink on the checks by "washing" them with a cleaning solvent, or alter what is already written on the check, e.g., by changing the payee name. A counterfeiter can also make new checks in the victim's name using a home computer and a printer. Consumers are advised to keep their checks in a secure place and write checks using a pen with thick, dark ink. It is also important to draw lines to fill in gaps in the payee and amount spaces so that the information cannot easily be altered. Consumers are also advised to order checks that have built-in security features that make them tamper-resistant to check washing or counterfeiting.

9. They obtain employment using the victim's identity.

10. They file false tax returns in the victim's name.

11. They obtain a driver's license in the victim's name.

12. They use the victim's identity if they are arrested or stopped for a traffic violation. When they subsequently fail to show up in court, an arrest warrant is issue in the victim's name.

The victim is usually unaware of the identity theft scheme until they find out that there is a fraudulent delinquent account being reported on their credit report, or they start to receive debt collection notices for accounts they never opened. This may not occur until the victim applies for credit and is unexpectedly denied. It may take months or even years before the victim becomes aware that their identity was stolen.

It is difficult, costly and time-consuming to undo all the damage identity theft can cause. It may be necessary to engage professional legal assistance because companies may be reluctant to accept the victim's representation that the account is fraudulent, and continue billing the victim and reporting delinquencies to credit reporting agencies. If the identity thief used the victim's identity in connection with a crime or arrest, as set forth below, it is always advisable to hire an attorney due to the seriousness of the offense.

IDENTITY THEFT TO AVOID CRIMINAL PROSECUTION

Fifteen percent of identity theft victims have reported that their personal information has been misused in connection with criminal activity. The most common use reported is when an identity thief gives another person's name and personal information, such as a driver's license, date of birth, or social security number, to a law enforcement officer during a criminal investigation or upon arrest in order to avoid criminal prosecution.

In many cases, the perpetrator is cited for a traffic violation or a misdemeanor offense, signs a citation requiring appearance in court, such as a desk appearance ticket, and is released from the arrest. If the identity thief appears in court on the violation, he or she may plead guilty to the offense, thus creating a criminal arrest record in the victim's name.

If the identity thief fails to appear in court, the judge will generally issue a bench warrant, which will be in the name of the victim. The victim is usually unaware that a warrant of arrest has been issued in his or her name and, if unexpectedly detained during a routine traffic stop, the victim may be arrested, booked and jailed on the outstanding bench warrant.

In some cases, the crime may be more serious, such as drunk driving or another felony offense. Again, if the identity thief provides law enforcement with the victim's name and personal information, this information may then be recorded in local and state criminal databases as well as the national database with the National Crime Information Center (NCIC).

This criminal activity is often conducted without the knowledge of the victim until some event occurs which uncovers the fraudulent misuse of the victim's name, such as a denial or termination of employment. For example, the employer may conduct a background investigation of the employee and discover the criminal record.

The burden of clearing one's name of this type of identity fraud is primarily on the victim. Once the victim's name and personal information is placed into all of the various local, state and federal crime databases, it is an extremely difficult task to make sure the records are completely cleared. The criminal justice system does not yet have any established and coordinated procedure for clearing this information from all of the various criminal computer systems.

LAW ENFORCEMENT RESPONSE

Law enforcement agencies have had difficulty tracking identity theft, in large part because there has been no clear definition of the criminal elements of identity theft. Rather, identity theft has been viewed as an element of many other crimes, such as bank fraud, credit card fraud, welfare fraud, tax fraud and mail fraud.

The mere possession of another's personal identifying information is not a crime. It is the unauthorized use of that information to fraudulently obtain financial benefit or otherwise deceive that constitutes a crime. For example, although identity theft may be an element of credit card fraud, law enforcement's focus is generally on the crime of credit card fraud rather than the identity theft as a crime in and of itself.

According to the Postal Inspection Service, the theft or diversion of mail contributes significantly to the problems of identity fraud. Nearly all mail-theft cases in which a financial transaction device, such as a credit card, or document is stolen can lead to a legitimate person's credit history and name being assumed.

Investigations conducted by the Postal Inspection Service show that organized criminal activity is largely responsible for the mail theft and credit card fraud components of identity theft crimes. The illegally diverted mail is often sent to private mail boxes located at commercial mail receiving agencies rented by the criminals. This mail theft and credit-card fraud activity frequently support drug trafficking because large amounts of money may be obtained through such fraud.

For example, a sophisticated crime ring involving the theft of identities of credit-worthy individuals in New York, and the subsequent use of fraudulently obtained credit cards, resulted in losses to the card-issuing banks of over $1.8 million. In another case, Postal inspectors participating in a Florida task force assisted in arresting 32 people in a credit card fraud ring that was responsible for losses of at least $1.5 million.

In addition, identity fraud schemes have a nationwide scope. Arrests for theft of mail and related offenses have been made in numerous major cities across the United States, including Atlanta, Boston, Chicago, Jacksonville, Houston, Miami, New Orleans, Newark, New York, Philadelphia, San Francisco, and Tampa.

A number of agencies work together to combat the growing problem of identity theft. The Postal Inspection Service has combined its resources with other law enforcement agencies to form task forces in many cities.

RECENT IDENTITY THEFT CASES

According to the U.S. Department of Justice, following are some recent cases which typify common identity theft crimes:

1. Central District of California—A woman plead guilty to federal charges for using a stolen social security number to obtain thousands of dollars in credit and then filing for bankruptcy in the name of her victim.

2. Central District of California—A man plead guilty to federal charges and was sentenced to 27 months in prison for obtaining private bank account information about an insurance company's policyholders and using that information to deposit $764,000 in counterfeit checks into a bank account he established.

3. Central District of California—Two defendants plead guilty to identity theft, bank fraud, and related charges for opening bank accounts with both real and fake identification documents, depositing U.S. Treasury checks that were stolen from the mail, and withdrawing funds from those accounts.

4. Middle District of Florida—A defendant plead guilty to bank fraud charges for obtaining names, addresses, and social security numbers from a website, and using the data to apply for a series of car loans over the internet.

5. Southern District of Florida—A woman plead guilty to federal charges for obtaining a fraudulent driver's license in the name of the victim, using the license to withdraw more than $13,000 from the victim's bank account, obtaining five department store credit cards in the victim's name, and charging approximately $4,000 on those cards.

6. District of Kansas—A defendant plead guilty to conspiracy, odometer fraud, and mail fraud for operating an odometer "rollback" scheme on used cars. The defendant used false and assumed identities, including the identities of deceased persons, to obtain false identification documents and fraudulent car titles.

CHAPTER 2:
IDENTITY THEFT STATISTICS

IN GENERAL

Identity theft is becoming the most expensive financial crime in the nation, costing consumers and the financial industry billions of dollars. Although statistics show that there has been a small but steady decrease in the number of victims, the costs resulting from identity theft and fraud has steadily risen. The decrease in the number of victims is likely due to legislation and safeguards established to prevent identity theft, and the public awareness efforts of various government agencies and private entities.

According to a 2006 survey released by Javelin Strategy and Research and the Better Business Bureau, the number of U.S. adult victims of identity fraud decreased from 10.1 million in 2003 and 9.3 million in 2005 to 8.9 million in 2006. Nevertheless, the total one-year fraud amount rose from 53.2 billon in 2004 and $54.4 billion in 2005, to $56.6 billion in 2006. In addition, the mean fraud amount per fraud victim rose from $5,249 in 2003 and $5,885 in 2005 to $6,383 in 2006.

IDENTITY THEFT COMPLAINT CATEGORIES

Identity theft victims reported more than one type of identity theft crime. Following is a breakdown of how the victims' information was misused during January 1, 2005 through December 31, 2005.

Credit Card Fraud

Credit card identity fraud accounted for 26% of the total identity theft complaints. New fraudulent credit card accounts were opened in the victim's name in 15.6% of the cases. Fraud using a victim's existing account occurred in 11.3% of the cases, and 0.2% of the credit card fraud complaints were unspecified as to sub-type.

Phone or Utilities Identity Fraud

Phone or utilities fraud accounted for 18% of the total identity theft complaints. New fraudulent wireless accounts were opened in the victim's name in 9.0% of all cases. New fraudulent telephone accounts were opened in 5.5% of all cases. New fraudulent utility accounts were opened in 5.2% of all cases. In 0.4% of all cases, unspecified phone/ utilities theft occurred, and in 0.7% of all cases, unauthorized charges were billed to a victim's existing account.

BANK FRAUD

Bank fraud accounted for 17% of the total identity theft complaints. New fraudulent bank accounts were opened in the victim's name in 3.3% of all cases. Fraud using a victim's existing bank account occurred in 7.4% of the cases. Fraud involving electronic fund transfers accounted for 7.9% of all cases, and 0.1% of the bank fraud complaints were unspecified as to sub-type.

LOAN FRAUD

Loan fraud accounted for 5% of the total identity theft complaints. Auto loans and leases accounted for 1.8% of all cases. Personal, business and student loans accounted for 2.6% of all cases. Real estate loans accounted for 1.2% of all cases, and 0.2% of the loan fraud complaints were unspecified as to sub-type.

EMPLOYMENT-RELATED FRAUD

Employment-related fraud accounted for 12% of the total identity theft complaints.

GOVERNMENT DOCUMENTS/BENEFITS IDENTITY FRAUD

Government Documents/Benefits fraud accounted for 9% of the total government fraud complaints. Driver's license issuance or forgery accounted for 1.8% of all cases. Fraudulent tax returns accounted for 4.7% of all cases. Social security card issuance or forgery accounted for 0.3% of all cases. Governmental benefits applied for or received accounted for 1.5% of all cases. Issuance or forgery of other government documents accounted for 0.6% of all cases, and <0.1% of the government fraud complaints were unspecified as to sub-type.

Other Identity Theft Crimes

Other types of identity theft accounted for 25% of the total identity theft complaints. Evasion of legal sanctions accounted for 2.2% of all cases. Internet and email-related fraud accounted for 1.9% of all cases.

Medical-related fraud accounted for 1.8% of all cases. Apartment and house rental fraud accounted for 0.9% of all cases. Internet and email-related fraud accounted for 1.0% of all cases. Insurance-related fraud accounted for 0.4% of all cases. Property rental fraud accounted for 0.3% of all cases. Bankruptcy accounted for 0.3% of all cases. Child support accounted for 0.2% of all cases. Magazines-related fraud accounted for 0.2% of all cases, and securities and investments-related fraud accounted for 0.2% of all cases. 17.6% of all other types of identity fraud were unspecified as to sub-type.

IDENTITY THEFT RELATED EXPENSES

Individuals whose information is misused bear only a small percentage of the cost of identity theft. For example, misuse of credit cards results in approximately $50 billion dollars in losses to businesses each year, with the average loss from the misuse of a victim's personal information approximately $4,800 dollars.

Nevertheless, the victim does incur certain out-of-pocket expenses including notary fees, copying costs, attorney fees, and other costs. In addition, the victim also suffers indirect expenses, such as wages lost, credit denied, or harm to reputation as a result of the fraud.

From January 1, 2005 through December 31, 2005, identity theft victims estimated that they had spent an average of $500 dealing with their identity theft problem. According to FTC statistics, the total annual cost of identity theft to victims is approximately $5 billion dollars.

Identity theft victims also spend a considerable amount of their own time resolving the various problems that occurred because of the misuse of their personal information. Victims reported that they spent approximately 30 hours resolving their problems, which means that Americans spent almost 300 million hours resolving identity theft-related problems. Studies also indicate that the emotional impact of identity theft has been found to parallel that of victims of violent crime.

AGE RANGE OF IDENTITY THEFT VICTIMS

According to FTC statistics for 2005, the largest group of consumers reporting an identity theft complaint ranged from ages 18-29, and represented 29% of all cases. 5% of all cases involve children under the age of 18; 24% of all cases involve individuals aged 30-39; 20% of all cases involve individuals age 40-49; 13% of all cases involve individuals age 50-59; 3% of all cases involve individuals age 60-64; and 6% of all cases involve individuals age 65 and over.

A table of identity theft victims, by age, in 2005, is set forth at Appendix 1.

LOCATION OF IDENTITY THEFT VICTIMS

According to FTC statistics for 2005, consumers contacted the FTC hotline from all 50 states, including the District of Columbia, with the largest number of complaints coming from California, Illinois, Pennsylvania, New York, Michigan, and Georgia. However, the highest concentration of complaints per 100,000 people came from Arizona, Nevada, California, Texas and Colorado.

A table of identity theft victims, by state, in 2005 is set forth at Appendix 1.

RELATIONSHIP TO VICTIM

According to FTC statistics for 2005, approximately 21 percent of all victims who provided relationship information had a personal relationship with the suspect. The types of relationship reported included family member (9.6%); roommate/cohabitant (2.4%); neighbor (1.3%); workplace coworker/employer/employee (1.8%); and unspecified relationship (5.6%).

LENGTH OF TIME BETWEEN IDENTITY THEFT AND KNOWLEDGE OF CRIME

According to FTC statistics for 2005, the amount of time between the date the identity theft occurred and the date it was noticed by the victim was less than 1 month in 43% of all reported cases. In 16% of cases, the amount of time was 6 to 12 months; in 7% of all cases, the amount of time was 7 to 12 months; in 8% of all cases, the amount of time was 13 to 24 months; in 12% of all cases, the amount of time was 25 to 48 months; in 3% of all cases, the amount of time was 49 to 60 months; and in 9% of all cases, the amount of time was over 60 months.

REPORTING

According to FTC statistics for 2005, at the time of their initial call to the FTC Hotline, 42 percent of victims had notified one or more of the credit reporting agencies and were able to place a fraud alert in their credit profile, and 58% of all victims had not contacted any credit reporting agency.

During the same time period, 61% of identity theft victims did not contact law enforcement; 30% notified the police and filed a report; and 9% notified the police but did not file a report.

CHAPTER 3:
CREDIT AND DEBIT CARDS

UNSOLICITED CREDIT CARDS

Due to the early practice of mailing unsolicited credit cards to individuals whose names had been taken from mass-mailing lists, many credit cards were stolen in the mail without the intended recipient ever knowing that a credit card was sent. To address this problem, in 1970, Congress enacted an amendment to the Truth In Lending Act (TILA) that placed an absolute ban on the distribution of unsolicited credit cards.

The prohibition against unsolicited cards was intended to increase consumer awareness by ensuring that consumers were given adequate information regarding their rights and obligations, and to make credit card issuers more responsible in the distribution of their credit cards.

A large number of states have enacted statutes which provide that a person who receives an unsolicited credit card, which he or she does not accept by use or authorization of use, is not responsible for any liability resulting from its loss or theft, and that failure to return or destroy an unsolicited card does not constitute acceptance.

These states include Alaska, California, Connecticut, Florida, Hawaii, Illinois, Kansas, Maryland, Massachusetts, Minnesota, New Mexico, New York, North Dakota, Ohio, Rhode Island, Tennessee, Vermont, Virginia, Wisconsin, and Wyoming.

In Connecticut, Delaware, Florida, Hawaii, New York and Rhode Island, the unauthorized issuance of credit cards is in itself a crime and, in Illinois, it is a business offense resulting in a maximum fine of $500.

Delaware law requires that an issuer of an unsolicited credit card must send the recipient fourteen days notice before the card is mailed to him. The notice must be accompanied by a conspicuous statement that the recipient has a right of refusal. Additionally, a prepaid return envelope must be included. But use of the card will constitute acceptance.

PRE-APPROVED CREDIT OFFERS

Credit card issuers often send creditworthy consumers pre-approved or pre-screened offers of credit. Identity thieves search for these types of credit card offers and will try to intercept them in the mail or retrieve them if discarded by the consumer. The companies do not advise the consumer that these offers are being sent to them, therefore, the consumer has no way of knowing whether they were the intended recipient of such an offer if the mail is intercepted.

The identity thief responds to the credit offer, changes the mailing address, receives the credit card and depletes the credit line before the consumer ever knows the card was issued. Consumers are advised, if they receive such an offer, to make sure the documents are shredded before discarding them. Of course, this does not help if the mail is intercepted. Consumers can also call 1-888-5-OPTOUT (1-888-557-8688) to "opt out" of receiving pre-screened credit card offers.

UNAUTHORIZED USE OF A CREDIT OR DEBIT CARD

Credit card issuers are required to provide a method whereby the user of the credit card can be identified as the person authorized to use it. In any action by a card issuer to enforce liability for the use of a credit card, the burden of proof is on the card issuer to show that the use was authorized, or that the conditions of liability for unauthorized use have been met.

Clearly, the statute applies to unauthorized use of another's credit card by a finder or a thief. This provision is not applicable in a situation where a cardholder voluntarily and knowingly allows another person to use his credit card and that other person subsequently misuses the card.

Unauthorized use of a credit card occurs only where there is no actual, implied, or apparent authority for such use by the cardholder. The Truth In Lending Act itself defines unauthorized use as "use by a person other than the cardholder who does not have actual, implied or apparent authority for such use, and from which the cardholder receives no benefit."

Thus, when a former spouse uses a credit card belonging to an account in the name of his or her former wife, even though the cardholder spouse previously notifies the credit card issuer that the other spouse is no longer authorized to use their card, the Courts have still held that the use of a credit card by a separated spouse after cardholder notification that the use is no longer authorized is not "unauthorized use" within the meaning of the Truth In Lending Act because such use is clothed with apparent authority.

Therefore, to avoid responsibility where a cardholder has previously given another authority to use his or her credit card, such as in the case of a former spouse, it is advisable for the cardholder to close the account, return the cards on the account, and ask the credit card issuer to open an entirely new account.

In addition, if a cardholder allows another person to use his or her credit card and that person exceeds the authority given by charging to the account more than he or she was authorized to charge against it, the cardholder remains responsible for those excessive purchases. That is because there is still apparent authority for the use.

LIABILITY LIMITATIONS

The Truth In Lending Act virtually eliminated cardholder liability for the unauthorized use of credit cards. The holder of a credit card is liable for its unauthorized use only if the card is an accepted card, and only to the extent of $50. This limited liability applies to all cardholders, including corporations as well as individuals. Many states have also enacted legislation limiting liability of cardholders for unauthorized use.

The Electronic Funds Transfer Act

The Electronic Funds Transfer Act limits the consumer's liability for unauthorized electronic fund transfers, including those transactions involving ATM and debit cards. If your ATM or debit card is lost or stolen, you must contact your bank immediately to limit your losses.

For example, your losses are limited to Fifty Dollars if you report the loss or theft of your card within two days of discovery, and up to Five Hundred Dollars if you report the loss or theft of your card after two business days but within sixty days after the unauthorized transaction appears on your bank statement. However, if you fail to report the loss or theft within the 60-day period, you risk losing all of the money stolen from your account.

An exception exists for Visa and MasterCard debit cards as those companies have voluntarily agreed to limit cardholder liability to Fifty Dollars regardless of the time between discovery and reporting the loss or theft.

CRIMES ASSOCIATED WITH STOLEN CREDIT CARDS

Larceny

The general criminal statutes of most states make credit purchases made with a stolen credit card or otherwise illegally obtained cards the offense of larceny. In addition, a person who obtains a credit card by misrepresentation and then uses the card to purchase goods or services on credit commits larceny the same as one who directly obtains property from its owner by false pretenses. It may be possible to prosecute someone who obtains a credit card by false pretenses even though he or she does not use it.

Forgery

Pursuant to most credit card plans, the cardholder is required to sign a check, invoice or other document for the merchandise or services received. If someone other than the legitimate cardholder signs the cardholder's name to such a document without the cardholder's authority the crime of forgery is also committed.

In addition, the material alteration of a credit card—e.g., by changing the name, number, or expiration—and the subsequent use of the card, would constitute a criminal offense in the areas of forgery and larceny.

STATE LAWS

North Carolina has a Financial Transaction Credit Card Theft statute which makes it a crime for anyone to take, keep, or use a credit card without the cardholder's consent, or to retain possession of a credit card with the intent to use a card that he or she knows to be lost, mislaid, or delivered to him or her by mistake. Under the law, the possession of a credit card that is not in the name of the person possessing the card, or in the name of a family member of the person possessing the card, is prima facie evidence of theft.

Most of the criminal codes drawn up among the states have included a separate offense covering theft or forgery of a credit card. Several states have not dealt separately with stealing a credit card or theft with a credit card, but have included offenses under general theft statutes.

THE MODEL PENAL CODE

Section 224.6 of the Model Penal Code provides that it is an offense to use a credit card for the purpose of obtaining property or services with knowledge that the card is stolen, forged, revoked, canceled, or for any other unauthorized reason. Some of the state codes have followed the Model Penal Code in not requiring any criminal state of mind beyond knowledge that use of the card is unauthorized. A number of the newer codes as well as many older ones require "intent to defraud."

Section 224.6 of the Model Penal Code distinguishes between the use of stolen, forged, revoked, or canceled cards, and the use of cards outside the authorization of the issuer. In grading credit card offenses, the Model Penal Code grades such offenses as a felony of the third degree where the amount involved is over $500 and otherwise as a misdemeanor. A few states have followed the Model Penal Code approach, although the dividing point between felony and misdemeanor varies.

For example, two states, Georgia and Texas, make the fraudulent use of a credit card an automatic felony. New Jersey grades all credit card fraud as a crime of the fourth degree, which carries a maximum term of 18 months. Utah has a four-tier scheme of grading that ranges from a class B misdemeanor for goods valued at less than $100 to a felony of the second degree for goods in excess of $2,500.

FEDERAL CRIMINAL STATUTES

The misuse of a credit card under certain circumstances may also give rise to a prosecution under various federal criminal statutes.

Mail Fraud

The federal mail fraud statute (18 U.S.C. §1341) prohibits the use or causing the use of the mails "for the purpose of executing" a scheme or artifice to defraud, This statute has been interpreted by the federal courts to be broad enough to cover the procurement of a credit card by misrepresentation in order to perpetrate a fraud, or to carry out a fraud through the use of a stolen or forged credit card, providing that the use of the mail was a significant step in the execution of the fraudulent scheme.

The Federal Truth in Lending Law

The Federal Truth in Lending Law also imposes criminal liability for the wrongful use of credit cards. The statute broadly proscribes fraudulent use of credit cards in interstate or foreign commerce, or transactions affecting such commerce. Counterfeit, fictitious, altered, forged, lost, stolen, or fraudulently obtained credit cards are dealt with by the statute in defining various offenses, the prescribed punishment for which is a fine of not more than $10,000 or imprisonment of not more than ten years, or both.

PROTECTING YOUR CREDIT CARDS

The best protection against credit card fraud is to know where your cards are at all times and to keep them secure. Carry only those cards that you anticipate you'll need. Be cautious about disclosing your account number over the phone unless you know you are dealing with a reputable company. Never put your account number on the outside of an envelope or on a postcard.

Open billing statements promptly and compare them with your receipts. Report mistakes or discrepancies as soon as possible to the special address listed on your statement for "billing inquiries." Under the Fair Credit Billing Act, the card issuer must investigate billing errors reported to them within 60 days of the date the statement was mailed. Keep a record of your account numbers, expiration dates, and the telephone numbers of each card issuer so you can report a loss quickly. These items should be kept in a safe place separate from your credit cards.

CREDIT CARD RECEIPTS

Following a transaction, draw a line through blank spaces above the total on your credit card receipt so the amount cannot be changed. Never sign a blank charge slip. Tear up carbons and save your receipts to check against your monthly billing statements.

Effective December 2006, companies will not be allowed to electronically print more than the last 5 digits of your credit or debit card number on your receipt. In addition, the electronic receipt will not show your card's expiration date. However, the law will still permit handwritten or mechanically printed receipts to contain the entire card number and expiration date.

CHAPTER 4:
INTERNET SAFETY

IN GENERAL

Although the Internet is a revolutionary tool for marketing, banking and communication, it has unfortunately spawned a whole new venue for identity thieves. The Internet enhances the availability and accessibility of personal identifying information, and thus creates greater risks for consumers and greater opportunities for criminal activity, including identity theft.

For example, consumers now use the Internet to handle their banking and make online purchases using credit cards and debit cards. Signing up for services generally requires the consumer to provide personal information, including financial information, in order to register. Identity thieves are constantly seeking to decode the massive amount of data being transmitted on the Internet.

In addition, there are many scams being perpetrated on the Internet which fool the consumer into revealing personal information. According to the Federal Trade Commission, in 2005, there were 196,503 internet-related fraud complaints filed. A fraud complaint is "Internet-related" if: (i) it concerns an Internet product or service; (ii) the company initially contacts the consumer via the Internet; or (iii) the consumer responds via the Internet.

A table setting forth the total number of Internet fraud complaints and the amounts paid (2003-2005) is set forth at Appendix 3.

All Internet users, regardless of age, have been victims of Internet-related fraud. Not surprisingly, however, the majority of victims are between the ages of 20 and 49, the group most likely to use computers for online banking, shopping, and other transactions. According to Consumer Sentinel, the Federal Trade Commission database, from January 1, 2005 through December 31, 2005, Internet-related fraud complaints were filed by 25% of persons aged 20-29; 25% of persons aged 30-39; and 24% of persons aged 40-49.

The least likely to be victimized over the Internet are children and senior citizens. During this same time period, only 3% of all Internet-related fraud complaints were reported for persons aged 19 and under; 16% for persons aged 50-59; 5% for persons aged 60-69; and a mere 2% for persons aged 70 and over.

A table setting forth the total number of Internet fraud complaints by consumer age (2003-2005) is set forth at Appendix 4.

Therefore, it is critical that Internet users become familiar with the most common Internet schemes and carefully safeguard their personal information to minimize the risk of being an identity theft victim.

SECURE TRANSACTIONS

Although it may be impossible to protect oneself completely from fraud and deception in both online and offline purchases, there are some steps the consumer can take to make it less likely they will be an identity theft victim. The consumer is advised to make sure that their online transactions are "secure,"—i.e., the consumer's personal information is protected against fraud.

A secure browser refers to software that encrypts or scrambles the purchase information sent over the Internet. The consumer should be sure that the browser they use has the latest encryption capabilities available and should comply with industry security standards. Most computers come with a browser installed. Some browsers are available for downloading over the Internet at no cost to the consumer.

In addition to making sure you use a secure browser before providing personal identifying or financial information on a particular website, it is important to review the site's privacy policy to ascertain the security features offered by the site. Do not divulge any private information if you are not satisfied that the website is secure.

One way of knowing whether or not a website is using a security system is to watch the address bar on the screen. At the point where the consumer enters their personal information, the prefix on the address should change to "shttp" or "https." Scroll left to determine whether the prefix changed. If you are unsure, contact the business directly to find out about their online security system and privacy policy.

If the website states that your personal identifying or financial information does not need to be encrypted, do not patronize the website. In addition, if the company does not have a physical address, and you are unfamiliar with it, do not conduct online business with the company, as it may be a fly-by-night operation set up for illegal purposes.

Electronic Payments

Most Internet consumers use credit cards to pay for their online purchases. However, the use of debit cards—e.g., automated teller machine (ATM) cards—for online purchases is becoming increasingly more common. A debit card authorizes the seller to debit the sale amount from the consumer's bank account electronically. Banks also issue debit cards that also "act" as credit cards—e.g., a "debit" MasterCard. The consumer chooses whether to select the debit or credit option at the point of purchase. Either way, the funds are deducted from the consumer's bank account. The attraction of the "debit/credit" card is that it is accepted more readily for purchases.

Another type of Internet-based payment system is called an "e-wallet." An e-wallet allows the consumer to establish an online account that is debited as the consumer makes online purchases. The consumer may use some form of stored value to establish the e-wallet account, or may set up an e-wallet account through a computer system connected to their credit or debit card account.

As discussed above, make sure that the online merchant's website uses a secure browser before providing personal identifying or financial information online. If you have any questions or concerns, contact the merchant directly to find about their security system and privacy policy.

Purchase Invoices and Receipts

Following your online purchase, the website usually generates a receipt or invoice which can be printed. The consumer should print out and retain this information and any other order confirmation sent by the merchant to the consumer's e-mail address. This information should be checked against the consumer's monthly credit card and bank statements. If there are any discrepancies, errors, or unauthorized purchases, the credit card issuer or bank should be notified immediately.

Anonymous Remailers

Consumers who are reluctant to provide any personal information online may use a program that masks their identity, such as an "anonymous remailer," by enabling the consumer to make their online transactions through third parties.

INTERNET BANKING

Internet banking is a rapidly growing technology now available through most banks. The service is generally offered to the customer for free or at a small monthly charge. Studies have indicated that there is substantial customer demand for these services and banks may have to offer this service in order to stay competitive.

Two-thirds of the 109 million households in the United States now have at least one computer connected to the Internet, and approximately 56% of those households conduct some type of online banking activity. However, fear of identity theft has deterred many from conducting their financial transactions online. This is because Internet banking customers must necessarily divulge a lot of their personal identifying and financial information in order to participate.

In order to sign up for Internet banking, the customer accesses their bank's website and follows the procedure for setting up the online banking account. After providing the account number and other identifying information, the customer is generally asked to choose a username and a password that they will use to access their existing accounts electronically.

Once registered, the customer can generally view their bank statements online, including recent activity, download their statements to their computer, and view imaged copies of individual items, without having to wait for their statements in the mail. In addition, most banks also offer the customer the ability to view the long-term activity on their account. The customer may also be able to link all of their bank accounts, transfer funds between accounts, open new accounts, apply for loans, order checks, make investments, and pay bills online.

Unfortunately, identity thieves who are able to obtain the consumer's username and password are also able to access this wealth of information and services. Further, if the website is not secure, as set forth above, identity thieves who are knowledgeable computer hackers may be able to access information through the bank's website.

Consumers should safeguard their Internet banking password very carefully. It is just as valuable as the PIN number assigned to the consumer's ATM card. Don't use a password that can easily be guessed by an identity thief. It is also wise to change your password from time to time to minimize the risk that your account will be accessed. In addition, if you get an e-mail asking you to confirm your password, do not respond without calling the bank directly.

Given the extensive amount of personal identifying and financial information involved in Internet banking, there are serious concerns relating to security issues, thus banks are very careful in selecting and developing an appropriate software system with a secure online server to process their customer's banking transactions. Customers should inquire about the bank's online security procedures to make sure that their information is secure and the risk of interception by identity thieves is minimized.

INTERNET SERVICE PROVIDER SCAM

According to information reported to the Federal Trade Commission, a common scam designed to obtain personal financial information from the consumer involves e-mail requests purportedly sent from the consumer's Internet service provider (ISP). The e-mail request generally advises the consumer that "your account information needs to be updated" or that "the credit card you signed up with is invalid or expired and the information needs to be reentered to keep your account active." Consumers are advised not to respond to any such e-mail request without first checking with their ISP.

SECURE E-MAIL

E-mail is generally not secure and can be intercepted and read by others. Therefore, it would be unwise to transmit any personal identifying or financial information by e-mail unless you use e-mail cryptography software to scramble your messages in code.

In addition, do not open unsolicited e-mails or download files from strangers. You could be opening a virus that can interfere with you computer's operation and destroy important files stored on your computer.

COOKIES

The term "cookies" refers to bits of electronic information that identify the computer used by a specific customer to a particular website. Cookies are placed on a consumer's computer when he or she visits various websites. Cookies are used by the website to tailor information to the particular customer, such as marketing information, preferences, etc. Cookies are also used so that customers can easily access the website without having to enter their password each time they visit the site.

The presence of cookies on a website can be detected using special software or particular browser settings. To check for cookie files on your computer, search the hard drive for a file labeled "cookies.txt." You can then delete the cookie files if you do not want to keep them on your computer's hard drive.

VIRUSES

From time to time, the media reports on "viruses" that are circulating in cyberspace, such as the infamous "Melissa" virus. A virus can do considerable damage to computer programs and files and can also reveal personal information stored on the computer. To protect yourself from accidentally downloading a virus to your computer, do not open any e-mail attachments from unknown senders. Even if you are familiar with the sender, if the subject matter appears suspicious, do not open it.

Those who circulate these viruses are able to access a computer user's mailing list and send the virus so that it appears to be coming from a known sender. Also be aware that certain programs available for download on the Internet may contain viruses. Check out the particular download carefully before accessing it. It is advisable to install and regularly update anti-virus software that will search your computer for viruses.

BROADBAND INTERNET ACCESS

Broadband Internet access has become available through cable, satellite and telephone companies. Broadband service is much faster than standard dial-up service, and keeps the consumer connected to the Internet whenever their computer is turned on as opposed to signing on and off each time they want to go online.

The problem with broadband Internet access is that it makes the consumer more vulnerable to identity thieves. Consider installing a "firewall," i.e., special software that provides a barrier and controls access to a computer by unauthorized users. Always remember to turn your computer off when it is not in use because a "hacker" cannot access information on a computer that is off.

THE CHILDREN'S ONLINE PRIVACY PROTECTION ACT (COPPA)

The Children's Online Privacy Protection Act (COPPA) and the FTC's implementing Rule took effect April 21, 2000. The primary goal of the Act and the Rule is to place parents in control over what information is collected from their children online.

The COPPA Rule applies to individually identifiable information about a child such as name, home address, e-mail address, telephone number or any other information that would allow someone to identify or contact the child. The Act also covers other types of information, such as hobbies, interests and information collected through cookies or other types of tracking mechanisms when they are tied to individually identifiable information.

The COPPA Rule applies to operators of commercial websites and online services directed to children under 13 that collect personal information from children, and operators of general audience sites with actual knowledge that they are collecting information from children under 13.

The COPPA Rule sets out a number of factors in determining whether a website is targeted to children, including: (i) the website's subject matter; (ii) the website's language; (iii) the website's use of animated characters; and (iv) whether advertising appearing on the website is directed to children. The Commission will also consider empirical evidence regarding the ages of the website's visitors. These standards are very similar to those previously established for TV, radio, and print advertising.

The COPPA Rule requires the website operator to post a link to a notice of its information practices on the home page of its website or online service and at each area where it collects personal information from children. An operator of a general audience site with a separate children's area must post a link to its notice on the home page of the children's area.

The link to the privacy notice must be clear and prominent. The notice must be clearly written and understandable. It should not include any unrelated or confusing materials. It must state the following information:

1. The name and contact information, including address, telephone number and e-mail address, of all operators collecting or maintaining children's personal information through the website or online service. If more than one operator is collecting information, the website may select and provide contact information for only one operator who will respond to all inquiries from parents about the website's privacy policies. However, the names of all operators must be listed in the notice.

2. The kinds of personal information collected from children and how the information is collected—e.g., directly from the child, or passively through cookies.

3. How the operator uses the personal information.

4. Whether the operator discloses information collected from children to third parties. If so, the operator also must disclose: (i) the kinds of businesses in which the third parties are engaged; (ii) the general purposes for which the information is used; and (iii) whether

the third parties have agreed to maintain the confidentiality and security of the information.

5. That the parent has the option to agree to the collection and use of the child's information without consenting to the disclosure of the information to third parties.

6. That the operator may not require a child to disclose more information than is reasonably necessary to participate in an activity as a condition of participation.

7. That the parent can review the child's personal information, ask to have it deleted and refuse to allow any further collection or use of the child's information. The notice also must state the procedures for the parent to follow to do so.

The notice to parents must contain the same information included on the notice on the website. In addition, an operator must notify a parent that it wishes to collect personal information from the child; that the parent's consent is required for the collection, use and disclosure of the information; and how the parent can provide consent. The notice to parents must be written clearly and understandably, and must not contain any unrelated or confusing information. An operator may use any one of a number of methods to notify a parent, including sending an e-mail message to the parent or a notice by regular mail.

Before collecting, using or disclosing personal information from a child, an operator must obtain verifiable parental consent from the child's parent. This means an operator must make reasonable efforts to ensure that the child's parent receives notice of the operator's information practices, and consents to those practices, before any personal information is collected from the child.

Operators may use e-mail to get parental consent for all internal uses of personal information, such as marketing back to a child based on his or her preferences or communicating promotional updates about site content, as long as they take additional steps to increase the likelihood that the parent has, in fact, provided the consent.

An operator must give a parent the option to agree to the collection and use of the child's personal information without agreeing to the disclosure of the information to third parties. However, when a parent agrees to the collection and use of their child's personal information, the operator may release that information to others who use it solely to provide support for the internal operations of the website or service, including technical support and order fulfillment.

The regulations include several exceptions that allow operators to collect a child's e-mail address without getting the parent's consent in advance. These exceptions cover many popular online activities for kids, including contests, online newsletters, homework help and electronic postcards. Prior parental consent is not required when:

1. an operator collects a child's or parent's e-mail address to provide notice and seek consent;

2. an operator collects an e-mail address to respond to a one-time request from a child and then deletes it;

3. an operator collects an e-mail address to respond more than once to a specific request in which case the operator must notify the parent that it is communicating regularly with the child and give the parent the opportunity to stop the communication before sending or delivering a second communication to a child;

4. an operator collects a child's name or online contact information to protect the safety of a child who is participating on the website in which case the operator must notify the parent and give him or her the opportunity to prevent further use of the information;

5. an operator collects a child's name or online contact information to protect the security or liability of the website or to respond to law enforcement, if necessary, and does not use it for any other purpose.

An operator is required to send a new notice and request for consent to parents if there are material changes in the collection, use or disclosure practices to which the parent had previously agreed.

At a parent's request, operators must disclose the general kinds of personal information they collect online from children as well as the specific information collected from children who visit their websites. Operators must use reasonable procedures to ensure they are dealing with the child's parent before they provide access to the child's specific information. They can use a variety of methods to verify the parent's identity, including:

1. obtaining a signed form from the parent via regular mail or fax;

2. accepting and verifying a credit card number;

3. taking calls from parents on a toll-free telephone number staffed by trained personnel;

4. e-mail accompanied by digital signature;

5. e-mail accompanied by a PIN or password obtained through one of the verification methods above.

Operators who follow one of these procedures acting in good faith to a request for parental access are protected from liability under federal and state law for inadvertent disclosures of a child's information to someone who purports to be a parent.

At any time, a parent may revoke his or her consent, refuse to allow an operator to further use or collect their child's personal information, and direct the operator to delete the information. In turn, the operator may terminate any service provided to the child, but only if the information at issue is reasonably necessary for the child's participation in that activity. If other activities on the website do not require the child's e-mail address, the operator must allow the child access to those activities.

The Federal Trade Commission (FTC) monitors the Internet for compliance with the Rule and brings law enforcement actions where appropriate to deter violations. Parents and other concerned individuals can submit complaints to the FTC for investigation. The FTC will also investigate referrals from consumer groups, industry, and approved safe harbor programs, as appropriate.

The FTC may impose civil penalties for violations of the Rule in the same manner as for other Rules under the FTC Act. The level of penalties assessed may turn on a number of factors including egregiousness of the violation. The factors considered may include: (i) the number of children involved; (ii) the amount and type of personal information collected; (iii) how the information was used; (iv) whether the information was shared with third parties; and (v) the size of the company.

The FTC has set up a special web page designed for children, parents, businesses, and educators (http://www.ftc.gov/kidzprivacy/).

In addition to providing compliance materials for businesses and parents, this web page features online safety tips for children and other useful education resources about the Children's Online Privacy Protection Act and related rules and online privacy in general.

The text of the Children's Online Privacy Protection Act (COPPA) is set forth at Appendix 5.

INTERNET PRIVACY POLICIES

Companies operating online often ask their customers personal information so that they can gather marketing information concerning the people who visit their website. The information gathered may also be shared with others for marketing and other purposes. Privacy policies vary among websites, therefore, the consumer is advised to read them carefully.

It is important to determine whether the website you visit has a privacy policy. If so, the privacy policy should detail the following:

1. The type of information collected;

2. How the information is used;

3. Whether the information is shared with third parties; and

4. What control the consumer has over their personal information.

Privacy policies also should advise the consumer how they can find out what information has been collected by the website so that erroneous information can be corrected or deleted. The privacy policy should also explain how the company restricts their employees' access to the consumer's personal information.

Consumers may also have the choice to "opt out" of having their information used in various ways. If there is such an "opt out" policy, the consumer must generally affirmatively state that they do not want their information used. Otherwise, the information will be disseminated, meaning that it will be used unless you say "no." If there is an "opt in" policy, this means that the consumer's personal information cannot be used unless they affirmatively state that they want their information used.

Many websites also ask the consumer's permission to contact them in the future by e-mail with notices, updates, offers and other information. The consumer should have the option of declining permission for future contact.

Privacy policies are discussed more fully in Chapter 5 of this Almanac.

CHAPTER 5:
PRIVACY POLICIES AND DIRECT MARKETING

IN GENERAL

As part of their daily transactions, consumers are continually being asked to provide personal information. It has become so commonplace, most consumers don't stop and ask how the information is going to be used. Activities such as ordering from catalogues, using credit cards, obtaining magazine subscriptions, and contributing to charitable causes, will often cause the consumer's name and personal information to be distributed among other companies.

In many cases, a consumer's personal information is used to create a profile about the individual so that future offers for products or services can be solicited. Direct marketing companies buy this information if they think the consumer fits into their target audience.

Direct marketing is broadly defined as any direct communication to a consumer or business recipient that is designed to generate a response in the form of an order, a request for further information, and/or a visit to a store or other place of business to purchase a specific product or service. The consumer may receive an unsolicited offer or other communication in the mail, by e-mail or through telemarketers.

Due to the growing problem of identity theft, consumers are becoming aware of the importance of safeguarding their personal information from these direct marketers. In response, more companies are offering the consumer choices on how their personal information may be used, and the consumer is given the choice of "opting out" of such uses in order to protect their personal information from theft and misuse.

THE DIRECT MARKETING ASSOCIATION

The Direct Marketing Association (DMA), established in 1917, is the oldest and largest national trade association serving the direct marketing field. It has approximately 4,800 corporate, affiliate and chapter members from the United States and 46 other nations, including 55 "Fortune 500" companies. Some of the most well-known member companies include AT&T, IBM, AOL Time Warner, Mellon Bank, Microsoft, Home Shopping Network, The New York Times, Prudential Insurance, Phillip Morris, Proctor & Gamble, and Experian.

The DMA members advertise their products and services directly to consumers by mail, telephone, magazine, Internet, radio and/or television, and include catalog companies, direct mailers, teleservice firms, internet marketers, and other marketers from every consumer and business-to-business segment.

The DMA provides consumers with the opportunity to "opt-out" of direct mail marketing from many national companies using the mail preference service (MPS); the telephone preference service (TPS); and the e-mail preference service (E-MPS). The DMA members are required to use these services, which are discussed more fully below.

The Mail Preference Service (MPS)

The DMA's Mail Preference Service (MPS) assists consumers in decreasing the amount of non-profit commercial mail they receive at home. Decreasing the amount of unsolicited mail, and the number of companies which share the consumer's personal information, minimizes the likelihood that the consumer's personal information will be intercepted and misused.

When the consumer registers with the MPS service, their name is placed on a "delete" file which is distributed to direct marketing companies four times a year. Registration is good for a period of five years. All DMA members are required to compare their list of prospective customers against the MPS records, and remove any individuals who have registered with MPS from their list. Non-members are also invited to use the service.

Although consumers will still receive commercial mailings from companies with which they do business, and charitable organizations, they should expect to see a decrease in most other commercial mailings within 3 months from the date they register with the service. Registration does not, however, cover mail sent to "resident" or "occupant."

Name deletion through MPS is a general service. You cannot select certain companies for deletion and keep your name on other mailing lists.

The only way to have your name deleted from a specific company's mailing list is to contact that company directly and request name deletion.

The consumer may register online, for a small fee (http://www.the-dma.org/) or register at no cost, in writing, in care of the following address:

Direct Marketing Association
P.O. Box 9008
Farmingdale, New York 11735-9014

The Telephone Preference Service (TPS)

Consumers are concerned about the increasing number of telemarketer calls being placed to their home, and are wary of providing personal information over the telephone. According to the DMA, more consumers than ever are requesting not to be called at home. In addition, as further set forth below, Federal legislation requires telemarketers to remove the name of any individual that tells them they do not want to be called, and state legislation restricting telemarketer's access to potential customers is also increasing.

In response, the DMA has instituted a telephone preference service (TPS). Consumers can register to have their phone numbers deleted from national marketing lists by sending their name, address and telephone number to:

DMA Telephone Preference Service
P.O. Box 9014
Farmingdale, New York 11735-9014

The E-Mail Preference Service (E-MPS)

The DMA also operates an E-Mail Preference Service (E-MPS) which assists the consumer by having their e-mail address removed from many national direct e-mail lists. According to DMA guidelines an unsolicited e-mail message should have two opt-out options:

1. Consumers may choose to opt-out of receiving e-mail from a specific marketer.

2. Consumers may opt-out of having their e-mail address rented or shared with other marketers.

For more information on the e-mail deletion service, the reader is advised to visit the DMA website (http://www.e-mps.org/).

DMA PRIVACY POLICIES

DMA member businesses all subscribe to the Direct Marketing Association Privacy Promise which assures consumers that American direct marketers will use the consumer's information in a manner that respects their wishes.

A proper privacy notice must contain the following nine items:

1. categories of personal information the company collects;

2. categories of personal information the company discloses;

3. categories of affiliates and nonaffiliated third parties to whom the company discloses the information;

4. an explanation of the consumer's right to opt out of disclosures to nonaffiliated third parties;

5. a description of the kind of disclosures to nonaffiliated parties that are exceptions to the rules and don't give the consumer the right to opt out;

6. an explanation of the ability to opt out of disclosures of information among affiliates under the Fair Credit Reporting Act (FCRA);

7. if the company discloses information to third parties, such as telemarketing agencies, to conduct marketing campaigns, etc., on the company's behalf, the company must include a separate statement of the categories of information disclosed and the categories of third parties to whom the information will be disclosed;

8. a description of the company's confidentiality and security policies and practices; and

9. categories of personal information about former customers that the company discloses, and to whom they disclose such information.

A sample Privacy Policy Outline is set forth at Appendix 6.

If the DMA Committee on Ethical Business Practice determines that a member appears not to be in compliance with the Privacy Promise, the company will be contacted and asked for immediate compliance. The member will then need to come into immediate compliance and/or demonstrate to the Committee that its practices are consistent with the Privacy Promise. Penalties for noncompliance include censure, suspension, or expulsion from The DMA, and publicity to that effect.

The Privacy Promise took effect on July 1, 1999 requires DMA members to adhere to certain privacy practices by:

1. providing customers with notice of their ability to opt out of information exchanges;

2. honoring customer opt out requests not to have their contact information transferred to others for marketing purposes;

3. accepting and maintaining consumer requests to be on an in-house suppress file to stop receiving solicitations from DMA member companies; and,

4. using The DMA Preference Service suppression files which now exist for mail (MPS), telephone (TPS), and e-mail (E-MPS) preference lists.

Notice

If the company is a business-to-consumer marketer that rents, sells or exchanges lists of customers, they must give the customers notice that they have a choice not to have their contact information rented, sold or exchanged. The first notice must take place when, or soon after, a "prospect" becomes a "customer."

A person is defined as a "prospect" if that person has not previously purchased from or donated to the company.

A person is defined as a "customer" if that person:

1. bought something from the company;

2. donated to the company;

3. is identified by the company as a "customer" on a list that the company rents or exchanges with someone else;

4. has inquired about the company's products, services or organization, and/or,

5. is a sweepstakes entrant, whether or not he or she has purchased anything from the company.

The company is required to give follow-up notices at least once a year unless they contact the customer less frequently than once a year, in which case the company need only give notice as frequently as they contact the customer.

A separate document is not necessary to provide the required notice. The company may place the notice in any routine communication with the customer. However, the notice must be prominent, and easy for the customer to read and understand.

Notice is required regardless of which medium the company uses to contact customers—e.g., mail, phone, fax, print or online—but need not be in the same medium as the solicitation. DMA examples of "opt out" notices include the following:

"We make our customer information available to other companies so they may contact you about products and services that may interest you. If you do not want your name passed on to other companies for the purpose of receiving marketing offers, just tell us by contacting us at [contact information], and we will be pleased to respect your wishes."

Alternative language:

"We make portions of our customer list available to carefully screened companies that offer products and services we believe you may enjoy. If you do not want to receive those offers and/or information, please let us know by contacting us at [contact information]."

Honoring Opt Out Requests

All direct marketers must promptly honor individual requests to opt out of the sale, rental or exchange of their contact information for marketing purposes. It is the list owner's responsibility to see that the "opt out" provision is offered and honored.

In-House Suppression Files

List owners and list users must honor individual requests for no future contact from both customers and prospects. Marketers must stop soliciting these individuals and flag them as "do-not-solicit" names in their customer file.

Generally, a marketer must not contact that person for at least five years after that individual makes a request not to be contacted in the future. In the case of telemarketing, the Telephone Consumer Protection Act requires that individuals who ask not to be called again be placed on the in-house suppression file for ten years.

DMA examples of in-house suppression notices include the following:

"If you decide you no longer wish to receive our catalog, send your mailing label with your request to [contact information]."

Alternative language:

"We would like to continue sending you information only on those subjects of interest to you. If you don't wish to continue to receive information on any of the following product lines, just let us know by [contact information]. If you would like to receive our catalog less frequently, let us know by [contact information]."

Use of DMA Mail, Telephone and E-mail Preference Services

Marketers that contact consumers are required to use MPS, TPS or E-MPS on all consumer marketing campaigns. The list user is the one responsible for using MPS/TPS before soliciting prospects. Usage by either the list owner or the list user, however, will satisfy the requirement. The goal is to ensure that the prospects' choices not to receive mail and telephone solicitations are respected.

The MPS and TPS files are updated monthly. As a minimum standard for complying with the Privacy Promise, the most recent quarterly release of the MPS/TPS file should be viewed by the company whenever contacting prospects. To ensure that consumers who requested name suppression see results as quickly as possible, the DMA recommends monthly processing.

CONSUMER OPT-OUT PROVISION

Companies must provide the consumer with a "reasonable opportunity to opt out" before they disclose personal information to nonaffiliated third parties. This obligation continues throughout the company's relationship with a customer. If the company sends the opt-out notice by mail, the customer must have at least 30 days to request the opt-out after the notice is sent.

The opt-out provisions may be communicated to the consumer by:

1. designating check-off boxes in a prominent position on the relevant forms with the opt-out notice;

2. including a reply form that provides the address to which the form should be mailed;

3. providing an electronic means to opt out, such as a form that can be sent via e-mail or an opt-out procedure at your Web site;

4. providing a toll-free number that consumers can call.

Nevertheless, there are exceptions to the company's requirement to provide notice and opt-out provisions, as follows:

1. where the disclosure is necessary to process or service a transaction;

2. to protect record security and confidentiality;

3. to provide information to legal counsel and to prove that the company is complying with industry standards;

4. to respond to requests from regulators, self-regulatory organizations, and law enforcement;

5. to report a customer's activities to a credit bureau;

6. to protect against fraud;

7. to individuals or businesses with a legal interest relating to the consumer;

8. in connection with a proposed or actual merger or acquisition; and

9. to comply with laws and legal process.

THE TELEMARKETING SALES RULE

In August 1994, the Telemarketing and Consumer Fraud and Abuse Prevention Act became law. The purpose of the Act is to combat the growth of telemarketing fraud by providing law enforcement agencies with powerful new tools, and to give consumers new protections and guidance on how to tell the difference between fraudulent and legitimate telemarketing.

Under the Act, the Federal Trade Commission (FTC) adopted the Telemarketing Sales Rule to achieve those goals. The key provisions of the Rule require specific disclosures, prohibit misrepresentations, set limits on the times telemarketers may call consumers, prohibit calls after a consumer asks not to be called, set payment restrictions for the sale of certain goods and services, and require that specific business records be kept for two years.

The Rule is not intended to affect any state or local telemarketing law. Therefore, an attorney general or other authorized state official may proceed with an action in state court to enforce any of that state's civil or criminal laws.

Covered Practices

The Telemarketing Sales Rule covers telemarketing—i.e., any plan, program, or campaign to sell goods or services through interstate telephone calls. With some important exceptions explained below, any persons or companies that take part in any plan, program, or campaign to sell goods or services through interstate telephone calls must comply with the Rule. This is true whether, as "telemarketers," they initiate or receive telephone calls to or from consumers, or whether, as "sellers," they provide, offer to provide, or arrange to provide goods or services to consumers in exchange for payment.

Some businesses and individuals are not covered by the Rule even though they may use interstate telephone calls to sell goods or services. The following four types of entities are not subject to the FTC's jurisdiction and therefore not covered by the Rule:

1. banks, federal credit unions, and federal savings and loans;

2. common carriers, such as long-distance telephone companies and airlines;

3. non-profit organizations—i.e., entities that are not organized to carry on business for their own profit or that of their members; and

4. companies engaged in the business of insurance, to the extent that this business is regulated by state law.

These four types of entities are not covered by the Rule only because they are specifically exempted from the FTC's jurisdiction; however, any other individual or company that contracts with one of these four types of entities to provide telemarketing services must comply with the Rule.

For example, although banks are not covered by the Rule, a nonbank company that contracts with a bank to provide telemarketing services on behalf of the bank is covered. Similarly, a non-airline company that contracts with an airline to provide telemarketing services on behalf of the airline is covered by the Rule, and a company that is acting for profit may be covered by the Rule if it sells goods or services of more than nominal value on behalf of a nonprofit corporation.

In addition, under the provisions of the Telemarketing and Consumer Fraud and Abuse Prevention Act, a number of entities and individuals subject to the jurisdiction of the Securities and Exchange Commission (SEC) or the Commodity Futures Trading Commission are not covered by the Rule, even if they engage in a plan, program, or campaign to sell through interstate telephone calls.

Certain types of calls are not covered by the Rule, regardless of whether the business or individual making the call is covered, including:

1. Calls placed by consumers in response to a catalog—Generally, the Rule does not apply to calls placed by consumers in response to a catalog provided: (a) the catalog contains a written description or illustration of the goods or services offered for sale; (b) the catalog includes the business address of the seller; (c) the catalog includes multiple pages of written material or illustrations; (d) the catalog has been issued not less frequently than once a year; and (e) the catalog seller does not solicit consumers by telephone but only receives calls initiated by consumers in response to the catalog, and during those calls from consumers takes orders only without further solicitation.

2. 900-number calls—The Rule does not apply to 900-Number pay-per-call telephone calls, however, providers of pay-per-call services must comply with the FTC's 900-Number Rule.

3. Calls related to the sale of franchises or certain business opportunities—The Rule does not apply to calls relating to sales of franchises or business opportunities that are covered by the FTC's Franchise Rule, however, the Rule does apply to the telemarketing of business ventures not covered by the FTC's Franchise Rule.

4. Unsolicited calls from consumers—Calls from consumers that are not the result of any solicitation by a seller or telemarketer are not

covered by the Rule because they are not considered to be part of a telemarketing plan, program, or campaign to sell goods or services.

5. Calls that are part of a transaction that involves a face-to-face sales presentation—The Rule does not cover telephone transactions that are not completed until after a face-to-face sales presentation by the seller and the consumer is not required to pay or authorize payment until after such a presentation. The goal of the Rule is to protect consumers against deceptive or abusive practices that can arise in situations where the consumer has no direct contact—other than the telephone sales call itself—with an invisible and anonymous seller.

6. Business-to-business calls that do not involve retail sales of nondurable office or cleaning supplies—Most telephone calls between a telemarketer and a business are exempt from the Rule's coverage, however, business-to-business calls involving the retail sale of nondurable office or cleaning supplies are covered by the Rule.

7. Calls made in response to general media advertising—The Rule generally does not apply to consumer calls made in response to general media advertising, such as television commercials, infomercials, home shopping programs, magazine and newspaper advertisements, Yellow Pages or similar general directory listings, and other forms of mass media advertising and solicitations, however, the Rule does cover calls from consumers in response to general media advertisements relating to credit repair, recovery services, advance-fee loans, or investment opportunities.

8. Calls made in response to direct mail advertising—Direct mail advertising includes any material—postcards, flyers, door hangers, brochures, "certificates," or letters—sent to a person urging that person to call a specified telephone number regarding an offer of some sort. However, there is no exemption for calls elicited by direct mail advertising that does not truthfully provide a consumer with the specific information required under the Rule nor is there any exemption for calls responding to any direct mail advertising that relates to credit repair, recovery services, advance-fee loans, investment opportunities, or prize promotions, regardless of whether the advertisement makes all the disclosures required by the Rule.

Disclosure Requirement

The Rule requires a seller or telemarketer, whether making outbound calls to consumers or receiving inbound calls from consumers, to provide certain material information before that consumer pays for goods or services that are the subject of the sales offer. Material information is information that would likely affect a person's choice of goods or services, or their conduct regarding them—i.e., information necessary for a consumer to make an informed purchasing decision.

Misrepresentation

The Rule generally prohibits a seller or telemarketer from making any false or misleading statement to induce anyone to pay for goods or services. For example, telemarketers cannot falsely claim that they need to obtain a consumer's bank account number or credit card number only for identification purposes, when in fact they use those numbers to obtain payment for the goods or services offered.

Credit Card Laundering

Credit card laundering is basically the misuse of what is known as a "merchant account" with a financial institution. A merchant account is a kind of bank account; it is what a seller or telemarketer needs in order to gain access to a credit card collection and payment system and to obtain cash for goods and services sold. Obtaining access to the credit card system through another's merchant account without the authorization of the financial institution is credit card laundering. Credit card laundering not only violates the Rule; it is a criminal offense under federal law, as well as the law of some states.

Calling Restrictions

The Rule imposes calling restrictions and prohibits telemarketers from:

1. calling consumers repeatedly or continuously, with the intent to annoy, abuse, or harass any person at the called number;

2. calling any consumer who previously has requested that he or she not be called again—the "do not call" provision as further discussed below; or

3. calling any consumer's residence before 8:00 A.M. or after 9:00 PM. local time at the consumer's location.

The "Do Not Call" Provision

A telemarketer may not call a consumer who previously has requested to receive no more calls from, or on behalf of, a particular seller whose goods or services are being offered. Similarly, a seller that has been requested by a consumer not to call again may not cause a telemarketer to call that consumer.

Sellers and telemarketers are responsible for keeping "do not call lists" of those consumers who have requested not to receive calls placed by, or on behalf of, a particular seller. Calling a consumer who has requested not to be called is a Rule violation and a telemarketer or seller that engages in the practice of making such calls risks a $10,000 civil penalty per violation.

If a consumer is called who has requested not to be called by or on behalf of a particular seller, the seller and telemarketer may be liable for a Rule violation. If an enforcement investigation finds that neither the seller nor the telemarketer had written "do not call" procedures in place, both would be liable for the Rule violation.

If the investigation reveals that the seller had written "do not call" procedures but the telemarketer ignored the procedures, the telemarketer would be liable for the Rule violation. The seller may also be liable if the investigation finds that the seller did not implement its written procedures. Ultimately a seller is responsible for keeping a current "do not call" list, whether it is through a telemarketing service it hires or through its own efforts.

If a seller or telemarketer has and implements written "do not call" procedures, it will not be liable for a Rule violation if a subsequent call is the result of error, but it may be subject to an enforcement investigation. The investigation would focus on the effectiveness of the procedures in place, how they are implemented, and if all personnel are trained in the "do not call" procedures. If there is a high incidence of "errors," it may be determined that the procedures are inadequate to comply with the Rule's "do not call " requirements and thus there is a Rule violation. On the other hand, if there is a low incidence of "errors," there may not be a Rule violation.

The National Do Not Call Registry

The National Do Not Call Registry is a free service established by the Federal government to protect consumers from unsolicited telemarketing calls. Consumers who do not wish to receive these calls simply register online (http://www.donotcall.gov/), or call the Registry toll-free (1-888-382-1222) from the telephone number they wish to register. The Registry accepts both cell phone and home phone numbers.

If you are still receiving unsolicited telemarketing calls 31 days after registering your telephone number, you can file a complaint with the Federal Trade Commission. Be prepared to provide the date of the call and the name and/or phone number of the company that called you. The telemarketer may be liable for a Rule violation.

Not all calls are covered by the Do Not Call Registry. For example, you may still receive calls from charities, political organizations, survey-takers, companies who you have given permission to call, and companies with whom you have an existing business relationship.

Recordkeeping Requirement

The Rule requires most sellers and telemarketers to keep certain records that relate to their telemarketing activities. The following records must be maintained for two years from the date that the record is produced:

1. advertising and promotional materials;

2. information about prize recipients;

3. sales records;

4. employee records; and

5. all verifiable authorizations for demand drafts.

Sellers and telemarketers may maintain the records in any manner, format, or place that they keep such records in the ordinary course of business, including in electronic storage, on microfiche, or on paper.

Absent a written agreement between the parties, or if the written agreement is unclear as to who must maintain the required records, the telemarketer must keep the employee records, while the seller is responsible for keeping the advertising and promotional materials, information on prize recipients, sales records, and verifiable authorizations.

Enforcement and Penalties

The Federal Trade Commission, the states, and private persons may bring civil law enforcement actions in federal district courts to enforce the Rule. Actions by the states may be brought by either the attorney general of the state or by any other state officer authorized by the state to bring actions on behalf of its residents. Private persons may bring an action to enforce the Rule if they have suffered $50,000 or more in actual damages.

Anyone who violates the Rule is subject to civil penalties of up to $10,000 per violation. In addition, violators may be subject to nation-wide injunctions that prohibit certain conduct, and may be required to pay redress to injured consumers.

CHAPTER 6:
IDENTITY THEFT LEGISLATION

FEDERAL LEGISLATION

The Identity Theft and Assumption Deterrence Act of 1998

In October 1998, Congress passed the Identity Theft and Assumption Deterrence Act to address the problem of identity theft. Specifically, the Act amended 18 U.S.C. § 1028 to make it a federal crime when anyone:

> knowingly transfers or uses, without lawful authority, a means of identification of another person with the intent to commit, or to aid or abet, any unlawful activity that constitutes a violation of Federal law, or that constitutes a felony under any applicable State or local law.

Under the Act, a name, social security number, credit card number, cellular telephone electronic serial number or any other piece of information that may be used alone or in conjunction with other information to identify a specific individual is considered a "means of identification."

Violations of the Act are investigated by federal investigative agencies such as the U.S. Secret Service, the FBI, and the U.S. Postal Inspection Service and prosecuted by the Department of Justice. In most instances, a conviction for identity theft carries a maximum penalty of 15 years imprisonment, a fine, and forfeiture of any personal property used or intended to be used to commit the crime.

The Act also directs the U.S. Sentencing Commission to review and amend the federal sentencing guidelines to provide appropriate penalties for those persons convicted of identity theft.

The text of the Identity Theft and Assumption Deterrence Act and 18 U.S.C. § 1028 is set forth at Appendices 7 and 8 respectively.

The Identity Theft Penalty Enhancement Act

The Identity Theft Penalty Enhancement Act was enacted in 2004. The Act establishes penalties for aggravated identity theft as defined in the statute.

The Gramm-Leach-Bliley Act

In its effort to prevent identity theft, the Federal Trade Commission (FTC) recognized that many financial institutions' transactions with customers involve the collection of personal information, including names, addresses and phone numbers; bank and credit card account numbers; income and credit histories; and social security numbers.

Under the Gramm-Leach-Bliley (GLB) Act, a federal law, financial institutions are required to take steps to ensure the security and confidentiality of this kind of customer data. Financial institutions are defined broadly as those entities engaged in "financial activities" such as banking, lending, insurance, loan brokering, and credit reporting.

In general, under the Act, financial institutions are prohibited from disclosing nonpublic personal information, including Social Security numbers, to non-affiliated third parties without first providing consumers with notice and the opportunity to opt out of the disclosure. However, the Act includes a number of statutory exceptions under which disclosure is permitted without having to provide notice and an opt-out. These exceptions include:

1. consumer reporting pursuant to the Fair Credit Reporting Act (FCRA);

2. fraud prevention;

3. law enforcement and regulatory or self-regulatory purposes;

4. compliance with judicial process; and

5. public safety investigations.

Nevertheless, entities that receive information under an exception to the Act are subject to the reuse and redisclosure restrictions of the Act's Privacy Rule, even if those entities are not themselves financial institutions. Specifically, the recipients may only use and disclose the information "in the ordinary course of business to carry out the activity covered by the exception under which . . . the information [was received]."

The Safeguards Rule

As part of its implementation of the Act, the Federal Trade Commission has issued a rule, which requires the financial institutions under its jurisdiction to safeguard customer records and information. This "Safeguards Rule" applies to individuals or organizations that are significantly engaged in providing financial products or services to consumers, including check-cashing businesses, data processors, mortgage brokers, nonbank lenders, personal property or real estate appraisers, and retailers that issue credit cards to consumers.

Under the Safeguards Rule, these financial institutions must develop a written information security plan that describes their program to protect customer information. All programs must be appropriate to the financial institution's size and complexity, the nature and scope of its activities, and the sensitivity of the customer information at issue. For example, covered financial institutions must accomplish the following:

1. designate the employees who are to coordinate the safeguards;

2. identify and assess the risks to customer information in each relevant area of the company's operation;

3. evaluate the effectiveness of current safeguards for controlling these risks;

4. design a safeguards program, and detail the plans to monitor it;

5. select appropriate service providers and contractually require them to implement the safeguards; and

6. evaluate the program and explain adjustments in light of changes to its business arrangements or the results of its security tests.

The Rule also requires financial institutions to be particularly careful in the areas of (i) employee training and management; (ii) information systems, including network and software design, and information, storage, transmission and retrieval; and (iii) security management, including the prevention, detection and response to system failures.

The text of the Safeguards Rule is set forth at Appendix 9.

The Fair Credit Reporting Act

The Fair Credit Reporting Act (FCRA) was enacted to promote accuracy, fairness and privacy of consumer information in the files of every credit reporting agency. In order to achieve this goal, the FCRA establishes procedures for correcting mistakes on one's credit report, and requires that a consumer's credit report only be provided for legitimate business needs.

A credit reporting agency (CRA) is in the business of gathering and selling information about consumers to creditors, employers, landlords and other entities. It advises those seeking this information on whether or not the consumer is "creditworthy," e.g., bill-paying habits, judgments, bankruptcies, etc.

An identity theft victim often finds that his or her credit report has been destroyed by the identity thief. The victim has the right to make sure their credit rating is restored and that any fraudulent credit information is deleted from their report.

In order to protect the consumer, the FCRA gives the consumer certain rights, as set forth below:

1. Consumers are entitled to receive a free copy of their credit report from each of the three nationwide credit-reporting agencies once every 12 months. Instructions on how to obtain your free annual credit report are set forth in Chapter 7 of this almanac.

2. The consumer must be told if information in their credit profile has been used against them, e.g., in denying credit, employment, etc. The consumer must be given the name, address and the phone number of the CRA that provided the report.

3. If the consumer needs to request a copy of their credit report more than once during a 12-month period, upon the consumer's request, the CRA must provide the consumer with a copy of their credit profile and a list of everyone who has requested a copy. Generally, the CRA may charge the consumer a fee for providing the report, with certain exceptions. If the consumer's request is in response to any adverse action taken against them as a result of the report, the CRA must provide the consumer with a copy of the report free of charge if the request is made within 60 days notice of the adverse action.

4. If the consumer disputes the accuracy of information contained in the credit profile, the CRA must investigate the consumer's allegations and evidence and provide the consumer with a written report. If an item is found to be inaccurate, it must be corrected or deleted. If the disputed item is not resolved, the consumer is allowed to include a brief statement on the credit report concerning the disputed item. The CRA is then obligated, upon the consumer's request, to send an amended copy of the report to anyone who recently received a copy of the report.

5. The CRA must remove or correct inaccurate information or unverified information from the file, usually within 30 days the dispute is made.

6. The consumer can notify the source of the disputed information that it is inaccurate. If the information is determined to be in error, the source cannot continue to report the information to the CRA.

7. A CRA is not allowed to report negative information that is more than seven years old, with the exception of bankruptcy, which may be reported for ten years.

8. Access to a consumer's credit profile is limited to those entities that have a legitimate need recognized by the Act, such as creditors, insurance companies, employers, etc.

9. The CRA is not permitted to provide information to a consumer's employer or prospective employer without the consumer's consent, nor can it report medical information to creditors, insurance companies or employers without the consumer's consent.

10. The consumer may request that their name be removed form the CRA's list for unsolicited credit and insurance offers.

11. The consumer may seek damages if their rights under the FCRA are violated.

Under the FCRA, violators are liable to the consumer for any actual damages suffered as a result of negligence. Actual damages generally include monetary losses and have also been held to include damages for mental anguish resulting from aggravation, embarrassment, humiliation and injury to reputation, etc. Further, if the violation is willful, punitive damages may also be available to the consumer.

The text of the Fair Credit Reporting Act is set forth at Appendix 10.

The FCRA Statute of Limitations—TRW vs. Andrews

The statute of limitations governing suits based on the Fair Credit Reporting Act is two years. An important United States Supreme Court decision addressed the statute of limitations in *TRW vs. Andrews*, a case involving identity theft. In *TRW*, the Supreme Court upheld the two-year time limitation for bringing identity theft lawsuits against credit reporting agencies.

The plaintiff in this case, Adelaide Andrews, claimed that she suffered damages as a result of the disclosure of inaccurate credit information by TRW, one of the three major consumer credit reporting agencies.

The Act provides that an action to enforce any liability created by thereunder may be brought "within two years from the date on which the liability arises." Andrews argued that the Act's two-year limitation commenced to run on her claims only after her *discovery* of defendant TRW's alleged violations of the Act.

On June 17, 1993, Andrews visited a radiologist's office in California. She filled out a new patient form listing certain basic information, including her name, birth date, and Social Security number. Andrews gave the form to the office receptionist, Andrea Andrews (the "identity thief"), who copied the information and subsequently moved to Las Vegas, Nevada.

In Las Vegas, the identity thief attempted to open credit accounts using Andrews' Social Security number and her own last name and address. On four of those occasions, the company from which the identity thief sought credit requested a report from TRW. Each time, TRW 's computers registered a match between Andrews ' Social Security number, last name, and first initial and furnished her file.

TRW thus disclosed Andrews' credit history at the identity thief's request to a bank on July 25, 1994; a cable television company on September 27, 1994; a department store on October 28, 1994; and to another credit provider on January 3, 1995. All recipients but the cable company rejected the identity thief's credit applications.

Andrews did not discover the TRW disclosures until May 31, 1995, when she sought to refinance her home mortgage and in the process received a copy of her credit report reflecting the identity thief's activity. Although TRW promptly corrected her file upon learning of its mistake, Andrews alleged in her complaint that the blemishes on her report not only caused her inconvenience and emotional distress, but also forced her to abandon her refinancing efforts and settle for an alternative line of credit on less favorable terms.

On October 21, 1996, almost 17 months after she discovered the identity thief's fraudulent conduct and more than two years after TRW's first two disclosures, Andrews filed suit in the United States District Court for the Central District of California.

Andrews alleged that TRW's four disclosures of her information in response to the identity thief's credit applications were improper because TRW failed to verify, before disclosing the information, that Andrews initiated the requests or was otherwise involved in the underlying transactions.

Andrews asserted that by processing requests that matched her profile on Social Security number, last name, and first initial but did not correspond to other key identifiers, such as birth date, address, and first name, TRW had facilitated the identity theft.

TRW moved for partial summary judgment, arguing that the Act's statute of limitations had expired on Andrews' claims based on the July 25 and September 27, 1994 disclosures because both occurred more than two years before she brought suit. Andrews countered that her claims as to all four disclosures were timely because the limitations period did not commence until May 31, 1995, the date she learned of TRW's alleged wrongdoing.

The District Court ruled for TRW, holding that relief stemming from the July and September 1994 disclosures was time barred. On appeal, the

Court of Appeals for the Ninth Circuit reversed this ruling, applying what it considered to be the "general federal rule . . . that a federal statute of limitations begins to run when a party knows or has reason to know that she was injured." The Court further opined that "[U]nless Congress has expressly legislated otherwise, the equitable doctrine of discovery is read into every federal statute of limitations." The court reinstated Andrews' improper disclosure claims and remanded them for trial.

On appeal, the United States Supreme Court reversed the Ninth Circuit ruling and held that the general discovery rule exception did not govern the Act because the Act was explicit as to its time limitations, with the only exception involving willful misrepresentation by the defendant, which was not relevant to the case.

The text of the TRW decision is set forth at Appendix 11.

The Fair and Accurate Credit Transactions Act of 2003

The Fair and Accurate Credit Transactions Act of 2003 (The FACT Act) amended the FCRA to include a number of provisions designed to increase the protection of sensitive consumer information, including Social Security numbers. One such provision requires the banking regulatory agencies and the Federal Trade Commission to promulgate a coordinated rule designed to prevent unauthorized access to consumer report information by requiring all users of such information to have reasonable procedures to dispose of it properly and safely.

This "Disposal Rule," which took effect on June 1, 2005, is designed to help minimize the risk of improper disclosure of Social Security numbers. In addition, the FACT Act requires credit-reporting agencies to truncate the Social Security number on consumer reports at the consumer's request. Eliminating the unnecessary display of this information could lessen the risk of it getting into the wrong hands.

In addition, the FACT Act requires credit reporting agencies, at the request of a consumer, to place a fraud alert on the consumer's credit report. Consumers may obtain an initial alert if they have a good faith suspicion that they have been or are about to become an identity theft victim. The initial alert must stay on the file for at least 90 days. Actual victims who submit an identity theft report can obtain an extended alert, which remains in effect for up to seven years. Fraud alerts require users of consumer reports who are extending credit or related services to take certain steps to verify the consumer's identity.

Section 5 of the FTC Act

Section 5 of the FTC Act prohibits "unfair or deceptive acts or practices in or affecting commerce." Under the FTC Act, the Federal Trade Commission (FTC) has broad jurisdiction over a wide variety of entities and individuals operating in commerce. Prohibited practices include making deceptive claims about one's privacy procedures, including claims about the security provided for consumer information.

In addition to deception, the FTC Act prohibits unfair practices. Practices are unfair if they cause or are likely to cause consumers substantial injury that is neither reasonably avoidable by consumers nor offset by countervailing benefits to consumers or competition. The FTC has used this authority to challenge a variety of injurious practices, including a company's failure to provide reasonable and appropriate security for sensitive customer data. The FTC can obtain injunctive relief for violations of Section 5, as well as consumer redress.

The Driver's Privacy Protection Act

The Driver's Privacy Protection Act (DPPA) prohibits state motor vehicle departments from disclosing personal information in motor vehicle records, subject to fourteen permissible uses, including law enforcement, motor vehicle safety, and insurance.

THE HEALTH INFORMATION PORTABILITY AND ACCOUNTABILITY ACT ("HIPAA")

The Health Information Portability and Accountability Act ("HIPAA") and its implementing privacy rule prohibit the disclosure to third parties of a consumer's medical information without prior consent, subject to a number of exceptions, e.g., disclosure of patient records between entities for purposes of routine treatment, insurance, or payment.

Like the Safeguards Rule discussed above, the HIPAA Privacy Rule also requires entities under its jurisdiction to have in place "appropriate administrative, technical, and physical safeguards to protect the privacy of protected health information."

The Fair Credit Billing Act

The Fair Credit Billing Act (FCBA) establishes procedures for resolving billing errors on credit card accounts and limiting the consumer's liability for fraudulent credit card charges. The FCBA is important to the identity theft victim who discovers that an identity thief has obtained fraudulent credit cards accounts in the victim's name, or who has made unauthorized charges to the victim's credit account. Under the FCBA, the victim's credit cannot be harmed while the investigation is under way, nor does the victim have to make payments on any of the unauthorized bills.

The FCBA applies to "open end" credit accounts such as credit cards and revolving charge accounts, and covers (i) unauthorized charges, in which case federal law limits the consumer's responsibility to $50; (ii) charges that list the wrong date or amount; (iii) charges for goods and services you didn't accept or weren't delivered as agreed; (iv) math errors; (v) failure to post payments and other credits, such as returns; (vi) failure to send bills to the consumer's current address; and (vii) charges for which the consumer asked for an explanation or written proof of purchase along with a claimed error or request for clarification.

The consumer must notify the creditor as to the disputed item and the creditor must acknowledge the dispute within 30 days, and resolve it within two billing cycles. In the meantime, the consumer is entitled to withhold payment on the disputed amount and the creditor cannot take any legal action to collect the disputed amount during the investigation.

In addition, the creditor may not report the consumer's account as delinquent or otherwise harm the consumer's credit rating while the bill is in dispute. A consumer may be awarded damages resulting from a violation of the FCBA, plus twice the amount of any finance charge (not less than $100 or more than $1,000). The court may also order the creditor to pay attorney's fees and costs.

The text of the Fair Credit Billing Act is set forth at Appendix 12.

The Fair Debt Collection Practices Act

The Fair Debt Collection Practices Act (FDCPA) prohibits debt collectors from using unfair or deceptive practices to collect overdue bills that the creditor has forwarded for collection. The identity theft victim is often subjected to debt collection after the identity thief has obtained credit and other debts in the victim's name and failed to pay the bills. The FDCPA ensures that the victim is not subjected to debt collection harassment while trying to resolve all of the credit problems the identity theft has caused.

Under the FDCPA, "debtors" must be treated fairly and cannot be subjected to harassment techniques. The debt collector is permitted to contact the debtor in person, by mail, telephone or fax, however; the contact must not take place at an inconvenient time or place. If the debtor writes a letter to the debt collector advising them to stop all contact, the debt collector may not make further contact with the debtor except to notify the debtor of any further action that will be taken, e.g. the filing of a lawsuit to recover the debt.

If the debtor is represented by an attorney, the debt collector must contact the attorney and not the debtor. Thus, victims of identity theft involving fraudulent debts should give all debt collectors written notice of the fraud and advise them to direct all correspondence to their attorney, assuming they have hired legal representation to assist them in resolving the situation. In addition, a debt collector may not contact a consumer who advises them in writing, within 30 days after receiving written notice of the debt, that the consumer does not owe the alleged debt.

In any event, among other things, a debt collector cannot: (i) harass or abuse the consumer or any third party contacts; (ii) use threats of violence or harm; (iii) publish a list of consumers who refuse to pay their debts; (iv) use obscene or profane language; (v) repeatedly telephone the debtor; (vi) make false or misleading statements to the consumer in an effort to collect the debt; (vii) send the consumer imitation court documents; or (viii) engage in unfair practices, such as collecting amounts greater than the debt or depositing post-dated checks prematurely.

Debt collectors who violate the prohibitions contained in the FDCPA may be sued in state or federal court within one year from the date the law was violated. Victims of unfair debt collection practices should contact the Federal Trade Commission, the state Attorney General's Office, or their local consumer protection agency.

The text of the Fair Debt Collection Practices Act is set forth at Appendix 13.

The Electronic Fund Transfer Act

The Electronic Fund Transfer Act (EFTA) provides consumers protection for all transactions using a debit card or electronic means to debit or credit an account, and other electronic banking transactions that can result in the withdrawal of cash from the consumer's bank account. The EFTA also limits a consumer's liability for unauthorized electronic fund transfers.

Electronic funds transfer systems under the EFTA include:

1. Automated Teller Machines, commonly referred to as ATMs, which permit customers to access banking services 24 hours per day;

2. Pay-by-Phone services;

3. Direct Deposit and Automatic Payment services; and

4. Point of Sale Transfer systems, which permit a consumer to pay for goods and services by transferring funds simultaneously out of the

consumer's account and into the seller's account at the time of purchase.

Under the EFTA, procedures have been established for resolving errors on bank account statements, including: electronic fund transfers that the consumer did not make; electronic fund transfers that are incorrectly identified or show the wrong amount or date; computation or similar errors; the failure to properly reflect payments, credits, or electronic fund transfers; electronic fund transfers for which the consumer requests an explanation or documentation, because of a possible error.

Under the EFTA, if there is a mistake or unauthorized withdrawal from your bank account through the use of a debit card, or other electronic fund transfers, you must notify your financial institution of the problem or error not later than 60 days after the statement containing the problem or error was sent. Although most financial institutions have a toll-free number to report the problem, you should follow up in writing.

For retail purchases, your financial institution has up to 10 business days to investigate after receiving your notice of the error. The financial institution must tell you the results of its investigation within three business days of completing its investigation. The error must be corrected within one business day after determining the error has occurred. If the institution needs more time, it may take up to 90 days to complete the investigation, but only if it returns the money in dispute to the customer's account within 10 business days after receiving notice of the error.

Under the EFTA, there are three levels of liability that may be assessed against the consumer for unauthorized transfers.

1. If an unauthorized withdrawal is made from the consumer's account prior to the consumer being aware that his or her access card was lost or stolen, the consumer may be held liable for amounts withdrawn from the consumer's account prior to his or her notification to the financial institution, up to a maximum of Fifty ($50.00) Dollars.

2. If the consumer fails to notify the financial institution that his or her access card was lost or stolen within two business days of the consumer being aware of the loss, the consumer may be held liable for amounts withdrawn from the consumer's account prior to his or her notification to the financial institution, up to a maximum of Five Hundred ($500.00) Dollars.

3. If the consumer fails to report unauthorized transfers within 60 days of receiving a statement on which the unauthorized transfer appears, the consumer may have unlimited liability for amounts with-

drawn from the consumer's account prior to his or her notification to the financial institution. That means the consumer could lose all the money in their account and the unused portion of their maximum line of credit established for overdrafts. The rationale for this apparently harsh rule is that the consumer would have to be unduly negligent for failing to notify the financial institution within that time period.

Some financial institutions may voluntarily cap a consumer's liability at $50 for certain types of transactions, regardless of when they report the loss or theft. However, because this protection is offered voluntarily, the policies could change at any time. Thus, the consumer is advised to ask their financial institution about its liability limits.

The EFTA may not cover stored-value cards or transactions involving them, so the consumer may not be covered for loss or misuse of such a card. Thus, a consumer should inquire as to whether the issuer offers any protection in the case of a lost, stolen, misused, or malfunctioning card.

If a financial institution or merchant does not fulfill its responsibilities under the EFTA, the consumer may file a complaint to the federal agency that has enforcement jurisdiction over the company, as follows:

State Member Banks of the Federal Reserve System

File a complaint with the Consumer and Community Affairs Board of Governors of the Federal Reserve System, 20th & C Sts., N.W., Mail Stop 800, Washington, D.C. 20551.

National Banks

File a complaint with the Office of the Comptroller of the Currency, Compliance Management, Mail Stop 7-5, Washington, D.C. 20219.

Federal Credit Unions

File a complaint with the National Credit Union Administration, 1776 G St., N.W., Washington, D.C. 20456.

Non-Member Federally Insured Banks

File a complaint with the Office of Consumer Programs, Federal Deposit Insurance Corporation, 550 Seventeenth St., N.W., Washington, D.C. 20429.

Federally Insured Savings and Loans, and Federally Chartered State Banks

File a complaint with the Consumer Affairs Program, Office of Thrift Supervision, 1700 G St., N.W., Washington, D.C. 20552.

Other Credit, Debit, or ATM Card Issuers Including Retailers

As more fully set forth in Chapter 7 of this almanac, a complaint may be filed with the Federal Trade Commission (FTC) online (http://www.ftc.gov), or you can call toll-free the FTC toll-free at 1-877-FTC-HELP (1-877-382-4357).

The text of the Electronic Fund Transfer Act is set forth at Appendix 14.

Related Federal Offenses

Schemes to commit identity theft may also involve violations of other federal statutes, such as credit card fraud; tax fraud, computer fraud; mail fraud; wire fraud; financial institution fraud; or Social Security fraud. Each of these federal offenses is a felony and carries substantial penalties, such as prison sentences as high as 15 to 30 years, significant fines and criminal forfeiture. At least three sections of the U.S. Code address identity fraud.

Under section 1028, title 18 of the U.S. Code, it is a criminal offense to, among other things, knowingly possess with intent to use unlawfully, or transfer unlawfully, five or more identification documents or false identification documents. As used in this section, the term "identification document" is defined to mean a document (1) made or issued by or under the authority of the U.S. government, a state, a political subdivision of a state, or certain other governmental and quasi-governmental entities and (2) which, when completed with information concerning a particular individual, is of a type intended or commonly accepted for the purpose of identification.

Under section 1029, title 18 of the U.S. Code, it is a criminal offense to, among other things, knowingly and with intent to defraud, traffic in or use one or more unauthorized access devices, such as credit cards, during any 1-year period and by such conduct obtain anything of value aggregating $1,000 or more during that period.

Under section 408(a)(7), title 42 of the U.S. Code, a penalty for up to 5 years in prison, or a fine, or both, can result from, among other things, falsely representing—with intent to deceive—a number as the Social Security account number assigned by the Commissioner of Social Security to him or to another person.

The above is not an all-inclusive listing of U.S. Code sections relating to identity fraud. For example, other statutory provisions that could involve elements of identity fraud include 18 U.S.C. § 287 which governs false, fictitious or fraudulent claims; 18 U.S.C. § 1341 which governs mail frauds and swindles; 18 § U.S.C. 1342 which governs fictitious names or address; 18 § U.S.C. 1343 which governs fraud by wire, radio, or television; and 18 § U.S.C. 1344 which governs bank fraud.

The federal mail fraud statute (18 U.S.C. § 1341) prohibits the use or causing the use of the mails "for the purpose of executing" a scheme or artifice to defraud. This statute has been interpreted by the federal courts to be broad enough to cover the procurement of a credit card by misrepresentation in order to perpetrate a fraud, or to carry out a fraud through the use of a stolen or forged credit card, providing that the use of the mails was a significant step in the execution of the fraudulent scheme.

In addition, the Internal Revenue Service's Criminal Investigation Division, which investigates tax fraud cases, has reported that they intercept thousands of questionable refund schemes annually, many of which involve personal and business identity fraud. For example, one scheme involved the fraudulent use of the actual social security numbers of 1,000 students in order to file for tax refunds.

The reader is advised to contact the agency with jurisdiction over the particular type of fraud involved with the identity theft, e.g., the United States Postal Inspection Service for mail fraud, the Internal Revenue Service for tax fraud, and the United States Secret Service for bank fraud.

STATE LEGISLATION

A number of states have passed legislation making identity theft a crime. Other states are considering such legislation. In states where there are no specific identity theft statutes, other state laws may govern such fraudulent practices.

Most of the state statutes prohibiting identity theft contain similar provisions. For example, they generally criminalize the act of obtaining another's records or other personal information, without that person's authorization or consent, with the intent to defraud. The degree of the crime is usually measured by the dollar amount in financial loss to the victim.

For example, Alabama's statute provides that where the financial loss to the victim is greater than $250, the crime is identity theft in the first degree—a Class C felony. A number of state statutes exempt the use of obtaining the identity of another person to misrepresent one's age for the sole purpose of obtaining alcoholic beverages, tobacco or another privilege unavailable to minors.

The following states have passed legislation relating to identity theft: Alabama; Alaska; Arizona; Arkansas; California; Colorado; Connecticut; Delaware; Florida; Georgia; Hawaii; Idaho; Illinois; Indiana; Iowa; Kansas; Kentucky; Louisiana; Maine; Maryland; Massachusetts; Michigan; Minnesota; Mississippi; Missouri; Montana; Nevada; New Hampshire; New Jersey; New Mexico; North Carolina; North Dakota; Ohio; Oklahoma; Oregon; Pennsylvania; Rhode Island; South Carolina; South Dakota; Tennessee; Texas; Utah; Virginia; Washington; West Virginia; Wisconsin and Wyoming.

A Table of State Identity Theft Statutes is set forth at Appendix 15.

The reader is advised to contact their State Attorney General's office or local consumer protection agency to find out whether there are any other state laws that address identity theft.

A Directory of State Consumer Protection Agencies is set forth at Appendix 16.

In addition, while there is no federal statute which limits one's losses if their bank checks are stolen and forged, most states have laws which hold the bank responsible for losses from a forged check. However, it is important for the victim to notify the bank as soon as possible after the theft is discovered to avoid responsibility for the loss. Most states require consumers to take reasonable care of their accounts. It would not likely be deemed reasonable if the consumer does not discover the loss in a timely manner.

CHAPTER 7:
MINIMIZING YOUR RISKS

IN GENERAL

Although it may be impossible to completely prevent identity theft, you can minimize the risk by keeping careful track of your financial affairs and by cautiously guarding your personal information. When personal information is requested, ask how it is to be used and whether it will be shared with others. If possible, request that your information be kept confidential.

Do not give out personal information over the telephone, through the mail, or over the Internet unless you have initiated the contact, and you know who you are communicating with concerning the transaction. If you receive a telephone call or unsolicited mailing or Internet contact, do not reveal any personal information.

It is also important to be familiar with your billing cycles and follow up with creditors if statements are missing or late. Make sure that your billing address has not been changed without your knowledge. Make sure that the passwords you use for your credit cards and bank cards are not easily guessed, such as your date of birth or phone number, etc.

When shopping, try to take only those credit cards which you expect to use or need so as to minimize the amount of identification information available to potential thieves. Do not carry your social security card with you in your wallet or purse. If your wallet is lost or stolen, take immediate action to minimize the potential for theft of your personal information. Close your bank and credit card accounts immediately and open new accounts. Place a preliminary fraud alert on your credit profile.

You should also contact the Department of Motor Vehicles and any other institution that issued identification cards, and follow their procedures for replacing lost or stolen identification. Report the incident to your local police department. You must take immediate action because experienced identity thieves are aware that they have a limited time to run up your credit cards and misuse your identification, and they will act quickly.

Make sure your mail is safe by emptying your mailbox as soon as possible after delivery. Have the mail held at the post office when leaving for vacation. Often, companies will send mailings to consumers that request the consumer to return postcards, such as warranty cards, customer surveys, etc. These postcards often contain personal information. Instead of returning the postcard, it is wiser to enclose the postcard in an envelope so that any personal information is not sent through the mail, and exposed to potential identity thieves.

When discarding trash that contains personal information, such as credit card receipts, bank statements, insurance information, etc., make sure these items are sufficiently shredded so that a potential identity thief cannot read the information. Also, before you dispose of your old computer, delete all of your personal information. Deleting files will not remove the files from your computer's hard drive; therefore, it is advisable to use a program that will overwrite the entire hard drive so your personal information cannot be retrieved.

In addition, find out who maintains the personnel files at your place of employment and verify that the information is secure. You should also make the same inquiries with any other entities that maintain a personal file on your behalf, such as your medical provider and insurance carrier. Ask that you be notified any time your personal information is requested by a third party so you can verify that the request is being made for a legitimate purpose that was authorized by you.

PROTECT YOUR SOCIAL SECURITY NUMBER

The Social Security Administration is the only government agency authorized to issue Social Security numbers. An individual's Social Security number is a unique identifier of that person. This uniqueness, paired with the broad applicability of the Social Security number, have made it the identifier of choice for government agencies and private businesses. In addition, the growth in computer technology over the past decades has prompted private businesses and government agencies to rely on Social Security numbers as a way to accumulate and identify information for their databases.

Therefore, the Social Security number is the most sought after piece of personal identification by individuals seeking to create false identities. Law enforcement officials and others consider the proliferation of false identities to be one of the fastest growing crimes today. According to the Social Security Administration, identity crime accounts for over

80 percent of social security number misuse allegations according to the SSA.

You should be careful about sharing your number with anyone who asks for it, even when you are provided with a benefit or service. Identity thieves are often able to intercept one's social security number by stealing wallets, purses, and mail; through unsecured websites on the Internet; from business or personnel records at work or in the home; by sorting through trash; by posing as someone who legitimately needs this information; by buying personal information from inside sources, such as a store employee where you do your shopping.

Stolen and counterfeit social security numbers have been used to gain employment, obtain benefits and services, establish credit, and to commit crimes. Using another's social security number, identity thieves have applied for and/or received government benefits such as supplemental security income, disability insurance, worker's compensation benefits, unemployment benefits, and public assistance. This has caused significant losses to government programs, credit card companies, and banks, and has caused consumers considerable time and out-of pocket expenses trying to clear their name and resolve the problems arising from the theft.

There are a limited number of people who really require an individual's Social Security number for business purposes. For example, employers need an employee's social security number for wage and tax reporting purposes. Banks require a Social Security number in order to report taxable interest income. Many companies request an individual's Social Security number to perform credit checks before extending credit.

However, some businesses request an individual's Social Security number merely for recordkeeping purposes. For example, colleges often use a student's social security number as their student identification number. Some states use the Social Security number as a driver's license identification number. Some companies ask consumers for their Social Security number in connection with a purchase.

Thus, it may not be necessary to divulge your Social Security number to everyone who asks for it, although, in some instances, a company will decline providing you with a service you request if you refuse to give them your social security number. Knowing why the company wants your Social Security number will make it easier to decide whether or not to share this information. The Federal Trade Commission (FTC) advises consumers to ask the following questions if a company asks for a Social Security number:

1. Why do you need my Social Security number?

2. How will my Social Security number be used?

3. What law requires me to give you my Social Security number?

4. What will happen if I don't give you my Social Security number?

According to the Social Security Administration, providing one's social security number, even if asked, is entirely voluntary. It is preferable to request companies that use your Social Security number merely for recordkeeping purposes, to provide you with an alternate number so that your social security number is not being circulated and subjected to potential interception by an identity thief.

In those jurisdictions where the driver's Social Security number is printed on their license, the consumer should inquire as to whether an alternate number can be provided. This is particularly important because one's driver's license is often required as a means of identification in a number of circumstances, e.g., when paying for goods or services by check. Alternate identification numbers offer some degree of protection of this most important piece of personal information.

CHECK YOUR CREDIT REPORT ON A REGULAR BASIS

It is wise to review your credit report regularly. Your credit report includes information on where you live, how you pay your bills, and whether you've been sued, arrested, or filed for bankruptcy. Nationwide credit reporting agencies sell the information in your report to creditors, insurers, employers, and other businesses that use it to evaluate your applications for credit, insurance, employment, or renting a home.

Under the Fair Credit Reporting Act (FCRA), consumers are entitled to receive a free copy of their credit report from each of the three nationwide consumer reporting agencies once every 12 months. The three consumer reporting agencies are Equifax, Experian and TransUnion. You should review all three reports as it is not unusual for there to be conflicting information on the reports. Your credit reports should be reviewed carefully to make sure that they are accurate, up-to-date, and contain only authorized accounts.

You can order your free annual credit report by calling 1-877-322-8228, or online at: http://www.annualcreditreport.com. Alternatively, you can download and complete the Annual Credit Report Request form and mail it to:

Annual Credit Report Request Service
P.O. Box 105281
Atlanta, Georgia 30348-5281

When you order, you need to provide your name, address, Social Security number, and date of birth. To verify your identity, you may need to provide some information that only you would know, like the amount of your monthly mortgage payment.

A sample Annual Credit Report Request form is set forth at Appendix 17.

The FTC advises consumers who order their free annual credit reports online to be sure to correctly spell the website address, or link to it from the FTC's website to avoid being misdirected to other websites that offer supposedly free reports, but only with the purchase of other products.

If you find errors in your report, or if you need to order a copy more than once during a 12-month period, you should contact the credit reporting agency directly. In order to order your credit reports, following is the contact information for the three major credit-reporting agencies:

EQUIFAX

> P.O. Box 740241
> Atlanta, GA 30374-0241
> Tel: 800-685-1111
> Website: http://www.equifax.com

EXPERIAN

To order a copy of your report:

> P.O. Box 2104
> Allen, TX 75013
> Tel: 888-EXPERIAN (888-397-3742)
> Website: http://www.experian.com

TRANSUNION

To order a copy of your report:

> P.O. Box 1000
> Chester, PA 19022
> Tel: 800-916-8800
> Website: http://www.transunion.com

Active Duty Military Personnel

If you are an active duty member of the military, amendments to the Fair Credit Reporting Act now allow you to place an "active duty alert" in your credit profile if you are stationed away from your usual duty station. This will help minimize the risk of identity theft while you are deployed.

According to the Federal Trade Commission, the active duty alert requires creditors to verify your identity before granting credit in your name. The business may try to contact you directly, but if you're on deployment, that may be impossible. As a result, the law allows you to use a personal representative to place or remove an alert. If your contact information changes before your alert expires, remember to update it.

An active duty alert is in effect on your report for one year unless you request the alert be removed sooner. If your deployment lasts longer than one year, you can place another alert on your credit report. In addition, an active duty alert will remove you from the credit reporting agency's marketing list for pre-screened credit card offers for two years. Prescreened offers—also referred to as "preapproved" offers—are based on information in your credit report that indicates you meet certain criteria set by the offeror.

To place an active duty alert in your credit profile, or to have it removed, call the toll-free fraud number of one of the three nationwide credit reporting agencies, as set forth above. The agency will require you to provide appropriate proof of your identity, which may include your Social Security number, your name, address, and other personal information. You only need to contact one of the agencies, which will in turn inform the other two agencies concerning the alert.

CREDIT CARD REGISTRATION SERVICES

Many companies, including credit card companies, offer a registration service for credit cards. For a fee, the company will notify all of your creditors in case your credit cards are lost or stolen. It is generally the consumer's responsibility to prepare a list of their credit cards and account numbers and submit them to the credit card registration service. If your credit cards are lost or stolen, instead of having to contact each individual creditor, the consumer makes one phone call to the registration service.

CHAPTER 8:
RESOLVING YOUR IDENTITY THEFT PROBLEMS

IN GENERAL

Victims of identity theft are often devastated by the personal nature of the crime and the amount of trouble it takes to resolve the problems resulting from the fraud. Identity theft victims are often forced to spend a considerable amount of time and expense repairing the damage done to their credit profile.

In addition, depending on the scope and nature of the identity theft, the victim may unjustly face arrest and detention, loss of employment, wage garnishment, driver's license revocation, all due to the illegal and fraudulent activities of the identity thief.

TAKING ACTION

If you suspect that your personal information has been stolen and used in order to commit fraud, it is important to take immediate action. You can expect to engage in numerous conversations with a variety of people, including customer service representatives, bank personnel, fraud investigators, government agencies, law enforcement agencies, etc.

It is advisable to keep a notebook with details of all of your contacts, including the dates, names, and substance of the conversations. It is virtually impossible to keep track of all of these contacts without a written record, which may prove helpful in resolving your unfortunate situation.

Identity theft may take many forms. However, in almost every identity theft case, there are basic steps the victim should take, as set forth below.

CREDIT REPORTING AGENCIES

According to one major credit reporting agency, identity theft accounts for many of the inquiries made to the agency's Fraud Department. The agency categorizes these identity theft inquiries as follows:

1. True Person Fraud—True person fraud involves incidents whereby someone assumes a "true" person's identity and applies for credit using that identity.

2. Account Takeover Fraud—Account takeover fraud involves the fraudulent access to an existing account.

3. Precautionary Inquiries—This category involves consumers who contacted the agency due to their concern over the growing problem of identity theft and sought information on minimizing their risk of being victimized.

If you are the victim of identity theft, it is important to contact the fraud department of each of the three major credit reporting agencies as soon as possible and request them to place a "fraud alert" in your file, as well as a victim's statement asking that creditors call you before opening any new accounts or changing information on existing accounts. This can help prevent an identity thief from opening additional accounts in your name.

A Sample Notification Letter to a Credit Reporting Agency is set forth at Appendix 18.

As set forth in Chapter 7, credit reporting agencies are required to give the consumer a free copy of their report annually, upon request. You are also entitled to a free copy of your credit report if it is inaccurate due to fraudulent activity.

Review your credit reports carefully to make sure no additional fraudulent accounts have been opened in your name or unauthorized changes made to your existing accounts. Also, check the "inquiries" section of the report. If any inquiries listed are from companies who opened fraudulent accounts, request that these inquiries be removed from your report.

After you have advised the credit reporting agencies of the fraud, and they have completed their investigation, order new copies of your reports to verify your corrections and changes have been made, and to make sure no new fraudulent activity has occurred.

Under normal circumstances, you should review your credit reports annually, however, victims of identity theft are advised to review their credit profile every 3 months for at least the first year following the identity theft.

Following is the contact information for the fraud departments of each of the three major credit reporting agencies:

EQUIFAX

Fraud Department
P.O. Box 740241
Atlanta, GA 30374-0241
Tel: 800-525-6285/TDD: 800-255-0056
Website: http://www.equifax.com

EXPERIAN

Fraud Department
P.O. Box 9532
Allen, TX 75013
Tel: 888-EXPERIAN (397-3742)/TDD: 800-972-0322
Website: http://www.experian.com

TRANSUNION

Fraud Department
P.O. Box 6790
Fullerton, CA 92634-6790
Tel: 800-680-7289/TDD: 877-553-7803
Website: http://www.transunion.com

CREDIT CARD ISSUERS

If you are the victim of identity theft, it is likely that the thief either used your existing accounts to run up credit card charges in your name, and/or opened new fraudulent credit card accounts. If your credit card is stolen, and you report the theft before any charges are incurred, you are not responsible. If your card is used before you report it missing, in most states, the most you will owe for unauthorized charges is $50. This is true even if a thief is able to use your credit card at an automated teller machine (ATM) to access your credit card account.

If your card is stolen, to minimize your liability, report the theft as soon as possible. Contact the fraud department of each credit card issuer for any accounts that have been tampered with or opened fraudulently. Some companies have toll-free numbers printed on their statements and 24-hour service to accept such emergency information. Note the name of the person you spoke with, and the date, time and substance of each conversation.

For your own protection, you should follow up your phone call with a letter to the credit card issuer. The letter should provide your credit card number, the date when you noticed your credit card was stolen, or that fraudulent accounts were opened in your name, and the date you reported the problem. This is particularly important because the consumer protection procedure for resolving errors on credit card billing statements requires that any **disputes** be in writing.

A Sample Notification Letter to a Credit Card Issuer is set forth at Appendix 19.

UNITED STATES POSTAL SERVICE

If the identity thief has stolen your mail for fraudulent purposes, e.g., to get new credit cards, bank and credit card statements, pre-screened credit offers or tax information, or if the identity thief has falsified change-of-address forms in order to divert billing statements, it should be reported to your local U.S. Postal Service Inspection Division immediately. You can find contact information for your local office by contacting the U.S. Postal Inspection Service by visiting the U.S. Postal Inspection Service's website (http://www.ups.gov/websites/depart/inspect/), and entering your city/state or zip code in the website's office locator. You can also file a report electronically on the website. All information submitted through the website is transmitted via a secure server.

If you prefer, you can mail your report and any correspondence to the following address:

U.S. Postal Inspection Service
Criminal Investigations Service Center
Attn: Mail Fraud
222 S. Riverside Plaza, Suite 1250
Chicago, Illinois 60606-6100

A sample U.S. Postal Service Mail Theft and Vandalism Complaint Form is set forth at Appendix 20.

BANKS

If the identity thief has tampered with your bank accounts, ATM card, or checks, close the accounts immediately and advise the appropriate bank authorities. Cancel all ATM cards and have new cards issued with new passwords that are not easily identifiable. You can contact the following major check verification companies to learn more about the services they provide in helping you track your stolen or misused checks.

SCAN: 1-800-262-7771
TeleCheck: 1-800-710-9898 or 1-800-927-0188
Certigy, Inc.: 1-800-437-5120
CrossCheck: 1-707-586-0431
International Check Services: 1-800-526-5380

INVESTMENT BROKER

If you believe that an identity thief has tampered with your securities investments or a brokerage account, immediately report the incident to your broker or account manager and to the Securities and Exchange Commission (SEC). You can also file a financial privacy complaint with the SEC if you believe your investment company has allowed someone to gain unauthorized access to your personal financial information, has improperly shared this information, or has failed to establish adequate safeguards to protect your personal financial information from unauthorized electronic access.

You can file a report electronically on the SEC website (http://www.sec.gov/complaint.shtml/). You should include as much information as possible regarding your complaint. All information submitted through the website is transmitted via a secure server.

If you prefer, you can mail or fax your complaint and any correspondence to the following address:

SEC Complaint Center
100 F Street N.E.
Washington, D.C. 20549-0213
Tel: 202-942-7040
Fax: 202-772-99295

UTILITIES/TELEPHONE SERVICE PROVIDER

If an identity thief has established a utility or telephone account in your name; is using your calling card number, or is making unauthorized calls that seem to come from—and are billed to—your cellular phone, you should contact your service provider and immediately cancel the account and open a new account.

If a service provider is reluctant to remove fraudulent charges from your account, you may need to contact the office that governs their operations. For a local service provider, contact your state Public Utility Commission. For a long-distance telephone or cellular service provider, contact the Federal Communications Commission (FCC). You can also file a complaint against your provider electronically on the FCC website (http://www.fcc.gov/cgb/complaints_general.html/).

If you prefer, you can mail your complaint and any correspondence to the following address:

Federal Communications Commission
445 12th Street S.W.
Washington, D.C. 20554
Tel: 1-888-CALL-FCC (1-888-225-5322)
Fax: 1-866-418-0232

If you mail your complaint, you should include the following information:

1. your name, address and the telephone numbers involved with your complaint;

2. a telephone number where you can be reached during business hours;

3. specific information about your complaint, including the name of the company involved with your complaint;

4. the names and telephone numbers of any company representatives that you contacted, the dates of contact, and the substance of any conversations;

5. a copy of the bill containing the charges you claim are fraudulent;

6. any additional information that will support your complaint; and

7. the resolution you are seeking, e.g., removal of the charges and any associated penalties or fees.

A sample FCC Complaint Form is set forth at Appendix 21.

SOCIAL SECURITY ADMINISTRATION

Your Social Security number and records are confidential. The Social Security Administration does not give your number to anyone, except when authorized by law. However, as set forth in Chapter 7, a social security number is one of the most sought after pieces of identification by identity thieves.

The use of your Social Security number by someone else to obtain credit, loans, telephone accounts, or other goods and services should be reported immediately to the Federal Trade Commission (FTC), as discussed more fully below.

If you think someone is using your number for employment purposes, you should contact the Social Security Administration. One way to find out whether someone is using your number in order to work is to check your Social Security Earnings Statement. The Earnings Statement lists earnings posted to your Social Security record. If you find an error on your Statement, contact the Social Security Administration immediately.

You can contact the Social Security Administration's general number at 1-800-772-1213 for information on verifying the accuracy of the earnings reported on your social security number, and to request a copy of your Social Security Earnings Statement.

If someone has used your Social Security number to obtain credit, the Social Security Administration cannot fix your credit record. To fix your credit record, you must call the creditors who approved the credit, file a police report, and contact the fraud departments at the three major credit reporting agencies, as set forth above. However, if you are having difficulty resolving all of the problems associated with the theft, the Social Security Administration, upon request, may assign you a new Social Security number.

Nevertheless, you should weigh this option carefully. Although it may appear that obtaining a new Social Security number will clear your name and permit you to establish a whole new credit profile, this is not always the case. In fact, a new Social Security number may actually cause more problems than it solves.

For example, a new credit profile will not show any credit history and may make it more difficult for you to obtain credit until you have built up an entirely new credit history. In addition, the credit reporting agencies may not create a new credit profile for you, but may simply compare personal information and combine the new Social Security number with the old file. This will only cause more confusion.

In any event, the Social Security Administration will not assign a new Social Security number to you if:

1. you filed for bankruptcy;

2. you intend to avoid the law or your legal responsibility;

3. you intend to avoid disclosure of a negative credit history or criminal record;

4. despite the theft of your Social Security number, there is no evidence that your number is being misused and causing you any harm that would necessitate a new number.

The Office of the Inspector General

According to the Social Security Administration's Office of the Inspector General, investigations relating to Social Security numbers fall into various categories that usually involve identity fraud. The largest such category involves program fraud, which almost always involves identity fraud. Other investigations entailing identity fraud involve counterfeiting social security cards; trafficking in counterfeit social security cards; trafficking in and selling social security number information; and trafficking in legitimate social security cards.

The Social Security Administration has been working to safeguard individual Social Security numbers. The Identity Theft and Assumption Deterrence Act provides some recourse in this area. As discussed in Chapter 6, under the Act, there are criminal penalties for any person who "knowingly transfers or uses another's 'means of identification' with the intent to commit, or to aid or abet, any unlawful activity . . . " Among other information, the Act specifically includes the Social Security number as one of the "means of identification" covered under the Act.

You can report social security fraud to:

> The Social Security Administration Fraud Hotline
> P.O. Box 17768
> Baltimore, MD 21235
> Tel: 1-800-269-0271
> Fax: 410-597-0118
> Email: oig.hotline@ssa.gov
> Website: http://www.ssa.gov

THE DEPARTMENT OF MOTOR VEHICLES

If you suspect that your name or Social Security number is being used by an identity thief to obtain a driver's license or a non-driver's identification card, contact your state Department of Motor Vehicles. If your state uses your Social Security number as your driver's license number, ask to substitute another identification number in its place. Request a copy of your driver's license record for review. Ask that a fraud alert be placed in your record.

IDENTITY THEFT TO AVOID CRIMINAL PROSECUTION

As set forth in Chapter 1, an identity thief may create a criminal record in your name, e.g., by using your name and/or identification if arrested. In order to clear your name, you should first contact the law enforcement agency that initiated the arrest and explain that your identity was used by the actual perpetrator. Have the law enforcement agency confirm your identity, e.g. through personal identification documents, fingerprints, photographs, etc., and then compare your information to the arrest and booking information of the actual perpetrator.

Once it has been established that your identity was misused, request the law enforcement agency to amend all arrest-related documents and records that contain your identity, and substitute the identity of the perpetrator, if known. They should also provide you with some type of documentation or certification establishing your innocence and cancel any warrants that may be outstanding in your name.

Based on the investigation of the law enforcement agency, the appropriate court should also issue an order establishing your innocence and amending any court records which incorrectly identify you as the defendant. If the law enforcement agency delays in investigating your claim, you should proceed directly to court to establish your innocence. The court will review all of the evidence provided, either by you or by the law enforcement agency, and make its determination of your innocence accordingly. You should keep a copy of the court's determination in case you encounter any related problems in the future, e.g. denial of employment, etc.

You will likely have to sign an affidavit that you did not give anyone the authority to use your name or personal identification, and that you agree to prosecute the offender. If the identity thief is caught, you may be asked to testify in court.

A problem may arise if the law enforcement agency does not believe that an identity thief is responsible for the original arrest, particularly if there were no fingerprints or photos taken, as is the case with traffic violations and some misdemeanors. If you encounter this type of resistance to your allegations of impersonation, it would be prudent to engage a criminal defense attorney to protect your rights while trying to clear your name.

In addition to the court and law enforcement agency records, there are other information gathering services that are in the business of compiling criminal histories and selling that information to potential employers, insurers, etc. It is important to find out which investigative agencies may have compiled erroneous information about you, and provide them with copies of the documentation establishing your innocence so that they can amend their databases.

THE FEDERAL TRADE COMMISSION

The Federal Trade Commission (FTC) serves as a federal clearinghouse for complaints by victims of identity theft. Although the FTC does not have the authority to bring criminal cases, their mission is to help victims of identity theft by providing them with information to help resolve the financial and other problems that can result from identity theft.

Consumers can obtain further information, by calling the FTC's toll-free hotline at 1-877-ID THEFT (1-877-438-4338)/TDD: 1-866-653-4261; by mail in care of The Identity Theft Clearinghouse, Federal Trade Commission, 600 Pennsylvania Avenue, NW, Washington, DC 20580; or electronically at http://www.consumer.gov/idtheft.

Consumer Sentinel

When an individual contacts the FTC with an Internet, telemarketing, identity theft or other fraud-related complaint, the FTC enters the information into Consumer Sentinel, the FTC's secure, online database. The Consumer Sentinel database is available to more than 1000 law enforcement agencies in the United States, Australia and Canada.

The database helps them build cases and detect trends in consumer fraud and identity theft. Consumer Sentinel gives law enforcement access to over one million complaints, including consumer complaints from numerous Better Business Bureaus and the National Fraud Information Center.

Victim complaints may also be referred to the appropriate government agencies and private organizations. The victim has the option of submitting their information anonymously, however, without contact information, law enforcement and other entities will not be able to speak with the victim to obtain additional information to assist in an identity theft investigation and prosecution.

According to the Federal Trade Commission, from January 1, 2005 through December 31, 2005, there were 686,683 complaints filed alleging identity theft and identity fraud.

A list of U.S. Agency and Office members of Consumer Sentinel is set forth at Appendix 22.

Consumer Sentinel maintains a website (http://www.consumer.gov/sentinel/) where the public is able to access helpful information, including the latest fraud trends and statistics, specific scams, and how to recognize and avoid identity theft. Consumers who visit the Consumer Sentinel website are able to obtain the following types of information:

1. the scams that garner the most frequent consumer complaints;

2. the scams that cost consumers most;

3. The location of companies complained about, by state and by province;

4. the number of identity theft complaints, by state; and

5. the types of identity theft most frequently reported.

In addition to the statistics about consumer fraud and identity theft, consumers can use the new site to find out whether their local law enforcement agencies are members of Consumer Sentinel, file a complaint about consumer fraud or identity theft, and learn what organizations contribute consumer data to the database.

THE ID THEFT AFFIDAVIT

The ID Theft Affidavit is a form developed by the FTC for victims of identity theft to complete and send to any company where a fraudulent account was opened in the victim's name by the identity thief. The ID Theft Affidavit simplifies the process of notifying companies by using one standard form.

A copy of the FTC ID Theft Affidavit and Instructions for completing the form are set forth at Appendix 23.

A number of organizations endorse the ID Theft Affidavit and, upon receipt, will investigate the fraud allegation on behalf of the consumer.

A list of organizations which accept and endorse the ID Theft Affidavit is set forth at Appendix 24.

PRIOR RELATIONSHIP WITH IDENTITY THIEF

A number of identity theft cases involve family members, friends, former spouses, co-workers or other individuals with whom the victim had a prior relationship. In such cases, particularly involving a family member, the victim is reluctant to contact law enforcement authorities because they do not want to see their relative arrested and prosecuted for the crime. However, the victim still wants to clear his or her name and reclaim their good reputation and credit rating.

The closer the relationship, the more difficult it is to report the offender to law enforcement authorities. However, without a police report, it may be very difficult to get the creditors to believe that an account is fraudulent. Many individuals make phony claims of identity theft simply to get out of debt. In order to protect themselves from unsubstantiated financial losses, the creditors have to sort through these claims and determine which claims are legitimate. Without a police report, the legitimacy of the claim is called into question.

If the identity thief agrees to take over the account, he or she should sign a letter acknowledging that they opened the account without authorization and agree to take over the payments. This letter should be provided to the creditor with a demand that the account be taken out of your name.

A sample letter from the identity thief to the creditor acknowledging responsibility for the fraudulent account is set forth at Appendix 25.

Because the creditor's concern is stopping losses, they may agree to this arrangement. However, if the identity thief does not have the money to pay the debt, the creditor may seek to keep the account in the victim's name. The victim should not agree to this.

If the identity thief will not acknowledge the fraudulent account, the creditor may determine that the account is not fraudulent. Although the creditor may not force the victim to file a police report against a family member, the victim may have no other recourse but to file a police report if they want the account removed from their credit profile, and do not want to be liable for the account balance.

In order to protect their own interest, the creditor may file their own police report if the victim refuses to file a report. In addition, if the creditor is particularly adamant about keeping the victim's name on the fraudulent account, the victim may have no choice but to hire an attorney to intervene on their behalf.

ASSISTING IN THE INVESTIGATION

Due to the nature of the identity theft crime, law enforcement resources available to investigate the rapidly growing number of identity theft cases are limited. In a world where murder, rape, robbery and assault take center stage in the courtroom, identity theft is not viewed as a priority. Therefore, the victim is often left to bear much of the responsibility of proving their innocence and resolving the damage done to their credit report and reputation. In many instances, the identity theft victim has to literally conduct their own investigation and hand the case over to law enforcement before they will act on the complaint.

Where fraudulent applications for credit cards, utility services, and bank accounts are concerned, the victim should request copies of the fraudulent credit applications from the companies. The victim may be able to determine the identity of the thief from the information listed on the application, thus making the investigation move along more swiftly. However, the victim is advised not to contact the suspected identity thief directly but to allow law enforcement to handle the situation.

Some companies will voluntarily agree to surrender this information to the victim. Other companies are reluctant to provide the documentation. Some states have enacted legislation requiring companies to surrender the documentation to the victim. The reader is advised to check the law of his or her jurisdiction to determine whether such legislation has been enacted.

Once the fraudulent documentation is obtained, the victim should review the documents carefully. Turn the evidence over to the law enforcement agency handling the complaint. If information contained in the documents places suspicion on someone known to the victim, the law enforcement agency should be advised of the perpetrator's identity. Law enforcement authorities may obtain a search warrant to search the suspect's home, which may lead to further evidence, followed by prosecution and conviction.

In addition to the fraudulent documentation, the victim should also maintain in their file a copy of the initial police report and any other updates to this report as the case works its way through the system and other law enforcement agencies become involved, e.g. Secret Service, Postal Inspection Service, etc. Also keep copies of any court documents generated as a result of the case.

All of the documentation you gather during your investigation should be kept in a safe place. You should also maintain copies of any documentation turned over to law enforcement agencies in case their copies are lost or misplaced, as well as copies of all correspondence sent and received in connection with the case.

It is also important to keep a journal of all of the activities related to the investigation, including the names, addresses, telephone and fax numbers, and date and summary of all conversations with contacts at law enforcement agencies, credit card companies, banks, etc. Insofar as a victim may seek restitution from the court, it is also important to keep receipts for all out-of-pocket costs associated with the identity theft and your efforts to clear your name.

Reasonable costs may include lost wages, telephone and fax expenses, copying costs, postage, notary fees, etc. The victim may even be able to recover the costs of therapy if the victim suffered emotional distress requiring counseling. Recent studies indicate that the emotional impact of identity theft has been found to parallel that of victims of violent crime, particularly in the context of criminal identity theft, where the victim was arrested or detained as a result of criminal activity having been committed by the identity thief in the name of the victim.

CHAPTER 9:
IDENTITY THEFT RISKS FOR BUSINESSES

IN GENERAL

In the ordinary course of doing business, most companies maintain personal information about employees, customers, business partners, etc. This information may include names and addresses, Social Security numbers, account numbers, banking information, and other identifying information that could result in identity theft. According to the Federal Trade Commission (FTC), all businesses should make sure they are in compliance with all of the federal and state laws concerning the maintenance and disposal of personal information.

THE SAFEGUARDS RULE

Pursuant to the Gramm-Leach-Bliley (GLB) Act, financial institutions are required to ensure the security and confidentiality of all personal information collected from their customers, including names and addresses, phone numbers, bank and credit card account numbers, income and credit histories, and Social Security numbers. This is known as the Safeguards Rule.

The Safeguards Rule requires companies to develop a written information security plan that describes their program to protect customer information. The plan must be appropriate to the company's size and complexity, the nature and scope of its activities, and the sensitivity of the customer information it handles.

As part of the security plan, each company must:

1. designate one or more employees to coordinate its information security program;

2. identify and assess the risks to customer information in each relevant area of the company's operation and evaluate the effectiveness of the current safeguards for controlling these risks;

3. design and implement a safeguards program, and regularly monitor and test it; and

4. select service providers that can maintain appropriate safeguards.

Implementing Safeguards

One of the first steps a company should take is to determine what information they are collecting and storing; whether they have a business need to maintain the information; and if not, to keep only what is needed. A company can further reduce the risks to its customer's information if it implements the following safeguards:

1. know where sensitive customer information is stored, and store it securely, preferably in a locked room, in an area protected from destruction or physical hazards;

2. make sure only authorized employees have access to customer information;

3. when customer information is stored on a server or other computer, ensure that the computer is accessible only with a "strong" password—i.e., a password that is not easily decoded;

4. where possible, avoid storing sensitive customer data on a computer with an Internet connection;

5. maintain secure backup records and keep archived data secure by storing it offline;

6. maintain a careful inventory of the company's computers and any other equipment on which customer information may be stored;

7. if you collect information online directly from customers, make sure secure transmission is automatic; and

8. dispose of customer information in a secure way and, where applicable, consistent with the FTC's Disposal Rule, as further discussed below.

Monitoring Employee Access to Customer Information

The success of any information security plan depends largely on the employees who implement it. Thus, the company should consider:

1. checking references or doing background checks before hiring employees who will have access to customer information;

2. asking every new employee to sign an agreement to follow the company's confidentiality and security standards for handling customer information;

3. limiting access to customer information to employees who have a business reason to see it;

4. controlling access to sensitive information by requiring employees to use strong passwords that must be changed on a regular basis;

5. using password-activated screen savers to lock employee computers after a period of inactivity;

6. developing policies for appropriate use and protection of laptops, PDAs, cell phones, or other mobile devices;

7. training employees to take basic steps to maintain the security, confidentiality, and integrity of customer information;

8. regularly reminding all employees of the company's policy—and the legal requirement—to keep customer information secure and confidential;

9. imposing disciplinary measures for security policy violations; and

10. preventing terminated employees from accessing customer information by immediately deactivating their passwords and user names, and taking other appropriate measures.

The company should also require all employees who use their personal computers to store or access customer information to use protections against viruses, spyware, and other unauthorized intrusions

DEALING WITH A BREACH

If, despite the company's best efforts, a data breach occurs, and information has been lost or stolen that could negatively impact the person whose information you maintained, you must immediately contact your local law enforcement agency. It is important to assess the potential risk for identity theft resulting from the breach as soon as possible. If your local police are not familiar with investigating information compromises, contact the local office of the FBI or the U.S. Secret Service. For incidents involving mail theft, contact the U.S. Postal Inspection Service. If necessary, hire trained security professionals to help assess the breach.

In addition, following a data breach, you should secure any information that has or may have been compromised. For example, if a computer connected to the Internet is compromised, disconnect the computer from the Internet. Also, preserve and review files or programs that may reveal how the breach occurred.

Early notification to customers whose personal information has been compromised allows them to take steps to mitigate the misuse of their information. In deciding if notification is warranted, consider: (i) the nature of the compromise; (ii) the type of information taken; (iii) the likelihood of misuse; and (iv) the potential damage arising from misuse. For example, thieves who have stolen names and Social Security numbers can use this information to cause significant damage to a victim's credit record. Individuals who are notified early can take some steps to prevent or limit any harm.

When notifying individuals, the FTC recommends that you: (i) consult with your law enforcement contact about the timing of the notification so it does not interfere with their investigation; (ii) designate a contact person within your organization for releasing information and give the contact person the latest information about the breach, your response, and how individuals should respond; (iii) consider using letters, websites, and toll-free numbers as methods of communication with those whose information may have been compromised.

Your notice should describe everything you know about the information compromise including: (i) how it happened; (ii) what information was taken; (iii) how the thieves have used the information, if known; and (iv) what actions you have taken already to remedy the situation. Explain how to reach the contact person in your organization. You should also explain possible actions the individual can take, such as contacting credit reporting agencies and placing a fraud alert on their credit profile, and filing a complaint with the FTC.

A model Notification of Data Breach is set forth at Appendix 26.

THE DISPOSAL RULE

On June 1, 2005, the Disposal Rule was established in order to reduce the risk of identity theft and protect the privacy of consumer information. The Disposal Rule is enforced by the Federal Trade Commission (FTC). Under the Rule, those who use consumer reports are required to properly dispose of all information contained in those reports in a manner designed to protect the information from unauthorized access or use.

The Rule does not spell out any particular manner in which the information must be disposed, but allows the business to decide the most "reasonable and appropriate" manner of disposal, taking into consideration the sensitivity of the information involved. For example, shredding may be considered a reasonable method of disposal provided it renders the information incapable of being read or reconstructed.

The Disposal Rule applies to any person or organization that uses consumer reports, including but not limited to:

1. consumer reporting companies;

2. lenders;

3. insurers;

4. employers;

5. landlords;

6. government agencies;

7. mortgage brokers;

8. automobile dealers;

9. attorneys or private investigators;

10. debt collectors;

11. individuals who obtain a credit report on prospective nannies, contractors, or tenants;

12. entities that maintain information in consumer reports as part of their role as service providers to other organizations covered by the Rule.

For purposes of the Rule, The Fair Credit Reporting Act defines the term "consumer report" as information obtained from a consumer reporting company that is used—or expected to be used—in establishing a consumer's eligibility for credit, employment, or insurance, among other purposes. Credit reports and credit scores are considered consumer reports. In addition, reports containing information relating to employment background, check-writing history, insurance claims, residential or tenant history, and medical history are also considered consumer reports subject to the Disposal Rule.

APPENDIX 1:
TRENDS IN IDENTITY THEFT
COMPLAINTS BY AGE
[JANUARY 1, 2005 – DECEMBER 31, 2005]

CONSUMER'S AGE	PERCENTAGE
65 and over	6%
60-64	3%
50-59	13%
40-49	20%
30-39	24%
18-29	29%
Under 18	5%

Source: Federal Trade Commission

APPENDIX 2:
IDENTITY THEFT VICTIMS, BY STATE
(JANUARY 1, 2005 – DECEMBER 31, 2005)

RANK	VICTIM STATE	VICTIMS PER 100,000	NUMBER OF VICTIMS
1	Arizona	156.9	9,320
2	Nevada	130.2	3,144
3	California	125	45,175
4	Texas	116.5	26,624
5	Colorado	97.2	4,535
6	Florida	95.8	17,048
7	Washington	92.4	5,810
8	New York	90.3	17,387
9	Georgia	87.3	7,918
10	Illinois	87.3	11,137
11	Maryland	86.6	4,848
12	New Mexico	84.7	1,634
13	Oregon	81.7	2,973
14	New Jersey	75.5	6,582
15	Michigan	70.5	7,139
16	Delaware	69.1	583
17	Virginia	68.2	5,163
18	Oklahoma	67.7	2,403
19	Missouri	67.6	3,920
20	Utah	67.5	1,668

RANK	VICTIM STATE	VICTIMS PER 100,000	NUMBER OF VICTIMS
21	North Carolina	67.1	5,830
22	Indiana	67.0	4,201
23	Connecticut	65.9	2,3113
24	Pennsylvania	63.6	7,908
25	Hawaii	63.5	810
26	Alaska	63.4	421
27	Louisiana	62.6	2,831
28	Massachusetts	62.5	3,999
29	Ohio	62.4	7,155
30	Minnesota	58.7	3,015
31	Alabama	58.7	2,675
32	Kansas	58.5	1,606
33	Arkansas	58.2	1,617
34	Rhode Island	58.2	626
35	Tennessee	57.2	3,412
36	South Carolina	56.8	2,416
37	Nebraska	52.3	919
38	Idaho	52.1	745
39	Wisconsin	50.3	2,782
40	Mississippi	49.9	1,458
41	New Hampshire	49.2	645
42	Wyoming	44.0	224
43	Kentucky	43.5	1,815
44	Montana	42.5	398
45	West Virginia	37.3	677
46	Maine	37.2	491
47	Iowa	36.7	1,090
48	Vermont	32.3	201
49	South Dakota	30.0	233
50	North Dakota	24.8	158

Source: Federal Trade Commission.

APPENDIX 3:
TOTAL NUMBER OF INTERNET-RELATED FRAUD COMPLAINTS AND AMOUNTS PAID (2003 – 2005)

YEAR	TOTAL NUMBER OF COMPLAINTS	COMPLAINTS REPORTING AMOUNT PAID	PERCENTAGE OF COMPLAINTS REPORTING AMOUNT PAID	AMOUNT PAID REPORTED	AVERAGE AMOUNT PAID	MEDIAN AMOUNT PAID
2003	176,754	158,534	90%	$205,550,456	$1,297	$1990
2004	210,727	188,675	90%	$271,305,849	$1,438	$215
2005	196,503	160,115	81%	$336,164,255	$2,100	$345

Source: Consumer Sentinel

APPENDIX 4:
TOTAL NUMBER OF INTERNET-RELATED
FRAUD COMPLAINTS BY CONSUMER AGE
(2003 – 2005)

CONSUMER AGE RANGE	2003	2004	2005
19 and Under	4,244	6,325	5,498
20-29	27,822	42,222	39,984
30-39	32,159	45,223	39,725
40-49	30,344	42,162	37,463
50-59	19,121	27,576	25,752
60-69	5,832	8,969	8,418
70 and Over	1,683	2,597	2,573
TOTAL	121,205	175,074	159,413

Source: Consumer Sentinel

APPENDIX 5:
THE CHILDREN'S ONLINE PRIVACY
PROTECTION ACT (COPPA)

SEC. 1301. SHORT TITLE.

This title may be cited as the "Children's Online Privacy Protection Act of 1998".

SEC. 1302. DEFINITIONS.

In this title:

(1) CHILD.—The term "child" means an individual under the age of 13.

(2) OPERATOR.—The term "operator"—

(A) means any person who operates a website located on the Internet or an online service and who collects or maintains personal information from or about the users of or visitors to such website or online service, or on whose behalf such information is collected or maintained, where such website or online service is operated for commercial purposes, including any person offering products or services for sale through that website or online service, involving commerce—

(i) among the several States or with 1 or more foreign nations;

(ii) in any territory of the United States or in the District of Columbia, or between any such territory and—

(I) another such territory; or

(II) any State or foreign nation; or

(iii) between the District of Columbia and any State, territory, or foreign nation; but

(B) does not include any nonprofit entity that would otherwise be exempt from coverage under section 5 of the Federal Trade Commission Act (15 U.S.C. 45).

(3) COMMISSION.—The term "Commission" means the Federal Trade Commission.

(4) DISCLOSURE.—The term "disclosure" means, with respect to personal information—

(A) the release of personal information collected from a child in identifiable form by an operator for any purpose, except where such information is provided to a person other than the operator who provides support for the internal operations of the website and does not disclose or use that information for any other purpose; and

(B) making personal information collected from a child by a website or online service directed to children or with actual knowledge that such information was collected from a child, publicly available in identifiable form, by any means including by a public posting, through the Internet, or through—

(i) a home page of a website;

(ii) a pen pal service;

(iii) an electronic mail service;

(iv) a message board; or

(v) a chat room.

(5) FEDERAL AGENCY.—The term "Federal agency" means an agency, as that term is defined in section 551(1) of title 5, United States Code.

(6) INTERNET.—The term "Internet" means collectively the myriad of computer and telecommunications facilities, including equipment and operating software, which comprise the interconnected world-wide network of networks that employ the Transmission Control Protocol/ Internet Protocol, or any predecessor or successor protocols to such protocol, to communicate information of all kinds by wire or radio.

(7) PARENT.—The term "parent" includes a legal guardian.

(8) PERSONAL INFORMATION.—The term "personal information" means individually identifiable information about an individual collected online, including—

(A) a first and last name;

(B) a home or other physical address including street name and name of a city or town;

(C) an e-mail address;

(D) a telephone number;

(E) a Social Security number;

(F) any other identifier that the Commission determines permits the physical or online contacting of a specific individual; or

(G) information concerning the child or the parents of that child that the website collects online from the child and combines with an identifier described in this paragraph.

(9) VERIFIABLE PARENTAL CONSENT.—The term "verifiable parental consent" means any reasonable effort (taking into consideration available technology), including a request for authorization for future collection, use, and disclosure described in the notice, to ensure that a parent of a child receives notice of the operator's personal information collection, use, and disclosure practices, and authorizes the collection, use, and disclosure, as applicable, of personal information and the subsequent use of that information before that information is collected from that child.

(10) WEBSITE OR ONLINE SERVICE DIRECTED TO CHILDREN.—

(A) IN GENERAL.—The term "website or online service directed to children" means—

(i) a commercial website or online service that is targeted to children; or

(ii) that portion of a commercial website or online service that is targeted to children.

(B) LIMITATION.—A commercial website or online service, or a portion of a commercial website or online service, shall not be deemed directed to children solely for referring or linking to a commercial website or online service directed to children by using information location tools, including a directory, index, reference, pointer, or hypertext link.

(11) PERSON.—The term "person" means any individual, partnership, corporation, trust, estate, cooperative, association, or other entity.

(12) ONLINE CONTACT INFORMATION.—The term "online contact information" means an e-mail address or an-other substantially similar identifier that permits direct contact with a person online.

SEC. 1303. REGULATION OF UNFAIR AND DECEPTIVE ACTS AND PRACTICES IN CONNECTION WITH THE COLLECTION AND USE OF PERSONAL INFORMATION FROM AND ABOUT CHILDREN ON THE INTERNET.

(a) ACTS PROHIBITED.—

(1) IN GENERAL.—It is unlawful for an operator of a website or online service directed to children, or any operator that has actual knowledge that it is collecting personal information from a child, to collect personal information from a child in a manner that violates the regulations prescribed under subsection (b).

(2) DISCLOSURE TO PARENT PROTECTED.—Notwithstanding paragraph (1), neither an operator of such a website or online service nor the operator's agent shall be held to be liable under any Federal or State law for any disclosure made in good faith and following reasonable procedures in responding to a request for disclosure of personal information under subsection (b)(1)(B)(iii) to the parent of a child.

(b) REGULATIONS.—

(1) IN GENERAL.—Not later than 1 year after the date of the enactment of this Act, the Commission shall promulgate under section 553 of title 5, United States Code, regulations that—

(A) require the operator of any website or online service directed to children that collects personal information from children or the operator of a website or online service that has actual knowledge that it is collecting personal information from a child—

(i) to provide notice on the website of what information is collected from children by the operator, how the operator uses such information, and the operator's disclosure practices for such information; and

(ii) to obtain verifiable parental consent for the collection, use, or disclosure of personal information from children;

(B) require the operator to provide, upon request of a parent under this subparagraph whose child has provided personal information to that website or online service, upon proper identification of that parent, to such parent—

(i) a description of the specific types of personal information collected from the child by that operator;

(ii) the opportunity at any time to refuse to permit the operator's further use or maintenance in retrievable form, or future online collection, of personal information from that child; and

(iii) notwithstanding any other provision of law, a means that is reasonable under the circumstances for the parent to obtain any personal information collected from that child;

(C) prohibit conditioning a child's participation in a game, the offering of a prize, or another activity on the child disclosing more personal information than is reasonably necessary to participate in such activity; and

(D) require the operator of such a website or online service to establish and maintain reasonable procedures to protect the confidentiality, security, and integrity of personal information collected from children.

(2) WHEN CONSENT NOT REQUIRED.—The regulations shall provide that verifiable parental consent under paragraph (1)(A)(ii) is not required in the case of—

(A) online contact information collected from a child that is used only to respond directly on a one-time basis to a specific request from the child and is not used to recontact the child and is not maintained in retrievable form by the operator;

(B) a request for the name or online contact information of a parent or child that is used for the sole purpose of obtaining parental consent or providing notice under this section and where such information is not maintained in retrievable form by the operator if parental consent is not obtained after a reasonable time;

(C) online contact information collected from a child that is used only to respond more than once directly to a specific request from the child and is not used to recontact the child beyond the scope of that request—

(i) if, before any additional response after the initial response to the child, the operator uses reasonable efforts to provide a parent notice of the online contact information collected from the child, the purposes for which it is to be used, and an opportunity for the parent to request that the operator make no further use of the information and that it not be maintained in retrievable form; or

(ii) without notice to the parent in such circumstances as the Commission may determine are appropriate, taking into consideration the benefits to the child of access to information and services, and risks to the security and privacy of the child, in regulations promulgated under this subsection;

(D) the name of the child and online contact information (to the extent reasonably necessary to protect the safety of a child participant on the site)—

(i) used only for the purpose of protecting such safety;

(ii) not used to recontact the child or for any other purpose; and

(iii) not disclosed on the site, if the operator uses reasonable efforts to provide a parent notice of the name and online contact information collected from the child, the purposes for which it is to be used, and an opportunity for the parent to request that the operator make no further use of the information and that it not be maintained in retrievable form; or

(E) the collection, use, or dissemination of such information by the operator of such a website or online service necessary—

(i) to protect the security or integrity of its website;

(ii) to take precautions against liability;

(iii) to respond to judicial process; or

(iv) to the extent permitted under other provisions of law, to provide information to law enforcement agencies or for an investigation on a matter related to public safety.

(3) TERMINATION OF SERVICE.—The regulations shall permit the operator of a website or an online service to terminate service provided to a child whose parent has refused, under the regulations prescribed under paragraph (1)(B)(ii), to permit the operator's further use or maintenance in retrievable form, or future online collection, of personal information from that child.

(c) ENFORCEMENT.—Subject to sections 1304 and 1306, a violation of a regulation prescribed under subsection (a) shall be treated as a violation of a rule defining an unfair or deceptive act or practice prescribed under section 18(a)(1)(B) of the Federal Trade Commission Act (15 U.S.C. 57a(a)(1)(B)).

(d) INCONSISTENT STATE LAW.—No State or local government may impose any liability for commercial activities or actions by operators in interstate or foreign commerce in connection with an activity or action described in this title that is inconsistent with the treatment of those activities or actions under this section.

SEC. 1304. SAFE HARBORS.

(a) GUIDELINES.—An operator may satisfy the requirements of regulations issued under section 1303(b) by following a set of self-regulatory guidelines, issued by representatives of the marketing or online indus-tries, or by other persons, approved under subsection (b).

(b) INCENTIVES.—

(1) SELF-REGULATORY INCENTIVES.—In prescribing regulations under section 1303, the Commission shall provide incentives for self-regulation by operators to implement the protections afforded children under the regulatory requirements described in subsection (b) of that section.

(2) DEEMED COMPLIANCE.—Such incentives shall include provi-sions for ensuring that a person will be deemed to be in compliance with the requirements of the regulations under section 1303 if that person complies with guidelines that, after notice and comment, are approved by the Commission upon making a determination that the guidelines meet the requirements of the regulations issued under section 1303.

(3) EXPEDITED RESPONSE TO REQUESTS.—The Commission shall act upon requests for safe harbor treatment within 180 days of the filing of the request, and shall set forth in writing its conclusions with regard to such requests.

(c) APPEALS.—Final action by the Commission on a request for ap-proval of guidelines, or the failure to act within 180 days on a request for approval of guidelines, submitted under subsection (b) may be ap-pealed to a district court of the United States of appropriate jurisdic-tion as provided for in section 706 of title 5, United States Code.

SEC. 1305. ACTIONS BY STATES.

(a) IN GENERAL.—

(1) CIVIL ACTIONS.—In any case in which the attorney general of a State has reason to believe that an interest of the residents of that State has been or is threatened or adversely affected by the engage-ment of any person in a practice that violates any regulation of the Commission prescribed under section 1303(b), the State, as parens patriae, may bring a civil action on behalf of the residents of the State in a district court of the United States of appropriate jurisdiction to—

(A) enjoin that practice;

(B) enforce compliance with the regulation;

(C) obtain damage, restitution, or other compensation on behalf of residents of the State; or

(D) obtain such other relief as the court may consider to be appropriate.

(2) NOTICE.—

(A) IN GENERAL.—Before filing an action under paragraph (1), the attorney general of the State involved shall provide to the Commission—

(i) written notice of that action; and

(ii) a copy of the complaint for that action.

(B) EXEMPTION.—

(i) IN GENERAL.—Subparagraph (A) shall not apply with respect to the filing of an action by an attorney general of a State under this subsection, if the attorney general determines that it is not feasible to provide the notice described in that subparagraph before the filing of the action.

(ii) NOTIFICATION.—In an action described in clause (i), the attorney general of a State shall provide notice and a copy of the complaint to the Commission at the same time as the attorney general files the action.

(b) INTERVENTION.—

(1) IN GENERAL.—On receiving notice under subsection (a)(2), the Commission shall have the right to intervene in the action that is the subject of the notice.

(2) EFFECT OF INTERVENTION.—If the Commission intervenes in an action under subsection (a), it shall have the right—

(A) to be heard with respect to any matter that arises in that action; and

(B) to file a petition for appeal.

(3) AMICUS CURIAE.—Upon application to the court, a person whose self-regulatory guidelines have been approved by the Commission and are relied upon as a defense by any defendant to a proceeding under this section may file amicus curiae in that proceeding.

(c) CONSTRUCTION.—For purposes of bringing any civil action under subsection (a), nothing in this title shall be construed to prevent an attorney general of a State from exercising the powers conferred on the attorney general by the laws of that State to—

(1) conduct investigations;

(2) administer oaths or affirmations; or

(3) compel the attendance of witnesses or the production of documentary and other evidence.

(d) ACTIONS BY THE COMMISSION.—In any case in which an action is instituted by or on behalf of the Commission for violation of any regulation prescribed under section 1303, no State may, during the pendency of that action, institute an action under subsection (a) against any defendant named in the complaint in that action for violation of that regulation.

(e) VENUE; SERVICE OF PROCESS.—

(1) VENUE.—Any action brought under subsection (a) may be brought in the district court of the United States that meets applicable requirements relating to venue under section 1391 of title 28, United States Code.

(2) SERVICE OF PROCESS.—In an action brought under subsection (a), process may be served in any district in which the defendant—

(A) is an inhabitant; or

(B) may be found.

SEC. 1306. ADMINISTRATION AND APPLICABILITY OF ACT.

(a) IN GENERAL.—Except as otherwise provided, this title shall be enforced by the Commission under the Federal Trade Commission Act (15 U.S.C. 41 et seq.).

(b) PROVISIONS.—Compliance with the requirements imposed under this title shall be enforced under—

(1) section 8 of the Federal Deposit Insurance Act (12 U.S.C. 1818), in the case of—

(A) national banks, and Federal branches and Federal agencies of foreign banks, by the Office of the Comptroller of the Currency;

(B) member banks of the Federal Reserve System (other than national banks), branches and agencies of foreign banks (other than Federal branches, Federal agencies, and insured State branches of foreign banks), commercial lending companies owned or controlled by foreign banks, and organizations operating under section 25 or 25(a) of the Federal Reserve Act (12 U.S.C. 601 et seq. and 611 et seq.), by the Board; and

(C) banks insured by the Federal Deposit Insurance Corporation (other than members of the Federal Reserve System) and insured

State branches of foreign banks, by the Board of Directors of the Federal Deposit Insurance Corporation;

(2) section 8 of the Federal Deposit Insurance Act (12 U.S.C. 1818), by the Director of the Office of Thrift Supervision, in the case of a savings association the deposits of which are insured by the Federal Deposit Insurance Corporation;

(3) the Federal Credit Union Act (12 U.S.C. 1751 et seq.) by the National Credit Union Administration Board with respect to any Federal credit union;

(4) part A of subtitle VII of title 49, United States Code, by the Secretary of Transportation with respect to any air carrier or foreign air carrier subject to that part;

(5) the Packers and Stockyards Act, 1921 (7 U.S.C. 181 et seq.) (except as provided in section 406 of that Act (7 U.S.C. 226, 227)), by the Secretary of Agriculture with respect to any activities subject to that Act; and

(6) the Farm Credit Act of 1971 (12 U.S.C. 2001 et seq.) by the Farm Credit Administration with respect to any Federal land bank, Federal land bank association, Federal intermediate credit bank, or production credit association.

(c) EXERCISE OF CERTAIN POWERS.—For the purpose of the exercise by any agency referred to in subsection (a) of its powers under any Act referred to in that subsection, a violation of any requirement imposed under this title shall be deemed to be a violation of a requirement imposed under that Act. In addition to its powers under any provision of law specifically referred to in subsection (a), each of the agencies referred to in that subsection may exercise, for the purpose of enforcing compliance with any requirement imposed under this title, any other authority conferred on it by law.

(d) ACTIONS BY THE COMMISSION.—The Commission shall prevent any person from violating a rule of the Commission under section 1303 in the same manner, by the same means, and with the same jurisdiction, powers, and duties as though all applicable terms and provisions of the Federal Trade Commission Act (15 U.S.C. 41 et seq.) were incorporated into and made a part of this title. Any entity that violates such rule shall be subject to the penalties and entitled to the privileges and immunities provided in the Federal Trade Commission Act in the same manner, by the same means, and with the same jurisdiction, power, and duties as though all applicable terms and provisions of the Federal Trade Commission Act were incorporated into and made a part of this title.

(e) EFFECT ON OTHER LAWS.—Nothing contained in the Act shall be construed to limit the authority of the Commission under any other provisions of law.

SEC. 1307. REVIEW.

Not later than 5 years after the effective date of the regulations initially issued under section 1303, the Commission shall—

(1) review the implementation of this title, including the effect of the implementation of this title on practices relating to the collection and disclosure of information relating to children, children's ability to obtain access to information of their choice online, and on the availability of websites directed to children; and

(2) prepare and submit to Congress a report on the results of the review under paragraph (1).

SEC. 1308. EFFECTIVE DATE.

Sections 1303(a), 1305, and 1306 of this title take effect on the later of—

(1) the date that is 18 months after the date of enactment of this Act; or

(2) the date on which the Commission rules on the first application filed for safe harbor treatment under section 1304 if the Commission does not rule on the first such application within one year after the date of enactment of this Act, but in no case later than the date that is 30 months after the date of enactment of this Act.

APPENDIX 6
SAMPLE PRIVACY POLICY OUTLINE

SECTION 1. IDENTITY OF THE WEBSITE ADMINISTRATORS

1. This is the website of [Company Name].

2. Our postal address is [Address].

3. We can be reached via e-mail at [e-mail address].

4. We can be reached by telephone at [telephone number].

SECTION 2. FOR EACH VISITOR TO OUR WEB PAGE, OUR WEB SERVER AUTOMATICALLY RECOGNIZES: (CHOOSE ONE)

1. The consumer's domain name and e-mail address (where possible);

2. Only the consumer's domain name, but not the e-mail address (where possible);

3. No information regarding the domain or e-mail address; or

4. Other [please explain].

SECTION 3. WE COLLECT: (CHOOSE ALL THAT APPLY)

1. Only the domain name, but not the e-mail address of visitors to our web page;

2. The domain name and e-mail address (where possible) of visitors to our web page;

3. The e-mail addresses of those who post messages to our bulletin board;

4. The e-mail addresses of those who communicate with us via e-mail;

5. The e-mail addresses of those who make postings to our chat areas;

6. Aggregate information on what pages consumers access or visit;

7. User-specific information on what pages consumers access or visit;

8. Information volunteered by the consumer, such as survey information and/or website registrations;

9. No information on consumers who browse our web page; and/or

10. Other [please explain].

SECTION 4. THE INFORMATION WE COLLECT IS: (CHOOSE ALL THAT APPLY)

1. Used for internal review and is then discarded;

2. Used to improve the content of our web page;

3. Used to customize the content and/or layout of our page for each individual visitor;

4. Used to notify visitors about updates to our website;

5. Used by us to contact consumers for marketing purposes;

6. Shared with other reputable organizations to help them contact consumers for marketing purposes;

7. Not shared with other organizations for commercial purposes; and/or

8. Other [please explain].

SECTION 5. WITH RESPECT TO COOKIES:

1. We do not set any cookies; or

2. We use cookies to: (choose all that apply)

(a) Store visitor preferences;

(b) Record session information, such as items that consumers add to their shopping cart;

(c) Record user-specific information on what pages users access or visit;

(d) Alert visitors to new areas that we think might be of interest to them when they return to our website;

(e) Record past activity at a website in order to provide better service when visitors return to our website;

(f) Ensure that visitors are not repeatedly sent the same banner ads;

(g) Customize Web page content on visitors' browser type or other information that the visitor sends; and/or

(h) Other [please explain].

SECTION 6. IF YOU DO NOT WANT TO RECEIVE E-MAIL FROM US IN THE FUTURE, PLEASE TELL US THAT YOU DO NOT WANT TO RECEIVE E-MAIL FROM OUR COMPANY AND PLEASE LET US KNOW BY: (CHOOSE ALL THAT APPLY)

1. Sending us an e-mail at the above address;

2. Calling us at the above telephone number;

3. Writing to us at the above address;

4. Visiting the following URL; and/or

5. Other [please explain].

SECTION 7. FROM TIME TO TIME, WE MAKE THE E-MAIL ADDRESSES OF THOSE WHO ACCESS OUR WEBSITE AVAILABLE TO OTHER REPUTABLE ORGANIZATIONS WHOSE PRODUCTS OR SERVICES WE THINK YOU MIGHT FIND INTERESTING. IF YOU DO NOT WANT US TO SHARE YOUR E-MAIL ADDRESS WITH OTHER COMPANIES OR ORGANIZATIONS, PLEASE TELL US THAT YOU DO NOT WANT US TO SHARE YOUR E-MAIL ADDRESS WITH OTHER COMPANIES, AND LET US KNOW BY: (CHOOSE ALL THAT APPLY)

1. Sending us an e-mail at the above address;

2. Calling us at the above telephone number;

3. Writing to us at the above address;

4. Visiting the following URL; and/or

5. Other [please explain].

SECTION 8. FROM TIME TO TIME, WE MAKE OUR CUSTOMER E-MAIL LIST AVAILABLE TO OTHER REPUTABLE ORGANIZATIONS WHOSE PRODUCTS OR SERVICES WE THINK YOU MIGHT FIND INTERESTING. IF YOU DO NOT WANT US TO SHARE YOUR E-MAIL ADDRESS WITH OTHER COMPANIES OR ORGANIZATIONS, PLEASE LET US KNOW BY: (CHOOSE ALL THAT APPLY)

1. Sending us an e-mail at the above address;

2. Calling us at the above telephone number;

3. Writing to us at the above address;

4. Visiting the following URL; and/or

5. Other (please explain).

SECTION 9. IF YOU SUPPLY US WITH YOUR POSTAL ADDRESS ONLINE: (CHOOSE EITHER OPTION 1 OR A COMBINATION OF OPTIONS 2 AND 3)

1. You will only receive the information for which you provided us your address;

2. You may receive periodic mailings from us with information on new products and services or upcoming events. If you do not wish to receive such mailings, please let us know by: (choose all that apply)

   (a) Sending us an e-mail at the above address;

   (b) Calling us at the above telephone number;

   (c) Writing to us at the above address;

   (d) Visiting the following URL; and/or

   (e) Other (please explain).

3. You may receive mailings from other reputable companies. You can, however, have your name put on our do-not-share list by: (choose all that apply)

   (a) Sending us an e-mail at the above address;

   (b) Calling us at the above telephone number;

   (c) Writing to us at the above address;

   (d) Visiting the following URL; and/or

   (e) Other (please explain).

Please provide us with your exact name and address. We will be sure your name is removed from the list we share with other organizations.

SECTION 10. PERSONS WHO SUPPLY US WITH THEIR TELEPHONE NUMBERS ON-LINE: (CHOOSE ALL THAT APPLY)

1. Will only receive telephone contact from us with information regarding orders they have placed online; and/or

2. May receive telephone contact from us with information regarding new products and services or upcoming events. If you do not wish to receive such telephone calls, please let us know by: (choose all that apply)

   (a) Sending us an e-mail at the above address;

   (b) Calling us at the above telephone number;

(c) Writing to us at the above address;

(d) Visiting the following URL; and/or

(e) Other (please explain)

3. May receive telephone contact from other reputable companies. You can, however, have your name put on our do-not-share list by: (choose all that apply)

(a) Sending us an e-mail at the above address;

(b) Calling us at the above telephone number;

(c) Writing to us at the above address;

(d) Visiting the following URL; and/or

(e) Other (please explain).

Please provide us with your name and phone number. We will be sure your name is removed from the list we share with other organizations.

SECTION 11. AD SERVERS: (CHOOSE ONE)

1. We do not partner with or have special relationships with any ad server companies; or

2. To try and bring you offers that are of interest to you, we have relationships with other companies that we allow to place ads on our web pages. As a result of your visit to our website, ad server companies may collect information such as your domain type, your IP address, and click stream information. For further information, consult the privacy policies of:

[List the URLs for the privacy statements of the ad server companies with whom you have contracted or partnered].

SECTION 12. FROM TIME TO TIME, WE MAY USE CUSTOMER INFORMATION FOR NEW, UNANTICIPATED USES NOT PREVIOUSLY DISCLOSED IN OUR PRIVACY NOTICE. IF OUR INFORMATION PRACTICES CHANGE AT SOME TIME IN THE FUTURE: (CHOOSE ALL THAT APPLY)

1. We will contact you before we use your data for these new purposes to notify you of the policy change and to provide you with the ability to opt out of these new uses;

2. We will post the policy changes to our website to notify you of these changes and provide you with the ability to opt out of these new uses. If you are concerned about how your information is used, you should check back at our website periodically;

3. We will use for these new purposes only data collected from the time of the policy change forward;

4. Customers may prevent their information from being used for purposes other than those for which it was originally collected by:

    (a) Sending us an e-mail at the above address;

    (b) Calling us at the above telephone number;

    (c) Writing to us at the above address;

    (c) Visiting the following URL; or

    (d) Other (please explain).

SECTION 13. UPON REQUEST WE PROVIDE WEBSITE VISITORS WITH ACCESS TO: (CHOOSE ALL THAT APPLY)

1. All information [including proprietary information] that we maintain about them;

2. Financial information (e.g., credit card account information) that we maintain about them;

3. Unique identifier information (e.g., customer number or password) that we maintain about them;

4. Transaction information (e.g., dates on which customers made purchases, amounts and types of purchases) that we maintain about them;

5. Communications that the consumer/visitor has directed to our website (e.g., e-mails, customer inquiries);

6. Contact information (e.g., name, address, phone number) that we maintain about them;

7. A description of information that we maintain about them;

8. No information that we have collected and that we maintain about them.

Consumers can access this information by (choose all that apply)

1. Sending us an e-mail at the above address;

2. Calling us at the above telephone number;

3. Writing to us at the above address;

4. Visiting the following URL; and/or

5. Other (please explain).

SECTION 14. UPON REQUEST WE OFFER VISITORS:

1. No ability to have factual inaccuracies corrected in information that we maintain about them; or

2. The ability to have inaccuracies corrected in: (choose all that apply)

(a) Contact information;

(b) Financial information;

(c) Unique identifiers;

(d) Transaction information;

(e) Communications that the consumer/visitor has directed to the website; and/or

(f) All information that we maintain.

Consumers can have this information corrected by: (choose all that apply)

1. Sending us an e-mail at the above address;

2. Calling us at the above telephone number;

3. Writing to us at the above address;

4. Visiting the following URL; and/or

5. Other (please explain).

SECTION 15. SECURITY: (CHOOSE ALL THAT APPLY)

1. We always use industry-standard encryption technologies when transferring and receiving consumer data exchanged with our website. When we transfer and receive certain types of sensitive information such as financial or health information, we redirect visitors to a secure server and will notify visitors through a pop-up screen on our website;

2. We have appropriate security measures in place in our physical facilities to protect against the loss, misuse, or alteration of information that we have collected from you at our website; and/or

3. Other (please explain).

SECTION 16. ENFORCEMENT:

If you feel that this website is not following its stated information policy, you may contact

1. [Company Name] at the above address or phone number;

2. The DMA's Committee on Ethical Business Practices;

3. State or local chapters of the Better Business Bureau;

4. State or local consumer protection office;

5. The Federal Trade Commission by telephone at: 202-FTC-HELP (202-382-4357); or electronically at http://www.ftc.gov/to/romap2.htm; and/or

6. Other [please explain].

Source: The Direct Marketing Association.

APPENDIX 7:
THE IDENTITY THEFT AND ASSUMPTION DETERRENCE ACT

§ 001. SHORT TITLE.

This Act may be cited as the "Identity Theft and Assumption Deterrence Act of 1998".

§ 002. CONSTITUTIONAL AUTHORITY TO ENACT THIS LEGISLATION.

The constitutional authority upon which this Act rests is the power of Congress to regulate commerce with foreign nations and among the several States, and the authority to make all laws which shall be necessary and proper for carrying into execution the powers vested by the Constitution in the Government of the United States or in any department or officer thereof, as set forth in article I, section 8 of the United States Constitution.

§ 003. IDENTITY THEFT.

(a) Establishment of Offense.—Section 1028(a) of title 18, United States Code, is amended—

(1) in paragraph (5), by striking "or" at the end;

(2) in paragraph (6), by adding "or" at the end;

(3) in the flush matter following paragraph (6), by striking "or attempts to do so,"; and

(4) by inserting after paragraph (6) the following:

"(7) knowingly transfers or uses, without lawful authority, a means of identification of another person with the intent to commit, or to aid or abet, any unlawful activity that constitutes a violation of Federal law, or that constitutes a felony under any applicable State or local law;".

(b) Penalties.—Section 1028(b) of title 18, United States Code, is amended—

    (1) in paragraph (1)—

        (A) in subparagraph (B), by striking "or" at the end;

        (B) in subparagraph (C), by adding "or" at the end; and

        (C) by adding at the end the following:

        "(D) an offense under paragraph (7) of such subsection that involves the transfer or use of 1 or more means of identification if, as a result of the offense, any individual committing the offense obtains anything of value aggregating $1,000 or more during any 1-year period;";

    (2) in paragraph (2)—

        (A) in subparagraph (A), by striking "or transfer of an identification document or" and inserting ", transfer, or use of a means of identification, an identification document, or a"; and

        (B) in subparagraph (B), by inserting "or (7)" after "(3)";

    (3) by amending paragraph (3) to read as follows:

        "(3) a fine under this title or imprisonment for not more than 20 years, or both, if the offense is committed—

        "(A) to facilitate a drug trafficking crime (as defined in section 929(a)(2));

        "(B) in connection with a crime of violence (as defined in section 924(c)(3)); or

        "(C) after a prior conviction under this section becomes final;";

    (4) in paragraph (4), by striking "and" at the end;

    (5) by redesignating paragraph (5) as paragraph (6); and

    (6) by inserting after paragraph (4) the following:

        "(5) in the case of any offense under subsection (a), forfeiture to the United States of any personal property used or intended to be used to commit the offense; and".

(c) Circumstances.—Section 1028(c) of title 18, United States Code, is amended by striking paragraph (3) and inserting the following:

    "(3) either—

"(A) the production, transfer, possession, or use prohibited by this section is in or affects interstate or foreign commerce; or

"(B) the means of identification, identification document, false identification document, or document- making implement is transported in the mail in the course of the production, transfer, possession, or use prohibited by this section.".

(d) Definitions.—Subsection (d) of section 1028 of title 18, United States Code, is amended to read as follows:

"(d) In this section—

"(1) the term 'document-making implement' means any implement, impression, electronic device, or computer hardware or software, that is specifically configured or primarily used for making an identification document, a false identification document, or another document-making implement;

"(2) the term 'identification document' means a document made or issued by or under the authority of the United States Government, a State, political subdivision of a State, a foreign government, political subdivision of a foreign government, an international governmental or an international quasi-governmental organization which, when completed with information concerning a particular individual, is of a type intended or commonly accepted for the purpose of identification of individuals;

"(3) the term 'means of identification' means any name or number that may be used, alone or in conjunction with any other information, to identify a specific individual, including any—

"(A) name, social security number, date of birth, official State or government issued driver's license or identification number, alien registration number, government passport number, employer or taxpayer identification number;

"(B) unique biometric data, such as fingerprint, voice print, retina or iris image, or other unique physical representation;

"(C) unique electronic identification number, address, or routing code; or

"(D) telecommunication identifying information or access device (as defined in section 1029(e));

"(4) the term 'personal identification card' means an identification document issued by a State or local government solely for the purpose of identification;

"(5) the term 'produce' includes alter, authenticate, or assemble; and

"(6) the term 'State' includes any State of the United States, the District of Columbia, the Commonwealth of Puerto Rico, and any other commonwealth, possession, or territory of the United States.".

(e) Attempt and Conspiracy.—Section 1028 of title 18, United States Code, is amended by adding at the end the following:

"(f) Attempt and Conspiracy.—Any person who attempts or conspires to commit any offense under this section shall be subject to the same penalties as those prescribed for the offense, the commission of which was the object of the attempt or conspiracy.".

(f) Forfeiture Procedures.—Section 1028 of title 18, United States Code, is amended by adding at the end the following:

"(g) Forfeiture Procedures.—The forfeiture of property under this section, including any seizure and disposition of the property and any related judicial or administrative proceeding, shall be governed by the provisions of section 413 (other than subsection (d) of that section) of the Comprehensive Drug Abuse Prevention and Control Act of 1970 (21 U.S.C. 853).".

(g) Rule of Construction.—Section 1028 of title 18, United States Code, is amended by adding at the end the following:

"(h) Rule of Construction.—For purpose of subsection (a)(7), a single identification document or false identification document that contains 1 or more means of identification shall be construed to be 1 means of identification.".

(h) Conforming Amendments.—Chapter 47 of title 18, United States Code, is amended—

(1) in the heading for section 1028, by adding "and information" at the end; and

(2) in the table of sections at the beginning of the chapter, in the item relating to section 1028, by adding "and information" at the end.

§ 004. AMENDMENT OF FEDERAL SENTENCING GUIDELINES FOR OFFENSES UNDER SECTION 1028.

(a) In General.—Pursuant to its authority under section 994(p) of title 28, United States Code, the United States Sentencing Commission shall review and amend the Federal sentencing guidelines and the policy statements of the Commission, as appropriate, to provide an appropriate penalty for each offense under section 1028 of title 18, United States Code, as amended by this Act.

(b) Factors for Consideration.—In carrying out subsection (a), the United States Sentencing Commission shall consider, with respect to each offense described in subsection (a)—

(1) the extent to which the number of victims (as defined in section 3663A(a) of title 18, United States Code) involved in the offense, including harm to reputation, inconvenience, and other difficulties resulting from the offense, is an adequate measure for establishing penalties under the Federal sentencing guidelines;

(2) the number of means of identification, identification documents, or false identification documents (as those terms are defined in section 1028(d) of title 18, United States Code, as amended by this Act) involved in the offense, is an adequate measure for establishing penalties under the Federal sentencing guidelines;

(3) the extent to which the value of the loss to any individual caused by the offense is an adequate measure for establishing penalties under the Federal sentencing guidelines;

(4) the range of conduct covered by the offense;

(5) the extent to which sentencing enhancements within the Federal sentencing guidelines and the court's authority to sentence above the applicable guideline range are adequate to ensure punishment at or near the maximum penalty for the most egregious conduct covered by the offense;

(6) the extent to which Federal sentencing guidelines sentences for the offense have been constrained by statutory maximum penalties;

(7) the extent to which Federal sentencing guidelines for the offense adequately achieve the purposes of sentencing set forth in section 3553(a)(2) of title 18, United States Code; and

(8) any other factor that the United States Sentencing Commission considers to be appropriate.

§ 005. CENTRALIZED COMPLAINT AND CONSUMER EDUCATION SERVICE FOR VICTIMS OF IDENTITY THEFT.

(a) In General.—Not later than 1 year after the date of enactment of this Act, the Federal Trade Commission shall establish procedures to—

(1) log and acknowledge the receipt of complaints by individuals who certify that they have a reasonable belief that 1 or more of their means of identification (as defined in section 1028 of title 18, United

States Code, as amended by this Act) have been assumed, stolen, or otherwise unlawfully acquired in violation of section 1028 of title 18, United States Code, as amended by this Act;

(2) provide informational materials to individuals described in paragraph (1); and

(3) refer complaints described in paragraph (1) to appropriate entities, which may include referral to—

(A) the 3 major national consumer reporting agencies; and

(B) appropriate law enforcement agencies for potential law enforcement action.

(b) Authorization of Appropriations.—There are authorized to be appropriated such sums as may be necessary to carry out this section.

§ 006. TECHNICAL AMENDMENTS TO TITLE 18, UNITED STATES CODE.

(a) Technical Correction Relating to Criminal Forfeiture Procedures.—Section 982(b)(1) of title 18, United States Code, is amended to read as follows:

"(1) The forfeiture of property under this section, including any seizure and disposition of the property and any related judicial or administrative proceeding, shall be governed by the provisions of section 413 (other than subsection (d) of that section) of the Comprehensive Drug Abuse Prevention and Control Act of 1970 (21 U.S.C. 853).".

(b) Economic Espionage and Theft of Trade Secrets as Predicate Offenses for Wire Interception.—Section 2516(1)(a) of title 18, United States Code, is amended by inserting "chapter 90 (relating to protection of trade secrets)," after "to espionage),".

§ 007. REDACTION OF ETHICS REPORTS FILED BY JUDICIAL OFFICERS AND EMPLOYEES.

Section 105(b) of the Ethics in Government Act of 1978 (5 U.S.C. App.) is amended by adding at the end the following new paragraph:

"(3)(A) This section does not require the immediate and unconditional availability of reports filed by an individual described in section 109(8) or 109(10) of this Act if a finding is made by the Judicial Conference, in consultation with United States Marshall Service, that revealing personal and sensitive information could endanger that individual.

"(3)(B) A report may be redacted pursuant to this paragraph only—

"(i) to the extent necessary to protect the individual who filed the report; and

"(ii) for as long as the danger to such individual exists.

"(C) The Administrative Office of the United States Courts shall submit to the Committees on the Judiciary of the House of Representatives and of the Senate an annual report with respect to the operation of this paragraph including—

"(i) the total number of reports redacted pursuant to this paragraph;

"(ii) the total number of individuals whose reports have been redacted pursuant to this paragraph; and

"(iii) the types of threats against individuals whose reports are redacted, if appropriate.

"(D) The Judicial Conference, in consultation with the Department of Justice, shall issue regulations setting forth the circumstances under which redaction is appropriate under this paragraph and the procedures for redaction.

"(E) This paragraph shall expire on December 31, 2001, and apply to filings through calendar year 2001.". [NOTE: Expiration date.]

APPENDIX 8:
FRAUD AND RELATED ACTIVITY IN CONNECTION WITH IDENTIFICATION DOCUMENTS AND INFORMATION (18 U.S.C. § 1028)

SEC. 1028.—FRAUD AND RELATED ACTIVITY IN CONNECTION WITH IDENTIFICATION DOCUMENTS AND INFORMATION

(a) Whoever, in a circumstance described in subsection (c) of this section—

(1) knowingly and without lawful authority produces an identification document or a false identification document;

(2) knowingly transfers an identification document or a false identification document knowing that such document was stolen or produced without lawful authority;

(3) knowingly possesses with intent to use unlawfully or transfer unlawfully five or more identification documents (other than those issued lawfully for the use of the possessor) or false identification documents;

(4) knowingly possesses an identification document (other than one issued lawfully for the use of the possessor) or a false identification document, with the intent such document be used to defraud the United States;

(5) knowingly produces, transfers, or possesses a document-making implement with the intent such document-making implement will be used in the production of a false identification document or another document-making implement which will be so used;

(6) knowingly possesses an identification document that is or appears to be an identification document of the United States which is stolen or produced without lawful authority knowing that such document was stolen or produced without such authority; or

(7) knowingly transfers or uses, without lawful authority, a means of identification of another person with the intent to commit, or to aid or abet, any unlawful activity that constitutes a violation of Federal law, or that constitutes a felony under any applicable State or local law; shall be punished as provided in subsection (b) of this section.

(b) the punishment for an offense under subsection (a) of this section is—

(1) except as provided in paragraphs (3) and (4), a fine under this title or imprisonment for not more than 15 years, or both, if the offense is—

(A) the production or transfer of an identification document or false identification document that is or appears to be—

(i) an identification document issued by or under the authority of the United States; or

(ii) a birth certificate, or a driver's license or personal identification card;

(B) the production or transfer of more than five identification documents or false identification documents;

(C) an offense under paragraph (5) of such subsection; or

(D) an offense under paragraph (7) of such subsection that involves the transfer or use of 1 or more means of identification if, as a result of the offense, any individual committing the offense obtains anything of value aggregating $1,000 or more during any 1-year period;

(2) except as provided in paragraphs (3) and (4), a fine under this title or imprisonment for not more than three years, or both, if the offense is—

(A) any other production, transfer, or use of a means of identification, an identification document, or a false identification document; or

(B) an offense under paragraph (3) or (7) of such subsection;

(3) a fine under this title or imprisonment for not more than 20 years, or both, if the offense is committed—

(A) to facilitate a drug trafficking crime (as defined in section 929(a)(2));

(B) in connection with a crime of violence (as defined in section 924(c)(3)); or

(C) after a prior conviction under this section becomes final;

(4) a fine under this title or imprisonment for not more than 25 years, or both, if the offense is committed to facilitate an act of international terrorism (as defined in section 2331(1) of this title);

(5) in the case of any offense under subsection (a), forfeiture to the United States of any personal property used or intended to be used to commit the offense; and

(6) a fine under this title or imprisonment for not more than one year, or both, in any other case.

(c) The circumstance referred to in subsection (a) of this section is that—

(1) the identification document or false identification document is or appears to be issued by or under the authority of the United States or the document-making implement is designed or suited for making such an identification document or false identification document;

(2) the offense is an offense under subsection (a)(4) of this section; or

(3) either—

(A) the production, transfer, possession, or use prohibited by this section is in or affects interstate or foreign commerce, including the transfer of a document by electronic means; or

(B) the means of identification, identification document, false identification document, or document-making implement is transported in the mail in the course of the production, transfer, possession, or use prohibited by this section.

(d) In this section—

(1) the term "document-making implement" means any implement, impression, template, computer file, computer disc, electronic device, or computer hardware or software, that is specifically configured or primarily used for making an identification document, a false identification document, or another document-making implement;

(2) the term "identification document" means a document made or issued by or under the authority of the United States Government, a State, political subdivision of a State, a foreign government, political subdivision of a foreign government, an international governmental or an international quasi-governmental organization which, when completed with information concerning a particular individual, is of a type intended or commonly accepted for the purpose of identification of individuals;

(3) the term "false identification document" means a document of a type intended or commonly accepted for the purposes of identification of individuals that—

(A) is not issued by or under the authority of a governmental entity; and

(B) appears to be issued by or under the authority of the United States Government, a State, a political subdivision of a State, a foreign government, a political subdivision of a foreign government, or an international governmental or quasi-governmental organization;

(4) the term "means of identification" means any name or number that may be used, alone or in conjunction with any other information, to identify a specific individual, including any—

(A) name, social security number, date of birth, official State or government issued driver's license or identification number, alien registration number, government passport number, employer or taxpayer identification number;

(B) unique biometric data, such as fingerprint, voice print, retina or iris image, or other unique physical representation;

(C) unique electronic identification number, address, or routing code; or

(D) telecommunication identifying information or access device (as defined in section 1029(e));

(5) the term "personal identification card" means an identification document issued by a State or local government solely for the purpose of identification;

(6) the term "produce" includes alter, authenticate, or assemble;

(7) the term "transfer" includes selecting an identification document, false identification document, or document-making implement and placing or directing the placement of such identification document, false identification document, or document-making implement on an online location where it is available to others; and

(8) the term "State" includes any State of the United States, the District of Columbia, the Commonwealth of Puerto Rico, and any other commonwealth, possession, or territory of the United States.

(e) This section does not prohibit any lawfully authorized investigative, protective, or intelligence activity of a law enforcement agency of the United States, a State, or a political subdivision of a State, or of an intelligence agency of the United States, or any activity authorized under chapter 224 of this title.

(f) Attempt and Conspiracy.—

Any person who attempts or conspires to commit any offense under this section shall be subject to the same penalties as those prescribed for the offense, the commission of which was the object of the attempt or conspiracy.

(g) Forfeiture Procedures.—

The forfeiture of property under this section, including any seizure and disposition of the property and any related judicial or administrative proceeding, shall be governed by the provisions of section 413 (other than subsection (d) of that section) of the Comprehensive Drug Abuse Prevention and Control Act of 1970 (21 U.S.C. 853).

(h) Rule of Construction.—

For purpose of subsection (a)(7), a single identification document or false identification document that contains 1 or more means of identification shall be construed to be 1 means of identification.

APPENDIX 9:
THE SAFEGUARDS RULE

FEDERAL TRADE COMMISSION

[16 CFR PART 314]

PART 314—STANDARDS FOR SAFEGUARDING CUSTOMER INFORMATION

§ 314.1 Purpose and scope.

(a) Purpose. This part ("rule"), which implements sections 501 and 505(b)(2) of the Gramm-Leach-Bliley Act, sets forth standards for developing, implementing, and maintaining reasonable administrative, technical, and physical safeguards to protect the security, confidentiality, and integrity of customer information.

(b) Scope. This rule applies to the handling of customer information by all financial institutions over which the Federal Trade Commission ("FTC" or "Commission") has jurisdiction. This rule refers to such entities as "you." The rule applies to all customer information in your possession, regardless of whether such information pertains to individuals with whom you have a customer relationship, or pertains to the customers of other financial institutions that have provided such information to you.

§ 314.2 Definitions.

(a) In general. Except as modified by this rule or unless the context otherwise requires, the terms used in this rule have the same meaning as set forth in the Commission's rule governing the Privacy of Consumer Financial Information, 16 CFR part 313.

(b) "Customer information" means any record containing nonpublic personal information as defined in 16 CFR 313.3(n), about a customer of a financial institution, whether in paper, electronic, or other form, that is handled or maintained by or on behalf of you or your affiliates.

(c) "Information security program" means the administrative, technical, or physical safeguards you use to access, collect, distribute, process, protect, store, use, transmit, dispose of, or otherwise handle customer information.

(d) "Service provider" means any person or entity that receives, maintains, processes, or otherwise is permitted access to customer information through its provision of services directly to a financial institution that is subject to the rule.

§ 314.3 Standards for safeguarding customer information.

(a) Information security program. You shall develop, implement, and maintain a comprehensive information security program that is written in one or more readily accessible parts and contains administrative, technical, and physical safeguards that are appropriate to your size and complexity, the nature and scope of your activities, and the sensitivity of any customer information at issue. Such safeguards shall include the elements set forth in section 314.4 and shall be reasonably designed to achieve the objectives of this rule, as set forth in paragraph (b) of this section.

(b) Objectives. The objectives of section 501(b) of the Act, and of this rule, are to:

(1) Insure the security and confidentiality of customer information;

(2) Protect against any anticipated threats or hazards to the security or integrity of such information; and

(3) Protect against unauthorized access to or use of such information that could result in substantial harm or inconvenience to any customer.

§ 314.4 Elements.

In order to develop, implement, and maintain your information security program, you shall:

(a) Designate an employee or employees to coordinate your information security program.

(b) Identify reasonably foreseeable internal and external risks to the security, confidentiality, and integrity of customer information that could result in the unauthorized disclosure, misuse, alteration, destruction or other compromise of such information, and assess the sufficiency of any safeguards in place to control these risks. At a minimum, such a risk assessment should include consideration of risks in each relevant area of your operations, including:

(1) employee training and management;

130   **Identity Theft and How to Protect Yourself**

(2) information systems, including network and software design, as well as information processing, storage, transmission and disposal; and

(3) detecting, preventing and responding to attacks, intrusions, or other systems failures.

(c) Design and implement information safeguards to control the risks you identify through risk assessment, and regularly test or otherwise monitor the effectiveness of the safeguards' key controls, systems, and procedures.

(d) Oversee service providers, by:

(1) taking reasonable steps to select and retain service providers that are capable of maintaining appropriate safeguards for the customer information at issue; and

(2) requiring your service providers by contract to implement and maintain such safeguards.

(e) Evaluate and adjust your information security program in light of the results of the testing and monitoring required by paragraph (c); any material changes to your operations or business arrangements; or any other circumstances that you know or have reason to know may have a material impact on your information security program.

§ 314.5 Effective date.

(a) Each financial institution subject to the Commission's jurisdiction must implement an information security program pursuant to this rule no later than one year from the date on which the Final Rule is published in the Federal Register.

(b) Two-year grandfathering of service contracts. Until two years from the date on which the Final Rule is published in the Federal Register, a contract you have entered into with a nonaffiliated third party to perform services for you or functions on your behalf satisfies the provisions of section 314.4(d) of this part, even if the contract does not include a requirement that the service provider maintain appropriate safeguards, as long as you entered into the contract not later than 30 days from the date on which the Final Rule is published in the Federal Register.

By direction of the Commission.

Donald S. Clark Secretary

APPENDIX 10:
THE FAIR CREDIT REPORTING ACT

§ 601. SHORT TITLE.

This title may be cited as the "Fair Credit Reporting Act".

§ 602. CONGRESSIONAL FINDINGS AND STATEMENT OF PURPOSE.
[15 U.S.C. § 1681]

(a) Accuracy and fairness of credit reporting. The Congress makes the following findings:

(1) The banking system is dependent upon fair and accurate credit reporting. Inaccurate credit reports directly impair the efficiency of the banking system, and unfair credit reporting methods undermine the public confidence which is essential to the continued functioning of the banking system.

(2) An elaborate mechanism has been developed for investigating and evaluating the credit worthiness, credit standing, credit capacity, character, and general reputation of consumers.

(3) Consumer reporting agencies have assumed a vital role in assembling and evaluating consumer credit and other information on consumers.

(4) There is a need to insure that consumer reporting agencies exercise their grave responsibilities with fairness, impartiality, and a respect for the consumer's right to privacy.

(b) Reasonable procedures. It is the purpose of this title to require that consumer reporting agencies adopt reasonable procedures for meeting the needs of commerce for consumer credit, personnel, insurance, and other information in a manner which is fair and equitable to the consumer, with regard to the confidentiality, accuracy, relevancy, and proper utilization of such information in accordance with the requirements of this title.

§ 603. DEFINITIONS; RULES OF CONSTRUCTION [OMITTED]

§ 604. PERMISSIBLE PURPOSES OF CONSUMER REPORTS.
[15 U.S.C. § 1681b]

(a) In general. Subject to subsection (c), any consumer reporting agency may furnish a consumer report under the following circumstances and no other:

(1) In response to the order of a court having jurisdiction to issue such an order, or a subpoena issued in connection with proceedings before a Federal grand jury.

(2) In accordance with the written instructions of the consumer to whom it relates.

(3) To a person which it has reason to believe:

(A) intends to use the information in connection with a credit transaction involving the consumer on whom the information is to be furnished and involving the extension of credit to, or review or collection of an account of, the consumer; or

(B) intends to use the information for employment purposes; or

(C) intends to use the information in connection with the underwriting of insurance involving the consumer; or

(D) intends to use the information in connection with a determination of the consumer's eligibility for a license or other benefit granted by a governmental instrumentality required by law to consider an applicant's financial responsibility or status; or

(E) intends to use the information, as a potential investor or servicer, or current insurer, in connection with a valuation of, or an assessment of the credit or prepayment risks associated with, an existing credit obligation; or

(F) otherwise has a legitimate business need for the information:

(i) in connection with a business transaction that is initiated by the consumer; or

(ii) to review an account to determine whether the consumer continues to meet the terms of the account.

(4) In response to a request by the head of a State or local child support enforcement agency (or a State or local government official au-

thorized by the head of such an agency), if the person making the request certifies to the consumer reporting agency that:

(A) the consumer report is needed for the purpose of establishing an individual's capacity to make child support payments or determining the appropriate level of such payments;

(B) the paternity of the consumer for the child to which the obligation relates has been established or acknowledged by the consumer in accordance with State laws under which the obligation arises (if required by those laws);

(C) the person has provided at least 10 days' prior notice to the consumer whose report is requested, by certified or registered mail to the last known address of the consumer, that the report will be requested; and

(D) the consumer report will be kept confidential, will be used solely for a purpose described in subparagraph (A), and will not be used in connection with any other civil, administrative, or criminal proceeding, or for any other purpose.

(5) To an agency administering a State plan under Section 454 of the Social Security Act (42 U.S.C. §654) for use to set an initial or modified child support award.

(b) Conditions for furnishing and using consumer reports for employment purposes.

(1) Certification from user. A consumer reporting agency may furnish a consumer report for employment purposes only if:

(A) the person who obtains such report from the agency certifies to the agency that:

(i) the person has complied with paragraph (2) with respect to the consumer report, and the person will comply with paragraph (3) with respect to the consumer report if paragraph (3) becomes applicable; and

(ii) information from the consumer report will not be used in violation of any applicable Federal or State equal employment opportunity law or regulation; and

(B) the consumer reporting agency provides with the report, or has previously provided, a summary of the consumer's rights under this title, as prescribed by the Federal Trade Commission under section 609(c)(3) [§1681g].

(2) Disclosure to consumer.

(A) In general. Except as provided in subparagraph (B), a person may not procure a consumer report, or cause a consumer report to be procured, for employment purposes with respect to any consumer, unless—

(i) a clear and conspicuous disclosure has been made in writing to the consumer at any time before the report is procured or caused to be procured, in a document that consists solely of the disclosure, that a consumer report may be obtained for employment purposes; and

(ii) the consumer has authorized in writing (which authorization may be made on the document referred to in clause (i)) the procurement of the report by that person.

(B) Application by mail, telephone, computer, or other similar means. If a consumer described in subparagraph (C) applies for employment by mail, telephone, computer, or other similar means, at any time before a consumer report is procured or caused to be procured in connection with that application—

(i) the person who procures the consumer report on the consumer for employment purposes shall provide to the consumer, by oral, written, or electronic means, notice that a consumer report may be obtained for employment purposes, and a summary of the consumer's rights under section 615(a)(3); and

(ii) the consumer shall have consented, orally, in writing, or electronically to the procurement of the report by that person.

(C) Scope. Subparagraph (B) shall apply to a person procuring a consumer report on a consumer in connection with the consumer's application for employment only if—

(i) the consumer is applying for a position over which the Secretary of Transportation has the power to establish qualifications and maximum hours of service pursuant to the provisions of section 31502 of title 49, or a position subject to safety regulation by a State transportation agency; and

(ii) as of the time at which the person procures the report or causes the report to be procured the only interaction between the consumer and the person in connection with that employment application has been by mail, telephone, computer, or other similar means.

(3) Conditions on use for adverse actions.

(A) In general. Except as provided in subparagraph (B), in using a consumer report for employment purposes, before taking any adverse action based in whole or in part on the report, the person intending to take such adverse action shall provide to the consumer to whom the report relates—

(i) a copy of the report; and

(ii) a description in writing of the rights of the consumer under this title, as prescribed by the Federal Trade Commission under section 609(c)(3).

(B) Application by mail, telephone, computer, or other similar means.

(i) If a consumer described in subparagraph (C) applies for employment by mail, telephone, computer, or other similar means, and if a person who has procured a consumer report on the consumer for employment purposes takes adverse action on the employment application based in whole or in part on the report, then the person must provide to the consumer to whom the report relates, in lieu of the notices required under subparagraph (A) of this section and under section 615(a), within 3 business days of taking such action, an oral, written or electronic notification—

(I) that adverse action has been taken based in whole or in part on a consumer report received from a consumer reporting agency;

(II) of the name, address and telephone number of the consumer reporting agency that furnished the consumer report (including a toll-free telephone number established by the agency if the agency compiles and maintains files on consumers on a nationwide basis);

(III) that the consumer reporting agency did not make the decision to take the adverse action and is unable to provide to the consumer the specific reasons why the adverse action was taken; and

(IV) that the consumer may, upon providing proper identification, request a free copy of a report and may dispute with the consumer reporting agency the accuracy or completeness of any information in a report.

(ii) If, under clause (B)(i)(IV), the consumer requests a copy of a consumer report from the person who procured the report, then, within 3 business days of receiving the consumer's request, together with proper identification, the person must send or provide to the consumer a copy of a report and a copy of the consumer's rights as prescribed by the Federal Trade Commission under section 609(c)(3).

(C) Scope. Subparagraph (B) shall apply to a person procuring a consumer report on a consumer in connection with the consumer's application for employment only if—

(i) the consumer is applying for a position over which the Secretary of Transportation has the power to establish qualifications and maximum hours of service pursuant to the provisions of section 31502 of title 49, or a position subject to safety regulation by a State transportation agency; and

(ii) as of the time at which the person procures the report or causes the report to be procured the only interaction between the consumer and the person in connection with that employment application has been by mail, telephone, computer, or other similar means.

(4) Exception for national security investigations.

(A) In general. In the case of an agency or department of the United States Government which seeks to obtain and use a consumer report for employment purposes, paragraph (3) shall not apply to any adverse action by such agency or department which is based in part on such consumer report, if the head of such agency or department makes a written finding that—

(i) the consumer report is relevant to a national security investigation of such agency or department;

(ii) the investigation is within the jurisdiction of such agency or department;

(iii) there is reason to believe that compliance with paragraph (3) will—

(I) endanger the life or physical safety of any person;

(II) result in flight from prosecution;

(III) result in the destruction of, or tampering with, evidence relevant to the investigation;

(IV) result in the intimidation of a potential witness relevant to the investigation;

(V) result in the compromise of classified information; or

(VI) otherwise seriously jeopardize or unduly delay the investigation or another official proceeding.

(B) Notification of consumer upon conclusion of investigation. Upon the conclusion of a national security investigation described in subparagraph (A), or upon the determination that the exception under subparagraph (A) is no longer required for the reasons set forth in such subparagraph, the official exercising the authority in such subparagraph shall provide to the consumer who is the subject of the consumer report with regard to which such finding was made—

(i) a copy of such consumer report with any classified information redacted as necessary;

(ii) notice of any adverse action which is based, in part, on the consumer report; and

(iii) the identification with reasonable specificity of the nature of the investigation for which the consumer report was sought.

(C) Delegation by head of agency or department. For purposes of subparagraphs (A) and (B), the head of any agency or department of the United States Government may delegate his or her authorities under this paragraph to an official of such agency or department who has personnel security responsibilities and is a member of the Senior Executive Service or equivalent civilian or military rank.

(D) Report to the congress. Not later than January 31 of each year, the head of each agency and department of the United States Government that exercised authority under this paragraph during the preceding year shall submit a report to the Congress on the number of times the department or agency exercised such authority during the year.

(E) Definitions. For purposes of this paragraph, the following definitions shall apply:

(i) Classified information. The term "classified information" means information that is protected from unauthorized disclosure under Executive Order No. 12958 or successor orders.

(ii) National security investigation. The term "national security investigation" means any official inquiry by an agency or department of the United States Government to determine the eligibility of a consumer to receive access or continued access to classified information or to determine whether classified information has been lost or compromised.

(c) Furnishing reports in connection with credit or insurance transactions that are not initiated by the consumer.

(1) In general. A consumer reporting agency may furnish a consumer report relating to any consumer pursuant to subparagraph (A) or (C) of subsection (a)(3) in connection with any credit or insurance transaction that is not initiated by the consumer only if:

(A) the consumer authorizes the agency to provide such report to such person; or

(B) (i) the transaction consists of a firm offer of credit or insurance;

(ii) the consumer reporting agency has complied with subsection (e); and

(iii) there is not in effect an election by the consumer, made in accordance with subsection (e), to have the consumer's name and address excluded from lists of names provided by the agency pursuant to this paragraph.

(2) Limits on information received under paragraph (1)(B). A person may receive pursuant to paragraph (1)(B) only:

(A) the name and address of a consumer;

(B) an identifier that is not unique to the consumer and that is used by the person solely for the purpose of verifying the identity of the consumer; and

(C) other information pertaining to a consumer that does not identify the relationship or experience of the consumer with respect to a particular creditor or other entity.

(3) Information regarding inquiries. Except as provided in section 609(a)(5) [§1681g], a consumer reporting agency shall not furnish to any person a record of inquiries in connection with a credit or insurance transaction that is not initiated by a consumer.

(d) Reserved.

(e) Election of consumer to be excluded from lists.

(1) In general. A consumer may elect to have the consumer's name and address excluded from any list provided by a consumer reporting agency under subsection (c)(1)(B) in connection with a credit or insurance transaction that is not initiated by the consumer, by notifying the agency in accordance with paragraph (2) that the consumer does not consent to any use of a consumer report relating to the consumer in connection with any credit or insurance transaction that is not initiated by the consumer.

(2) Manner of notification. A consumer shall notify a consumer reporting agency under paragraph (1):

(A) through the notification system maintained by the agency under paragraph (5); or

(B) by submitting to the agency a signed notice of election form issued by the agency for purposes of this subparagraph.

(3) Response of agency after notification through system. Upon receipt of notification of the election of a consumer under paragraph (1) through the notification system maintained by the agency under paragraph (5), a consumer reporting agency shall:

(A) inform the consumer that the election is effective only for the 2-year period following the election if the consumer does not submit to the agency a signed notice of election form issued by the agency for purposes of paragraph (2)(B); and

(B) provide to the consumer a notice of election form, if requested by the consumer, not later than 5 business days after receipt of the notification of the election through the system established under paragraph (5), in the case of a request made at the time the consumer provides notification through the system.

(4) Effectiveness of election. An election of a consumer under paragraph (1):

(A) shall be effective with respect to a consumer reporting agency beginning 5 business days after the date on which the consumer notifies the agency in accordance with paragraph (2);

(B) shall be effective with respect to a consumer reporting agency:

(i) subject to subparagraph (C), during the 2-year period beginning 5 business days after the date on which the consumer notifies the agency of the election, in the case of an election for which a consumer notifies the agency only in accordance with paragraph (2)(A); or

(ii) until the consumer notifies the agency under subparagraph (C), in the case of an election for which a consumer notifies the agency in accordance with paragraph (2)(B);

(C) shall not be effective after the date on which the consumer notifies the agency, through the notification system established by the agency under paragraph (5), that the election is no longer effective; and

(D) shall be effective with respect to each affiliate of the agency.

(5) Notification system.

(A) In general. Each consumer reporting agency that, under subsection (c)(1)(B), furnishes a consumer report in connection with a credit or insurance transaction that is not initiated by a consumer, shall:

(i) establish and maintain a notification system, including a toll-free telephone number, which permits any consumer whose consumer report is maintained by the agency to notify the agency, with appropriate identification, of the consumer's election to have the consumer's name and address excluded from any such list of names and addresses provided by the agency for such a transaction; and

(ii) publish by not later than 365 days after the date of enactment of the Consumer Credit Reporting Reform Act of 1996, and not less than annually thereafter, in a publication of general circulation in the area served by the agency:

(I) a notification that information in consumer files maintained by the agency may be used in connection with such transactions; and

(II) the address and toll-free telephone number for consumers to use to notify the agency of the consumer's election under clause (I).

(B) Establishment and maintenance as compliance. Establishment and maintenance of a notification system (including a toll-free telephone number) and publication by a consumer reporting agency on the agency's own behalf and on behalf of any of its affiliates in accordance with this paragraph is deemed to be compliance with this paragraph by each of those affiliates.

(6) Notification system by agencies that operate nationwide.

Each consumer reporting agency that compiles and maintains files on consumers on a nationwide basis shall establish and maintain a notification system for purposes of paragraph (5) jointly with other such consumer reporting agencies.

(f) Certain use or obtaining of information prohibited. A person shall not use or obtain a consumer report for any purpose unless:

(1) the consumer report is obtained for a purpose for which the consumer report is authorized to be furnished under this section; and

(2) the purpose is certified in accordance with section 607 [§1681e] by a prospective user of the report through a general or specific certification.

(g) Protection of Medical Information

(1) Limitation on consumer reporting agencies. A consumer reporting agency shall not furnish for employment purposes, or in connection with a credit or insurance transaction, a consumer report that contains medical information (other than medical contact information treated in the manner required under section 605(a)(6)) about a consumer, unless—

(A) if furnished in connection with an insurance transaction, the consumer affirmatively consents to the furnishing of the report;

(B) if furnished for employment purposes or in connection with a credit transaction—

(i) the information to be furnished is relevant to process or effect the employment or credit transaction; and

(ii) the consumer provides specific written consent for the furnishing of the report that describes in clear and conspicuous language the use for which the information will be furnished; or

(C) the information to be furnished pertains solely to transactions, accounts, or balances relating to debts arising from the receipt of medical services, products, or devises, where such information, other than account status or amounts, is restricted or reported using codes that do not identify, or do not provide information sufficient to infer, the specific provider or the nature of such services, products, or devices, as provided in section 605(a)(6).

(2) Limitation on creditors. Except as permitted pursuant to paragraph (3)(C) or regulations prescribed under paragraph (5)(A), a creditor shall not obtain or use medical information (other than medical contact information treated in the manner required under section 605(a)(6)) pertaining to a consumer in connection with any determination of the consumer's eligibility, or continued eligibility, for credit.

(3) Actions authorized by federal law, insurance activities and regulatory determinations. Section 603(d)(3) shall not be construed so as to treat information or any communication of information as a consumer report if the information or communication is disclosed—

(A) in connection with the business of insurance or annuities, including the activities described in section 18B of the model Privacy of

Consumer Financial and Health Information Regulation issued by the National Association of Insurance Commissioners (as in effect on January 1, 2003);

(B) for any purpose permitted without authorization under the Standards for Individually Identifiable Health Information promulgated by the Department of Health and Human Services pursuant to the Health Insurance Portability and Accountability Act of 1996, or referred to under section 1179 of such Act, or described in section 502(e) of Public Law 106-102; or

(C) as otherwise determined to be necessary and appropriate, by regulation or order and subject to paragraph (6), by the Commission, any Federal banking agency or the National Credit Union Administration (with respect to any financial institution subject to the jurisdiction of such agency or Administration under paragraph (1), (2), or (3) of section 621(b), or the applicable State insurance authority (with respect to any person engaged in providing insurance or annuities).

(4) Limitation on redisclosure of medical information. Any person that receives medical information pursuant to paragraph (1) or (3) shall not disclose such information to any other person, except as necessary to carry out the purpose for which the information was initially disclosed, or as otherwise permitted by statute, regulation, or order.

(5) Regulations and Effective Date for Paragraph (2)

(A) Regulations required. Each Federal banking agency and the National Credit Union Administration shall, subject to paragraph (6) and after notice and opportunity for comment, prescribe regulations that permit transactions under paragraph (2) that are determined to be necessary and appropriate to protect legitimate operational, transactional, risk, consumer, and other needs (and which shall include permitting actions necessary for administrative verification purposes), consistent with the intent of paragraph (2) to restrict the use of medical information for inappropriate purposes.

(B) Final regulations required. The Federal banking agencies and the National Credit Union Administration shall issue the regulations required under subparagraph (A) in final form before the end of the 6-month period beginning on the date of enactment of the Fair and Accurate Credit Transactions Act of 2003.

(6) Coordination with other laws. No provision of this subsection shall be construed as altering, affecting, or superseding the applicability of any other provision of Federal law relating to medical confidentiality.

§ 605. REQUIREMENTS RELATING TO INFORMATION CONTAINED IN CONSUMER REPORTS [15 U.S.C. § 1681c]

(a) Information excluded from consumer reports. Except as authorized under subsection (b) of this section, no consumer reporting agency may make any consumer report containing any of the following items of information:

(1) Cases under title 11 [United States Code] or under the Bankruptcy Act that, from the date of entry of the order for relief or the date of adjudication, as the case may be, antedate the report by more than 10 years.

(2) Civil suits, civil judgments, and records of arrest that from date of entry, antedate the report by more than seven years or until the governing statute of limitations has expired, whichever is the longer period.

(3) Paid tax liens which, from date of payment, antedate the report by more than seven years.

(4) Accounts placed for collection or charged to profit and loss which antedate the report by more than seven years.*

(5) Any other adverse item of information, other than records of convictions of crimes which antedates the report by more than seven years.*

---

*The reporting periods have been lengthened for certain adverse information pertaining to certain U.S. Government insured or guaranteed student loans, or pertaining to national direct student loans. See Section 430A(f) and 463(c)(3) of the Higher Education Act of 1965, 20 U.S.C. 1080a(f) and 20 U.S.C. 1087cc(c)(3), respectively.

(b) Exempted cases. The provisions of subsection (a) of this section are not applicable in the case of any consumer credit report to be used in connection with

(1) a credit transaction involving, or which may reasonably be expected to involve, a principal amount of $150,000 or more;

(2) the underwriting of life insurance involving, or which may reasonably be expected to involve, a face amount of $150,000 or more; or

(3) the employment of any individual at an annual salary which equals, or which may reasonably be expected to equal $75,000, or more.

(c) Running of reporting period.

(1) In general. The 7-year period referred to in paragraphs (4) and (6) [(4) and (5)] of subsection (a) shall begin, with respect to any delin-

quent account that is placed for collection (internally or by referral to a third party, whichever is earlier), charged to profit and loss, or subjected to any similar action, upon the expiration of the 180-day period beginning on the date of the commencement of the delinquency which immediately preceded the collection activity, charge to profit and loss, or similar action.

(2) Effective date. Paragraph (1) shall apply only to items of information added to the file of a consumer on or after the date that is 455 days after the date of enactment of the Consumer Credit Reporting Reform Act of 1996.

(d) Information Required to be Disclosed

(1) Title 11 information. Any consumer reporting agency that furnishes a consumer report that contains information regarding any case involving the consumer that arises under title 11, United States Code, shall include in the report an identification of the chapter of such title 11 under which such case arises if provided by the source of the information. If any case arising or filed under title 11, United States Code, is withdrawn by the consumer before a final judgment, the consumer reporting agency shall include in the report that such case or filing was withdrawn upon receipt of documentation certifying such withdrawal.

(2) Key factor in credit score information. Any consumer reporting agency that furnishes a consumer report that contains any credit score or any other risk score or predictor on any consumer shall include in the report a clear and conspicuous statement that a key factor (as defined in section 609(f)(2)(B)) that adversely affected such score or predictor was the number of enquiries, if such a predictor was in fact a key factor that adversely affected such score. This paragraph shall not apply to a check services company, acting as such, which issues authorizations for the purpose of approving or processing negotiable instruments, electronic fund transfers, or similar methods of payments, but only to the extent that such company is engaged in such activities.

(e) Indication of closure of account by consumer. If a consumer reporting agency is notified pursuant to section 623(a)(4) [§ 1681s-2] that a credit account of a consumer was voluntarily closed by the consumer, the agency shall indicate that fact in any consumer report that includes information related to the account.

(f) Indication of dispute by consumer. If a consumer reporting agency is notified pursuant to section 623(a)(3) [§ 1681s-2] that information regarding a consumer who was furnished to the agency is disputed by the consumer, the agency shall indicate that fact in each consumer report that includes the disputed information.

(g) Truncation of Credit Card and Debit Card Numbers

(1) In general. Except as otherwise provided in this subsection, no person that accepts credit cards or debit cards for the transaction of business shall print more than the last 5 digits of the card number or the expiration date upon any receipt provided to the cardholder at the point of the sale or transaction.

(2) Limitation. This subsection shall apply only to receipts that are electronically printed, and shall not apply to transactions in which the sole means of recording a credit card or debit card account number is by handwriting or by an imprint or copy of the card.

(3) Effective date. This subsection shall become effective—

(A) 3 years after the date of enactment of this subsection, with respect to any cash register or other machine or device that electronically prints receipts for credit card or debit card transactions that is in use before January 1, 2005; and

(B) 1 year after the date of enactment of this subsection, with respect to any cash register or other machine or device that electronically prints receipts for credit card or debit card transactions that is first put into use on or after January 1, 2005.

(h) Notice of Discrepancy in Address

(1) In general. If a person has requested a consumer report relating to a consumer from a consumer reporting agency described in section 603(p), the request includes an address for the consumer that substantially differs from the addresses in the file of the consumer, and the agency provides a consumer report in response to the request, the consumer reporting agency shall notify the requester of the existence of the discrepancy.

(2) Regulations

(A) Regulations required. The Federal banking agencies, the National Credit Union Administration, and the Commission shall jointly, with respect to the entities that are subject to their respective enforcement authority under section 621, prescribe regulations providing guidance regarding reasonable policies and procedures that a user of a consumer report should employ when such user has received a notice of discrepancy under paragraph (1).

(B) Policies and procedures to be included. The regulations prescribed under subparagraph (A) shall describe reasonable policies and procedures for use by a user of a consumer report—

(i) to form a reasonable belief that the user knows the identity of the person to whom the consumer report pertains; and

(ii) if the user establishes a continuing relationship with the consumer, and the user regularly and in the ordinary course of business furnishes information to the consumer reporting agency from which the notice of discrepancy pertaining to the consumer was obtained, to reconcile the address of the consumer with the consumer reporting agency by furnishing such address to such consumer reporting agency as part of information regularly furnished by the user for the period in which the relationship is established.

§ 605A. IDENTITY THEFT PREVENTION; FRAUD ALERTS AND ACTIVE DUTY ALERTS [15 U.S.C. §1681C-1]

(a) One-call Fraud Alerts

(1) Initial alerts. Upon the direct request of a consumer, or an individual acting on behalf of or as a personal representative of a consumer, who asserts in good faith a suspicion that the consumer has been or is about to become a victim of fraud or related crime, including identity theft, a consumer reporting agency described in section 603(p) that maintains a file on the consumer and has received appropriate proof of the identity of the requester shall—

(A) include a fraud alert in the file of that consumer, and also provide that alert along with any credit score generated in using that file, for a period of not less than 90 days, beginning on the date of such request, unless the consumer or such representative requests that such fraud alert be removed before the end of such period, and the agency has received appropriate proof of the identity of the requester for such purpose; and

(B) refer the information regarding the fraud alert under this paragraph to each of the other consumer reporting agencies described in section 603(p), in accordance with procedures developed under section 621(f).

(2) Access to free reports. In any case in which a consumer reporting agency includes a fraud alert in the file of a consumer pursuant to this subsection, the consumer reporting agency shall—

(A) disclose to the consumer that the consumer may request a free copy of the file of the consumer pursuant to section 612(d); and

(B) provide to the consumer all disclosures required to be made under section 609, without charge to the consumer, not later than 3 business days after any request described in subparagraph (A).

(b) Extended Alerts

(1) In general. Upon the direct request of a consumer, or an individual acting on behalf of or as a personal representative of a consumer, who submits an identity theft report to a consumer reporting agency described in section 603(p) that maintains a file on the consumer, if the agency has received appropriate proof of the identity of the requester, the agency shall—

(A) include a fraud alert in the file of that consumer, and also provide that alert along with any credit score generated in using that file, during the 7-year period beginning on the date of such request, unless the consumer or such representative requests that such fraud alert be removed before the end of such period and the agency has received appropriate proof of the identity of the requester for such purpose;

(B) during the 5-year period beginning on the date of such request, exclude the consumer from any list of consumers prepared by the consumer reporting agency and provided to any third party to offer credit or insurance to the consumer as part of a transaction that was not initiated by the consumer, unless the consumer or such representative requests that such exclusion be rescinded before the end of such period; and

(C) refer the information regarding the extended fraud alert under this paragraph to each of the other consumer reporting agencies described in section 603(p), in accordance with procedures developed under section 621(f).

(2) Access to free reports. In any case in which a consumer reporting agency includes a fraud alert in the file of a consumer pursuant to this subsection, the consumer reporting agency shall—

(A) disclose to the consumer that the consumer may request 2 free copies of the file of the consumer pursuant to section 612(d) during the 12-month period beginning on the date on which the fraud alert was included in the file; and

(B) provide to the consumer all disclosures required to be made under section 609, without charge to the consumer, not later than 3 business days after any request described in subparagraph (A).

(c) Active duty alerts. Upon the direct request of an active duty military consumer, or an individual acting on behalf of or as a personal representative of an active duty military consumer, a consumer reporting agency described in section 603(p) that maintains a file on the active duty military consumer and has received appropriate proof of the identity of the requester shall—

(1) include an active duty alert in the file of that active duty military consumer, and also provide that alert along with any credit score generated in using that file, during a period of not less than 12 months, or such longer period as the Commission shall determine, by regulation, beginning on the date of the request, unless the active duty military consumer or such representative requests that such fraud alert be removed before the end of such period, and the agency has received appropriate proof of the identity of the requester for such purpose;

(2) during the 2-year period beginning on the date of such request, exclude the active duty military consumer from any list of consumers prepared by the consumer reporting agency and provided to any third party to offer credit or insurance to the consumer as part of a transaction that was not initiated by the consumer, unless the consumer requests that such exclusion be rescinded before the end of such period; and

(3) refer the information regarding the active duty alert to each of the other consumer reporting agencies described in section 603(p), in accordance with procedures developed under section 621(f).

(d) Procedures. Each consumer reporting agency described in section 603(p) shall establish policies and procedures to comply with this section, including procedures that inform consumers of the availability of initial, extended, and active duty alerts and procedures that allow consumers and active duty military consumers to request initial, extended, or active duty alerts (as applicable) in a simple and easy manner, including by telephone.

(e) Referrals of alerts. Each consumer reporting agency described in section 603(p) that receives a referral of a fraud alert or active duty alert from another consumer reporting agency pursuant to this section shall, as though the agency received the request from the consumer directly, follow the procedures required under—

(1) paragraphs (1)(A) and (2) of subsection (a), in the case of a referral under subsection (a)(1)(B);

(2) paragraphs (1)(A), (1)(B), and (2) of subsection (b), in the case of a referral under subsection (b)(1)(C); and

(3) paragraphs (1) and (2) of subsection (c), in the case of a referral under subsection (c)(3).

(f) Duty of reseller to reconvey alert. A reseller shall include in its report any fraud alert or active duty alert placed in the file of a consumer pursuant to this section by another consumer reporting agency.

(g) Duty of other consumer reporting agencies to provide contact information. If a consumer contacts any consumer reporting agency that is not described in section 603(p) to communicate a suspicion that the consumer has been or is about to become a victim of fraud or related crime, including identity theft, the agency shall provide information to the consumer on how to contact the Commission and the consumer reporting agencies described in section 603(p) to obtain more detailed information and request alerts under this section.

(h) Limitations on Use of Information for Credit Extensions

(1) Requirements for initial and active duty alerts—

(A) Notification. Each initial fraud alert and active duty alert under this section shall include information that notifies all prospective users of a consumer report on the consumer to which the alert relates that the consumer does not authorize the establishment of any new credit plan or extension of credit, other than under an open-end credit plan (as defined in section 103(i)), in the name of the consumer, or issuance of an additional card on an existing credit account requested by a consumer, or any increase in credit limit on an existing credit account requested by a consumer, except in accordance with subparagraph (B).

(B) Limitation on Users

(i) In general. No prospective user of a consumer report that includes an initial fraud alert or an active duty alert in accordance with this section may establish a new credit plan or extension of credit, other than under an open-end credit plan (as defined in section 103(i)), in the name of the consumer, or issue an additional card on an existing credit account requested by a consumer, or grant any increase in credit limit on an existing credit account requested by a consumer, unless the user utilizes reasonable policies and procedures to form a reasonable belief that the user knows the identity of the person making the request.

(ii) Verification. If a consumer requesting the alert has specified a telephone number to be used for identity verification purposes, before authorizing any new credit plan or extension described in clause (i) in the name of such consumer, a user of such consumer report shall contact the consumer using that telephone number or take reasonable steps to verify the consumer's identity and confirm that the application for a new credit plan is not the result of identity theft.

(2) Requirements for Extended Alerts

(A) Notification. Each extended alert under this section shall include information that provides all prospective users of a consumer report relating to a consumer with—

(i) notification that the consumer does not authorize the establishment of any new credit plan or extension of credit described in clause (i), other than under an open-end credit plan (as defined in section 103(i)), in the name of the consumer, or issuance of an additional card on an existing credit account requested by a consumer, or any increase in credit limit on an existing credit account requested by a consumer, except in accordance with subparagraph (B); and

(ii) a telephone number or other reasonable contact method designated by the consumer.

(B) Limitation on users. No prospective user of a consumer report or of a credit score generated using the information in the file of a consumer that includes an extended fraud alert in accordance with this section may establish a new credit plan or extension of credit, other than under an open-end credit plan (as defined in section 103(i)), in the name of the consumer, or issue an additional card on an existing credit account requested by a consumer, or any increase in credit limit on an existing credit account requested by a consumer, unless the user contacts the consumer in person or using the contact method described in subparagraph (A)(ii) to confirm that the application for a new credit plan or increase in credit limit, or request for an additional card is not the result of identity theft.

§ 605B. BLOCK OF INFORMATION RESULTING FROM IDENTITY THEFT [15 U.S.C. §1681c-2]

(a) Block. Except as otherwise provided in this section, a consumer reporting agency shall block the reporting of any information in the file of a consumer that the consumer identifies as information that resulted from an alleged identity theft, not later than 4 business days after the date of receipt by such agency of—

(1) appropriate proof of the identity of the consumer;

(2) a copy of an identity theft report;

(3) the identification of such information by the consumer; and

(4) a statement by the consumer that the information is not information relating to any transaction by the consumer.

(b) Notification. A consumer reporting agency shall promptly notify the furnisher of information identified by the consumer under subsection (a)—

(1) that the information may be a result of identity theft;

(2) that an identity theft report has been filed;

(3) that a block has been requested under this section; and

(4) of the effective dates of the block.

(c) Authority to Decline or Rescind

(1) In general. A consumer reporting agency may decline to block, or may rescind any block, of information relating to a consumer under this section, if the consumer reporting agency reasonably determines that—

(A) the information was blocked in error or a block was requested by the consumer in error;

(B) the information was blocked, or a block was requested by the consumer, on the basis of a material misrepresentation of fact by the consumer relevant to the request to block; or

(C) the consumer obtained possession of goods, services, or money as a result of the blocked transaction or transactions.

(2) Notification to consumer. If a block of information is declined or rescinded under this subsection, the affected consumer shall be notified promptly, in the same manner as consumers are notified of the reinsertion of information under section 611(a)(5)(B).

(3) Significance of block. For purposes of this subsection, if a consumer reporting agency rescinds a block, the presence of information in the file of a consumer prior to the blocking of such information is not evidence of whether the consumer knew or should have known that the consumer obtained possession of any goods, services, or money as a result of the block.

(d) Exception for Resellers

(1) No reseller file. This section shall not apply to a consumer reporting agency, if the consumer reporting agency—

(A) is a reseller;

(B) is not, at the time of the request of the consumer under subsection (a), otherwise furnishing or reselling a consumer report concerning the information identified by the consumer; and

(C) informs the consumer, by any means, that the consumer may report the identity theft to the Commission to obtain consumer information regarding identity theft.

(2) Reseller with file. The sole obligation of the consumer reporting agency under this section, with regard to any request of a consumer under this section, shall be to block the consumer report maintained by the consumer reporting agency from any subsequent use, if—

(A) the consumer, in accordance with the provisions of subsection (a), identifies, to a consumer reporting agency, information in the file of the consumer that resulted from identity theft; and

(B) the consumer reporting agency is a reseller of the identified information.

(3) Notice. In carrying out its obligation under paragraph (2), the reseller shall promptly provide a notice to the consumer of the decision to block the file. Such notice shall contain the name, address, and telephone number of each consumer reporting agency from which the consumer information was obtained for resale.

(e) Exception for verification companies. The provisions of this section do not apply to a check services company, acting as such, which issues authorizations for the purpose of approving or processing negotiable instruments, electronic fund transfers, or similar methods of payments, except that, beginning 4 business days after receipt of information described in paragraphs (1) through (3) of subsection (a), a check services company shall not report to a national consumer reporting agency described in section 603(p), any information identified in the subject identity theft report as resulting from identity theft.

(f) Access to blocked information by law enforcement agencies. No provision of this section shall be construed as requiring a consumer reporting agency to prevent a Federal, State, or local law enforcement agency from accessing blocked information in a consumer file to which the agency could otherwise obtain access under this title.

§ 606. DISCLOSURE OF INVESTIGATIVE CONSUMER REPORTS.
[15 U.S.C. § 1681d]

(a) Disclosure of fact of preparation. A person may not procure or cause to be prepared an investigative consumer report on any consumer unless—

(1) it is clearly and accurately disclosed to the consumer that an investigative consumer report including information as to his character, general reputation, personal characteristics and mode of living, whichever are applicable, may be made, and such disclosure

(A) is made in a writing mailed, or otherwise delivered, to the consumer, not later than three days after the date on which the report was first requested, and

(B) includes a statement informing the consumer of his right to request the additional disclosures provided for under subsection (b) of this section and the written summary of the rights of the consumer prepared pursuant to section 609(c) [§1681g]; and

(2) the person certifies or has certified to the consumer reporting agency that:

(A) the person has made the disclosures to the consumer required by paragraph (1); and

(B) the person will comply with subsection (b).

(b) Disclosure on request of nature and scope of investigation. Any person who procures or causes to be prepared an investigative consumer report on any consumer shall, upon written request made by the consumer within a reasonable period of time after the receipt by him of the disclosure required by subsection (a)(1) of this section, make a complete and accurate disclosure of the nature and scope of the investigation requested. This disclosure shall be made in a writing mailed, or otherwise delivered, to the consumer not later than five days after the date on which the request for such disclosure was received from the consumer or such report was first requested, whichever is the later.

(c) Limitation on liability upon showing of reasonable procedures for compliance with provisions. No person may be held liable for any violation of subsection (a) or (b) of this section if he shows by a preponderance of the evidence that at the time of the violation he maintained reasonable procedures to assure compliance with subsection (a) or (b) of this section.

(d) Prohibitions.

(1) Certification. A consumer reporting agency shall not prepare or furnish investigative consumer report unless the agency has re-

ceived a certification under subsection (a)(2) from the person who requested the report.

(2) Inquiries. A consumer reporting agency shall not make an inquiry for the purpose of preparing an investigative consumer report on a consumer for employment purposes if the making of the inquiry by an employer or prospective employer of the consumer would violate any applicable Federal or State equal employment opportunity law or regulation.

(3) Certain public record information. Except as otherwise provided in section 613 [§1681k], a consumer reporting agency shall not furnish an investigative consumer report that includes information that is a matter of public record and that relates to an arrest, indictment, conviction, civil judicial action, tax lien, or outstanding judgment, unless the agency has verified the accuracy of the information during the 30-day period ending on the date on which the report is furnished.

(4) Certain adverse information. A consumer reporting agency shall not prepare or furnish an investigative consumer report on a consumer that contains information that is adverse to the interest of the consumer and that is obtained through a personal interview with a neighbor, friend, or associate of the consumer or with another person with whom the consumer is acquainted or who has knowledge of such item of information, unless:

(A) the agency has followed reasonable procedures to obtain confirmation of the information, from an additional source that has independent and direct knowledge of the information; or

(B) the person interviewed is the best possible source of the information.

§ 607. COMPLIANCE PROCEDURES [15 U.S.C. §1681e]

(a) Identity and purposes of credit users. Every consumer reporting agency shall maintain reasonable procedures designed to avoid violations of section 605 [§1681c] and to limit the furnishing of consumer reports to the purposes listed under section 604 [§1681b] of this title. These procedures shall require that prospective users of the information identify themselves, certify the purposes for which the information is sought, and certify that the information will be used for no other purpose. Every consumer reporting agency shall make a reasonable effort to verify the identity of a new prospective user and the uses certified by such prospective user prior to furnishing such user a consumer report. No consumer reporting agency may furnish a consumer report to any person if it has reasonable grounds for believing that the consumer report will not be used for a purpose listed in section 604 [§1681b] of this title.

(b) Accuracy of report. Whenever a consumer reporting agency prepares a consumer report it shall follow reasonable procedures to assure maximum possible accuracy of the information concerning the individual about whom the report relates.

(c) Disclosure of consumer reports by users allowed. A consumer reporting agency may not prohibit a user of a consumer report furnished by the agency on a consumer from disclosing the contents of the report to the consumer, if adverse action against the consumer has been taken by the user based in whole or in part on the report.

(d) Notice to users and furnishers of information.

(1) Notice requirement. A consumer reporting agency shall provide to any person:

(A) who regularly and in the ordinary course of business furnishes information to the agency with respect to any consumer; or

(B) to whom a consumer report is provided by the agency; a notice of such person's responsibilities under this title.

(2) Content of notice. The Federal Trade Commission shall prescribe the content of notices under paragraph (1), and a consumer reporting agency shall be in compliance with this subsection if it provides a notice under paragraph (1) that is substantially similar to the Federal Trade Commission prescription under this paragraph.

(e) Procurement of consumer report for resale.

(1) Disclosure. A person may not procure a consumer report for purposes of reselling the report (or any information in the report) unless the person discloses to the consumer reporting agency that originally furnishes the report:

(A) the identity of the end-user of the report (or information); and

(B) each permissible purpose under section 604 [§1681b] for which the report is furnished to the end-user of the report (or information).

(2) Responsibilities of procurers for resale. A person who procures a consumer report for purposes of reselling the report (or any information in the report) shall:

(A) establish and comply with reasonable procedures designed to ensure that the report (or information) is resold by the person only for a purpose for which the report may be furnished under section 604 [§1681b], including by requiring that each person to which the report (or information) is resold and that resells or provides the report (or information) to any other person:

(i) identifies each end user of the resold report (or information);

(ii) certifies each purpose for which the report (or information) will be used; and

(iii) certifies that the report (or information) will be used for no other purpose; and

(B) before reselling the report, make reasonable efforts to verify the identifications and certifications made under subparagraph (A).

(3) Resale of consumer report to a federal agency or department. Notwithstanding paragraph (1) or (2), a person who procures a consumer report for purposes of reselling the report (or any information in the report) shall not disclose the identity of the end-user of the report under paragraph (1) or (2) if —

(A) the end user is an agency or department of the United States Government which procures the report from the person for purposes of determining the eligibility of the consumer concerned to receive access or continued access to classified information (as defined in section 604(b)(4)(E)(i)); and

(B) the agency or department certifies in writing to the person reselling the report that nondisclosure is necessary to protect classified information or the safety of persons employed by or contracting with, or undergoing investigation for work or contracting with the agency or department.

§ 608. DISCLOSURES TO GOVERNMENTAL AGENCIES [15 U.S.C. §1681f]

Notwithstanding the provisions of section 604 [§1681b] of this title, a consumer reporting agency may furnish identifying information respecting any consumer, limited to his name, address, former addresses, places of employment, or former places of employment, to a governmental agency.

§ 609. DISCLOSURES TO CONSUMERS. [15 U.S.C. § 1681g]

(a) Information on file; sources; report recipients. Every consumer reporting agency shall, upon request, and subject to 610(a)(1) [§ 1681h], clearly and accurately disclose to the consumer:

(1) All information in the consumer's file at the time of the request except that—

(A) if the consumer to whom the file relates requests that the first five digits of the social security number (or similar identification number) of the consumer not be included in the disclosure and the consumer reporting agency has received appropriate proof of the identity of the requester, the consumer reporting agency shall so truncate such number in such disclosure; and

(B) nothing in this paragraph shall be construed to require a consumer reporting agency to disclose to a consumer any information concerning credit scores or any other risk scores or predictors relating to the consumer.

(2) The sources of the information; except that the sources of information acquired solely for use in preparing an investigative consumer report and actually use for no other purpose need not be disclosed: Provided, That in the event an action is brought under this title, such sources shall be available to the plaintiff under appropriate discovery procedures in the court in which the action is brought.

(3)(A) Identification of each person (including each end-user identified under section 607(e)(1) [§ 1681e]) that procured a consumer report

(i) for employment purposes, during the 2-year period preceding the date on which the request is made; or

(ii) for any other purpose, during the 1-year period preceding the date on which the request is made.

(B) An identification of a person under subparagraph (A) shall include

(i) the name of the person or, if applicable, the trade name (written in full) under which such person conducts business; and

(ii) upon request of the consumer, the address and telephone number of the person.

(C) Subparagraph (A) does not apply if—

(i) the end user is an agency or department of the United States Government that procures the report from the person for purposes of determining the eligibility of the consumer to whom the report relates to receive access or continued access to classified information (as defined in section 604(b)(4)(E)(i)); and

(ii) the head of the agency or department makes a written finding as prescribed under section 604(b)(4)(A).

(4) The dates, original payees, and amounts of any checks upon which is based any adverse characterization of the consumer, included in the file at the time of the disclosure.

(5) A record of all inquiries received by the agency during the 1-year period preceding the request that identified the consumer in connection with a credit or insurance transaction that was not initiated by the consumer.

(6) If the consumer requests the credit file and not the credit score, a statement that the consumer may request and obtain a credit score.

(b) Exempt information. The requirements of subsection (a) of this section respecting the disclosure of sources of information and the recipients of consumer reports do not apply to information received or consumer reports furnished prior to the effective date of this title except to the extent that the matter involved is contained in the files of the consumer reporting agency on that date.

(c) Summary of Rights to Obtain and Dispute Information in Consumer Reports and to Obtain Credit Scores

(1) Commission Summary of Rights Required

(A) In general. The Commission shall prepare a model summary of the rights of consumers under this title.

(B) Content of summary. The summary of rights prepared under subparagraph (A) shall include a description of–

(i) the right of a consumer to obtain a copy of a consumer report under subsection (a) from each consumer reporting agency;

(ii) the frequency and circumstances under which a consumer is entitled to receive a consumer report without charge under section 612;

(iii) the right of a consumer to dispute information in the file of the consumer under section 611;

(iv) the right of a consumer to obtain a credit score from a consumer reporting agency, and a description of how to obtain a credit score;

(v) the method by which a consumer can contact, and obtain a consumer report from, a consumer reporting agency without charge, as provided in the regulations of the Commission prescribed under section 211(c) of the Fair and Accurate Credit Transactions Act of 2003; and

(vi) the method by which a consumer can contact, and obtain a consumer report from, a consumer reporting agency described in section 603(w), as provided in the regulations of the Commission prescribed under section 612(a)(1)(C).

(C) Availability of summary of rights. The Commission shall—

(i) actively publicize the availability of the summary of rights prepared under this paragraph;

(ii) conspicuously post on its Internet website the availability of such summary of rights; and

(iii) promptly make such summary of rights available to consumers, on request.

(2) Summary of rights required to be included with agency disclosures. A consumer reporting agency shall provide to a consumer, with each written disclosure by the agency to the consumer under this section—

(A) the summary of rights prepared by the Commission under paragraph (1);

(B) in the case of a consumer reporting agency described in section 603(p), a toll-free telephone number established by the agency, at which personnel are accessible to consumers during normal business hours;

(C) a list of all Federal agencies responsible for enforcing any provision of this title, and the address and any appropriate phone number of each such agency, in a form that will assist the consumer in selecting the appropriate agency;

(D) a statement that the consumer may have additional rights under State law, and that the consumer may wish to contact a State or local consumer protection agency or a State attorney general (or the equivalent thereof) to learn of those rights; and

(E) a statement that a consumer reporting agency is not required to remove accurate derogatory information from the file of a consumer, unless the information is outdated under section 605 or cannot be verified.

(d) Summary of Rights of Identity Theft Victims

(1) In general. The Commission, in consultation with the Federal banking agencies and the National Credit Union Administration, shall prepare a model summary of the rights of consumers under this title with respect to the procedures for remedying the effects of fraud or identity theft involving credit, an electronic fund transfer, or an account or transaction at or with a financial institution or other creditor.

(2) Summary of rights and contact information. Beginning 60 days after the date on which the model summary of rights is prescribed in

final form by the Commission pursuant to paragraph (1), if any consumer contacts a consumer reporting agency and expresses a belief that the consumer is a victim of fraud or identity theft involving credit, an electronic fund transfer, or an account or transaction at or with a financial institution or other creditor, the consumer reporting agency shall, in addition to any other action that the agency may take, provide the consumer with a summary of rights that contains all of the information required by the Commission under paragraph (1), and information on how to contact the Commission to obtain more detailed information.

(e) Information Available to Victims

(1) In general. For the purpose of documenting fraudulent transactions resulting from identity theft, not later than 30 days after the date of receipt of a request from a victim in accordance with paragraph (3), and subject to verification of the identity of the victim and the claim of identity theft in accordance with paragraph (2), a business entity that has provided credit to, provided for consideration products, goods, or services to, accepted payment from, or otherwise entered into a commercial transaction for consideration with, a person who has allegedly made unauthorized use of the means of identification of the victim, shall provide a copy of application and business transaction records in the control of the business entity, whether maintained by the business entity or by another person on behalf of the business entity, evidencing any transaction alleged to be a result of identity theft to—

(A) the victim;

(B) any Federal, State, or local government law enforcement agency or officer specified by the victim in such a request; or

(C) any law enforcement agency investigating the identity theft and authorized by the victim to take receipt of records provided under this subsection.

(2) Verification of identity and claim. Before a business entity provides any information under paragraph (1), unless the business entity, at its discretion, otherwise has a high degree of confidence that it knows the identity of the victim making a request under paragraph (1), the victim shall provide to the business entity—

(A) as proof of positive identification of the victim, at the election of the business entity—

(i) the presentation of a government-issued identification card;

(ii) personally identifying information of the same type as was provided to the business entity by the unauthorized person; or

(iii) personally identifying information that the business entity typically requests from new applicants or for new transactions, at the time of the victim's request for information, including any documentation described in clauses (i) and (ii); and

(B) as proof of a claim of identity theft, at the election of the business entity—

(i) a copy of a police report evidencing the claim of the victim of identity theft; and

(ii) a properly completed—

(I) copy of a standardized affidavit of identity theft developed and made available by the Commission; or

(II) an affidavit of fact that is acceptable to the business entity for that purpose.

(3) Procedures. The request of a victim under paragraph (1) shall—

(A) be in writing;

(B) be mailed to an address specified by the business entity, if any; and

(C) if asked by the business entity, include relevant information about any transaction alleged to be a result of identity theft to facilitate compliance with this section including–

(i) if known by the victim (or if readily obtainable by the victim), the date of the application or transaction; and

(ii) if known by the victim (or if readily obtainable by the victim), any other identifying information such as an account or transaction number.

(4) No charge to victim. Information required to be provided under paragraph (1) shall be so provided without charge.

(5) Authority to decline to provide information. A business entity may decline to provide information under paragraph (1) if, in the exercise of good faith, the business entity determines that—

(A) this subsection does not require disclosure of the information;

(B) after reviewing the information provided pursuant to paragraph (2), the business entity does not have a high degree of confidence in knowing the true identity of the individual requesting the information;

(C) the request for the information is based on a misrepresentation of fact by the individual requesting the information relevant to the request for information; or

(D) the information requested is Internet navigational data or similar information about a person's visit to a website or online service.

(6) Limitation on liability. Except as provided in section 621, sections 616 and 617 do not apply to any violation of this subsection.

(7) Limitation on civil liability. No business entity may be held civilly liable under any provision of Federal, State, or other law for disclosure, made in good faith pursuant to this subsection.

(8) No new recordkeeping obligation. Nothing in this subsection creates an obligation on the part of a business entity to obtain, retain, or maintain information or records that are not otherwise required to be obtained, retained, or maintained in the ordinary course of its business or under other applicable law.

(9) Rule of Construction

(A) In general. No provision of subtitle A of title V of Public Law 106-102, prohibiting the disclosure of financial information by a business entity to third parties shall be used to deny disclosure of information to the victim under this subsection.

(B) Limitation. Except as provided in subparagraph (A), nothing in this subsection permits a business entity to disclose information, including information to law enforcement under subparagraphs (B) and (C) of paragraph (1), that the business entity is otherwise prohibited from disclosing under any other applicable provision of Federal or State law.

(10) Affirmative defense. In any civil action brought to enforce this subsection, it is an affirmative defense (which the defendant must establish by a preponderance of the evidence) for a business entity to file an affidavit or answer stating that—

(A) the business entity has made a reasonably diligent search of its available business records; and

(B) the records requested under this subsection do not exist or are not reasonably available.

(11) Definition of victim. For purposes of this subsection, the term "victim" means a consumer whose means of identification or financial information has been used or transferred (or has been alleged to have been used or transferred) without the authority of that con-

sumer, with the intent to commit, or to aid or abet, an identity theft or a similar crime.

(12) Effective date. This subsection shall become effective 180 days after the date of enactment of this subsection.

(13) Effectiveness study. Not later than 18 months after the date of enactment of this subsection, the Comptroller General of the United States shall submit a report to Congress assessing the effectiveness of this provision.

* * *

§ 610. CONDITIONS AND FORM OF DISCLOSURE TO CONSUMERS. [15 U.S.C. § 1681h]

(a) In general.

(1) Proper identification. A consumer reporting agency shall require, as a condition of making the disclosures required under section 609 [§1681g], that the consumer furnish proper identification.

(2) Disclosure in writing. Except as provided in subsection (b), the disclosures required to be made under section 609 [§1681g] shall be provided under that section in writing.

(b) Other forms of disclosure.

(1) In general. If authorized by a consumer, a consumer reporting agency may make the disclosures required under 609 [§1681g]:

(A) other than in writing; and

(B) in such form as may be:

(i) specified by the consumer in accordance with paragraph (2); and

(ii) available from the agency.

(2) Form. A consumer may specify pursuant to paragraph (1) that disclosures under section 609 [§1681g] shall be made:

(A) in person, upon the appearance of the consumer at the place of business of the consumer reporting agency where disclosures are regularly provided, during normal business hours, and on reasonable notice;

(B) by telephone, if the consumer has made a written request for disclosure by telephone;

(C) by electronic means, if available from the agency; or

(D) by any other reasonable means that is available from the agency.

(c) Trained personnel. Any consumer reporting agency shall provide trained personnel to explain to the consumer any information furnished to him pursuant to section 609 [§1681g] of this title.

(d) Persons accompanying consumer. The consumer shall be permitted to be accompanied by one other person of his choosing, who shall furnish reasonable identification. A consumer reporting agency may require the consumer to furnish a written statement granting permission to the consumer reporting agency to discuss the consumer's file in such person's presence.

(e) Limitation of liability. Except as provided in sections 616 and 617 [§§1681n and 1681o] of this title, no consumer may bring any action or proceeding in the nature of defamation, invasion of privacy, or negligence with respect to the reporting of information against any consumer reporting agency, any user of information, or any person who furnishes information to a consumer reporting agency, based on information disclosed pursuant to section 609, 610, or 615 [§§1681g, 1681h, or 1681m] of this title or based on information disclosed by a user of a consumer report to or for a consumer against whom the user has taken adverse action, based in whole or in part on the report, except as to false information furnished with malice or willful intent to injure such consumer.

§ 611. PROCEDURE IN CASE OF DISPUTED ACCURACY. [15 U.S.C. § 1681i]

(a) Reinvestigations of Disputed Information

(1) Reinvestigation Required

(A) In general. Subject to subsection (f), if the completeness or accuracy of any item of information contained in a consumer's file at a consumer reporting agency is disputed by the consumer and the consumer notifies the agency directly, or indirectly through a reseller, of such dispute, the agency shall, free of charge, conduct a reasonable reinvestigation to determine whether the disputed information is inaccurate and record the current status of the disputed information, or delete the item from the file in accordance with paragraph (5), before the end of the 30-day period beginning on the date on which the agency receives the notice of the dispute from the consumer or reseller.

(B) Extension of period to reinvestigate. Except as provided in subparagraph (C), the 30-day period described in subparagraph (A) may be extended for not more than 15 additional days if the consumer reporting agency receives information from the consumer during that 30-day period that is relevant to the reinvestigation.

(C) Limitations on extension of period to reinvestigate. Subparagraph (B) shall not apply to any reinvestigation in which, during the 30-day period described in subparagraph (A), the information that is the subject of the reinvestigation is found to be inaccurate or incomplete or the consumer reporting agency determines that the information cannot be verified.

(2) Prompt notice of dispute to furnisher of information.

(A) In general. Before the expiration of the 5-business-day period beginning on the date on which a consumer reporting agency receives notice of a dispute from any consumer or a reseller in accordance with paragraph (1), the agency shall provide notification of the dispute to any person who provided any item of information in dispute, at the address and in the manner established with the person. The notice shall include all relevant information regarding the dispute that the agency has received from the consumer or reseller.

(B) Provision of other information. The consumer reporting agency shall promptly provide to the person who provided the information in dispute all relevant information regarding the dispute that is received by the agency from the consumer or the reseller after the period referred to in subparagraph (A) and before the end of the period referred to in paragraph (1)(A).

(3) Determination that dispute is frivolous or irrelevant.

(A) In general. Notwithstanding paragraph (1), a consumer reporting agency may terminate a reinvestigation of information disputed by a consumer under that paragraph if the agency reasonably determines that the dispute by the consumer is frivolous or irrelevant, including by reason of a failure by a consumer to provide sufficient information to investigate the disputed information.

(B) Notice of determination. Upon making any determination in accordance with subparagraph (A) that a dispute is frivolous or irrelevant, a consumer reporting agency shall notify the consumer of such determination not later than 5 business days after making such determination, by mail or, if authorized by the consumer for that purpose, by any other means available to the agency.

(C) Contents of notice. A notice under subparagraph (B) shall include:

(i) the reasons for the determination under subparagraph (A); and

(ii) identification of any information required to investigate the disputed information, which may consist of a standardized form describing the general nature of such information.

(4) Consideration of consumer information. In conducting any reinvestigation under paragraph (1) with respect to disputed information in the file of any consumer, the consumer reporting agency shall review and consider all relevant information submitted by the consumer in the period described in paragraph (1)(A) with respect to such disputed information.

(5) Treatment of inaccurate or unverifiable information.

(A) In general. If, after any reinvestigation under paragraph (1) of any information disputed by a consumer, an item of the information is found to be inaccurate or incomplete or cannot be verified, the consumer reporting agency shall—

(i) promptly delete that item of information from the file of the consumer, or modify that item of information, as appropriate, based on the results of the reinvestigation; and

(ii) promptly notify the furnisher of that information that the information has been modified or deleted from the file of the consumer.

(B) Requirements relating to reinsertion of previously deleted material.

(i) Certification of accuracy of information. If any information is deleted from a consumer's file pursuant to subparagraph (A), the information may not be reinserted in the file by the consumer reporting agency unless the person who furnishes the information certifies that the information is complete and accurate.

(ii) Notice to consumer. If any information that has been deleted from a consumer's file pursuant to subparagraph (A) is reinserted in the file, the consumer reporting agency shall notify the consumer of the reinsertion in writing not later than 5 business days after the reinsertion or, if authorized by the consumer for that purpose, by any other means available to the agency.

(iii) Additional information. As part of, or in addition to, the notice under clause (ii), a consumer reporting agency shall provide to a consumer in writing not later than 5 business days after the date of the reinsertion:

(I) a statement that the disputed information has been reinserted;

(II) the business name and address of any furnisher of information contacted and the telephone number of such furnisher, if reasonably available, or of any furnisher of information that contacted the consumer reporting agency, in connection with the reinsertion of such information; and

(III) a notice that the consumer has the right to add a statement to the consumer's file disputing the accuracy or completeness of the disputed information.

(C) Procedures to prevent reappearance. A consumer reporting agency shall maintain reasonable procedures designed to prevent the reappearance in a consumer's file, and in consumer reports on the consumer, of information that is deleted pursuant to this paragraph (other than information that is reinserted in accordance with subparagraph (B)(i)).

(D) Automated reinvestigation system. Any consumer reporting agency that compiles and maintains files on consumers on a nationwide basis shall implement an automated system through which furnishers of information to that consumer reporting agency may report the results of a reinvestigation that finds incomplete or inaccurate information in a consumer's file to other such consumer reporting agencies.

(6) Notice of results of reinvestigation.

(A) In general. A consumer reporting agency shall provide written notice to a consumer of the results of a reinvestigation under this subsection not later than 5 business days after the completion of the reinvestigation, by mail or, if authorized by the consumer for that purpose, by other means available to the agency.

(B) Contents. As part of, or in addition to, the notice under subparagraph (A), a consumer reporting agency shall provide to a consumer in writing before the expiration of the 5-day period referred to in subparagraph (A):

(i) a statement that the reinvestigation is completed;

(ii) a consumer report that is based upon the consumer's file as that file is revised as a result of the reinvestigation;

(iii) a notice that, if requested by the consumer, a description of the procedure used to determine the accuracy and completeness of the information shall be provided to the consumer by the agency, including the business name and address of any furnisher of information contacted in connection with such information and the telephone number of such furnisher, if reasonably available;

(iv) a notice that the consumer has the right to add a statement to the consumer's file disputing the accuracy or completeness of the information; and

(v) a notice that the consumer has the right to request under subsection (d) that the consumer reporting agency furnish notifications under that subsection.

(7) Description of reinvestigation procedure. A consumer reporting agency shall provide to a consumer a description referred to in paragraph (6)(B)(iii) by not later than 15 days after receiving a request from the consumer for that description.

(8) Expedited dispute resolution. If a dispute regarding an item of information in a consumer's file at a consumer reporting agency is resolved in accordance with paragraph (5)(A) by the deletion of the disputed information by not later than 3 business days after the date on which the agency receives notice of the dispute from the consumer in accordance with paragraph (1)(A), then the agency shall not be required to comply with paragraphs (2), (6), and (7) with respect to that dispute if the agency:

(A) provides prompt notice of the deletion to the consumer by telephone;

(B) includes in that notice, or in a written notice that accompanies a confirmation and consumer report provided in accordance with subparagraph (C), a statement of the consumer's right to request under subsection (d) that the agency furnish notifications under that subsection; and

(C) provides written confirmation of the deletion and a copy of a consumer report on the consumer that is based on the consumer's file after the deletion, not later than 5 business days after making the deletion.

(b) Statement of dispute. If the reinvestigation does not resolve the dispute, the consumer may file a brief statement setting forth the nature of the dispute. The consumer reporting agency may limit such statements to not more than one hundred words if it provides the consumer with assistance in writing a clear summary of the dispute.

(c) Notification of consumer dispute in subsequent consumer reports. Whenever a statement of a dispute is filed, unless there is reasonable grounds to believe that it is frivolous or irrelevant, the consumer reporting agency shall, in any subsequent consumer report containing the information in question, clearly note that it is disputed by the consumer and provide either the consumer's statement or a clear and accurate codification or summary thereof.

(d) Notification of deletion of disputed information. Following any deletion of information which is found to be inaccurate or whose accuracy can no longer be verified or any notation as to disputed information, the consumer reporting agency shall, at the request of the consumer, furnish notification that the item has been deleted or the statement, codification or summary pursuant to subsection (b) or (c) of this section to any person specifically designated by the consumer who has within two years prior thereto received a consumer report for employment purposes, or within six months prior thereto received a consumer report for any other purpose, which contained the deleted or disputed information.

(e) Treatment of Complaints and Report to Congress

(1) In general. The Commission shall—

(A) compile all complaints that it receives that a file of a consumer that is maintained by a consumer reporting agency described in section 603(p) contains incomplete or inaccurate information, with respect to which, the consumer appears to have disputed the completeness or accuracy with the consumer reporting agency or otherwise utilized the procedures provided by subsection (a); and

(B) transmit each such complaint to each consumer reporting agency involved.

(2) Exclusion. Complaints received or obtained by the Commission pursuant to its investigative authority under the Federal Trade Commission Act shall not be subject to paragraph (1).

(3) Agency responsibilities. Each consumer reporting agency described in section 603(p) that receives a complaint transmitted by the Commission pursuant to paragraph (1) shall—

(A) review each such complaint to determine whether all legal obligations imposed on the consumer reporting agency under this title (including any obligation imposed by an applicable court or administrative order) have been met with respect to the subject matter of the complaint;

(B) provide reports on a regular basis to the Commission regarding the determinations of and actions taken by the consumer reporting agency, if any, in connection with its review of such complaints; and

(C) maintain, for a reasonable time period, records regarding the disposition of each such complaint that is sufficient to demonstrate compliance with this subsection.

(4) Rulemaking authority. The Commission may prescribe regulations, as appropriate to implement this subsection.

(5) Annual report. The Commission shall submit to the Committee on Banking, Housing, and Urban Affairs of the Senate and the Committee on Financial Services of the House of Representatives an annual report regarding information gathered by the Commission under this subsection.

(f) Reinvestigation Requirement Applicable to Resellers

(1) Exemption from general reinvestigation requirement. Except as provided in paragraph (2), a reseller shall be exempt from the requirements of this section.

(2) Action required upon receiving notice of a dispute. If a reseller receives a notice from a consumer of a dispute concerning the completeness or accuracy of any item of information contained in a consumer report on such consumer produced by the reseller, the reseller shall, within 5 business days of receiving the notice, and free of charge—

(A) determine whether the item of information is incomplete or inaccurate as a result of an act or omission of the reseller; and

(B) if (i) the reseller determines that the item of information is incomplete or inaccurate as a result of an act or omission of the reseller, not later than 20 days after receiving the notice, correct the information in the consumer report or delete it; or

(ii) if the reseller determines that the item of information is not incomplete or inaccurate as a result of an act or omission of the reseller, convey the notice of the dispute, together with all relevant information provided by the consumer, to each consumer reporting agency that provided the reseller with the information that is the subject of the dispute, using an address or a notification mechanism specified by the consumer reporting agency for such notices.

(3) Responsibility of consumer reporting agency to notify consumer through reseller. Upon the completion of a reinvestigation under this section of a dispute concerning the completeness or accuracy of any in-

formation in the file of a consumer by a consumer reporting agency that received notice of the dispute from a reseller under paragraph (2)—

(A) the notice by the consumer reporting agency under paragraph (6), (7), or (8) of subsection (a) shall be provided to the reseller in lieu of the consumer; and

(B) the reseller shall immediately reconvey such notice to the consumer, including any notice of a deletion by telephone in the manner required under paragraph (8)(A).

(4) Reseller reinvestigations. No provision of this subsection shall be construed as prohibiting a reseller from conducting a reinvestigation of a consumer dispute directly.

§ 612. CHARGES FOR CERTAIN DISCLOSURES. [15 U.S.C. § 1681j]

(a) Free Annual Disclosure

(1) Nationwide Consumer Reporting Agencies

(A) In general. All consumer reporting agencies described in subsections (p) and (w) of section 603 shall make all disclosures pursuant to section 609 once during any 12-month period upon request of the consumer and without charge to the consumer.

(B) Centralized source. Subparagraph (A) shall apply with respect to a consumer reporting agency described in section 603(p) only if the request from the consumer is made using the centralized source established for such purpose in accordance with section 211(c) of the Fair and Accurate Credit Transactions Act of 2003.

(C) Nationwide Specialty Consumer Reporting Agency

(i) In general. The Commission shall prescribe regulations applicable to each consumer reporting agency described in section 603(w) to require the establishment of a streamlined process for consumers to request consumer reports under subparagraph (A), which shall include, at a minimum, the establishment by each such agency of a toll-free telephone number for such requests.

(ii) Considerations. In prescribing regulations under clause (i), the Commission shall consider–

(I) the significant demands that may be placed on consumer reporting agencies in providing such consumer reports;

(II) appropriate means to ensure that consumer reporting agencies can satisfactorily meet those demands, including the efficacy of a system of staggering the availability to consumers of such consumer reports; and

(III) the ease by which consumers should be able to contact consumer reporting agencies with respect to access to such consumer reports.

(iii) Date of issuance. The Commission shall issue the regulations required by this subparagraph in final form not later than 6 months after the date of enactment of the Fair and Accurate Credit Transactions Act of 2003.

(iv) Consideration of ability to comply. The regulations of the Commission under this subparagraph shall establish an effective date by which each nationwide specialty consumer reporting agency (as defined in section 603(w)) shall be required to comply with subsection (a), which effective date—

(I) shall be established after consideration of the ability of each nationwide specialty consumer reporting agency to comply with subsection (a); and

(II) shall be not later than 6 months after the date on which such regulations are issued in final form (or such additional period not to exceed 3 months, as the Commission determines appropriate).

(2) Timing. A consumer reporting agency shall provide a consumer report under paragraph (1) not later than 15 days after the date on which the request is received under paragraph (1).

(3) Reinvestigations. Notwithstanding the time periods specified in section 611(a)(1), a reinvestigation under that section by a consumer reporting agency upon a request of a consumer that is made after receiving a consumer report under this subsection shall be completed not later than 45 days after the date on which the request is received.

(4) Exception for first 12 months of operation. This subsection shall not apply to a consumer reporting agency that has not been furnishing consumer reports to third parties on a continuing basis during the 12-month period preceding a request under paragraph (1), with respect to consumers residing nationwide.

(b) Free disclosure after adverse notice to consumer. Each consumer reporting agency that maintains a file on a consumer shall make all disclosures pursuant to section 609 [§ 1681g] without charge to the consumer if, not later than 60 days after receipt by such consumer of a notification pursuant to section 615 [§ 1681m], or of a notification from a debt collection agency affiliated with that consumer reporting agency stating that the consumer's credit rating may be or has been adversely affected, the consumer makes a request under section 609 [§ 1681g].

(c) Free disclosure under certain other circumstances. Upon the request of the consumer, a consumer reporting agency shall make all disclosures pursuant to section 609 [§ 1681g] once during any 12-month period without charge to that consumer if the consumer certifies in writing that the consumer:

(1) is unemployed and intends to apply for employment in the 60-day period beginning on the date on which the certification is made;

(2) is a recipient of public welfare assistance; or

(3) has reason to believe that the file on the consumer at the agency contains inaccurate information due to fraud.

(d) Free disclosures in connection with fraud alerts. Upon the request of a consumer, a consumer reporting agency described in section 603(p) shall make all disclosures pursuant to section 609 without charge to the consumer, as provided in subsections (a)(2) and (b)(2) of section 605A, as applicable.

(e) Other charges prohibited A consumer reporting agency shall not impose any charge on a consumer for providing any notification required by this title or making any disclosure required by this title, except as authorized by subsection (f).

(f) Reasonable Charges Allowed for Certain Disclosures

(1) In general. In the case of a request from a consumer other than a request that is covered by any of subsections (a) through (d), a consumer reporting agency may impose a reasonable charge on a consumer

(A) for making a disclosure to the consumer pursuant to section 609 [§ 1681g], which charge

(i) shall not exceed $8;4 and

(ii) shall be indicated to the consumer before making the disclosure; and

(B) for furnishing, pursuant to 611(d) [§ 1681i], following a reinvestigation under section 611(a) [§ 1681i], a statement, codification, or summary to a person designated by the consumer under that section after the 30-day period beginning on the date of notification of the consumer under paragraph (6) or (8) of section 611(a) [§ 1681i] with respect to the reinvestigation, which charge

(i) shall not exceed the charge that the agency would impose on each designated recipient for a consumer report; and

(ii) shall be indicated to the consumer before furnishing such information.

(2) Modification of amount. The Federal Trade Commission shall increase the amount referred to in paragraph (1)(A)(I) on January 1 of each year, based proportionally on changes in the Consumer Price Index, with fractional changes rounded to the nearest fifty cents.

§ 613. PUBLIC RECORD INFORMATION FOR EMPLOYMENT PURPOSES [15 U.S.C. §1681k]

(a) In general. A consumer reporting agency which furnishes a consumer report for employment purposes and which for that purpose compiles and reports items of information on consumers which are matters of public record and are likely to have an adverse effect upon a consumer's ability to obtain employment shall:

(1) at the time such public record information is reported to the user of such consumer report, notify the consumer of the fact that public record information is being reported by the consumer reporting agency, together with the name and address of the person to whom such information is being reported; or

(2) maintain strict procedures designed to insure that whenever public record information which is likely to have an adverse effect on a consumer's ability to obtain employment is reported it is complete and up to date. For purposes of this paragraph, items of public record relating to arrests, indictments, convictions, suits, tax liens, and outstanding judgments shall be considered up to date if the current public record status of the item at the time of the report is reported.

(b) Exemption for national security investigations. Subsection (a) does not apply in the case of an agency or department of the United States Government that seeks to obtain and use a consumer report for employment purposes, if the head of the agency or department makes a written finding as prescribed under section 604(b)(4)(A).

§ 614. RESTRICTIONS ON INVESTIGATIVE CONSUMER REPORTS. [15 U.S.C. § 1681l]

Whenever a consumer reporting agency prepares an investigative consumer report, no adverse information in the consumer report (other than information which is a matter of public record) may be included in a subsequent consumer report unless such adverse information has been verified in the process of making such subsequent consumer report, or the adverse information was received within the three-month period preceding the date the subsequent report is furnished.

§ 615. REQUIREMENTS ON USERS OF CONSUMER REPORTS
[15 U.S.C. §1681m]

(a) Duties of users taking adverse actions on the basis of information contained in consumer reports. If any person takes any adverse action with respect to any consumer that is based in whole or in part on any information contained in a consumer report, the person shall:

(1) provide oral, written, or electronic notice of the adverse action to the consumer;

(2) provide to the consumer orally, in writing, or electronically:

(A) the name, address, and telephone number of the consumer reporting agency (including a toll-free telephone number established by the agency if the agency compiles and maintains files on consumers on a nationwide basis) that furnished the report to the person; and

(B) a statement that the consumer reporting agency did not make the decision to take the adverse action and is unable to provide the consumer the specific reasons why the adverse action was taken; and

(3) provide to the consumer an oral, written, or electronic notice of the consumer's right:

(A) to obtain, under section 612 [§1681j], a free copy of a consumer report on the consumer from the consumer reporting agency referred to in paragraph (2), which notice shall include an indication of the 60-day period under that section for obtaining such a copy; and

(B) to dispute, under section 611 [§1681i], with a consumer reporting agency the accuracy or completeness of any information in a consumer report furnished by the agency.

(b) Adverse action based on information obtained from third parties other than consumer reporting agencies.

(1) In general. Whenever credit for personal, family, or household purposes involving a consumer is denied or the charge for such credit is increased either wholly or partly because of information obtained from a person other than a consumer reporting agency bearing upon the consumer's credit worthiness, credit standing, credit capacity, character, general reputation, personal characteristics, or mode of

living, the user of such information shall, within a reasonable period of time, upon the consumer's written request for the reasons for such adverse action received within sixty days after learning of such adverse action, disclose the nature of the information to the consumer. The user of such information shall clearly and accurately disclose to the consumer his right to make such written request at the time such adverse action is communicated to the consumer.

(2) Duties of person taking certain actions based on information provided by affiliate.

(A) Duties, generally. If a person takes an action described in subparagraph (B) with respect to a consumer, based in whole or in part on information described in subparagraph (C), the person shall:

(i) notify the consumer of the action, including a statement that the consumer may obtain the information in accordance with clause (ii); and

(ii) upon a written request from the consumer received within 60 days after transmittal of the notice required by clause (I), disclose to the consumer the nature of the information upon which the action is based by not later than 30 days after receipt of the request.

(B) Action described. An action referred to in subparagraph (A) is an adverse action described in section 603(k)(1)(A) [§ 1681a], taken in connection with a transaction initiated by the consumer, or any adverse action described in clause (i) or (ii) of section 603(k)(1)(B) [§1681a].

(C) Information described. Information referred to in subparagraph (A):

(i) except as provided in clause (ii), is information that:

(I) is furnished to the person taking the action by a person related by common ownership or affiliated by common corporate control to the person taking the action; and

(II) bears on the credit worthiness, credit standing, credit capacity, character, general reputation, personal characteristics, or mode of living of the consumer; and

(ii) does not include:

(I) information solely as to transactions or experiences between the consumer and the person furnishing the information; or

(II) information in a consumer report.

(c) Reasonable procedures to assure compliance. No person shall be held liable for any violation of this section if he shows by a preponderance of the evidence that at the time of the alleged violation he maintained reasonable procedures to assure compliance with the provisions of this section.

(d) Duties of users making written credit or insurance solicitations on the basis of information contained in consumer files.

(1) In general. Any person who uses a consumer report on any consumer in connection with any credit or insurance transaction that is not initiated by the consumer, that is provided to that person under section 604(c)(1)(B) [§1681b], shall provide with each written solicitation made to the consumer regarding the transaction a clear and conspicuous statement that:

(A) information contained in the consumer's consumer report was used in connection with the transaction;

(B) the consumer received the offer of credit or insurance because the consumer satisfied the criteria for credit worthiness or insurability under which the consumer was selected for the offer;

(C) if applicable, the credit or insurance may not be extended if, after the consumer responds to the offer, the consumer does not meet the criteria used to select the consumer for the offer or any applicable criteria bearing on credit worthiness or insurability or does not furnish any required collateral;

(D) the consumer has a right to prohibit information contained in the consumer's file with any consumer reporting agency from being used in connection with any credit or insurance transaction that is not initiated by the consumer; and

(E) the consumer may exercise the right referred to in subparagraph (D) by notifying a notification system established under section 604(e) [§1681b].

(2) Disclosure of address and telephone number; format. A statement under paragraph (1) shall—

(A) include the address and toll-free telephone number of the appropriate notification system established under section 604(e); and (B) be presented in such format and in such type size and manner as to be simple and easy to understand, as established by the Commission, by rule, in consultation with the Federal banking agencies and the National Credit Union Administration.

(3) Maintaining criteria on file. A person who makes an offer of credit or insurance to a consumer under a credit or insurance transaction

described in paragraph (1) shall maintain on file the criteria used to select the consumer to receive the offer, all criteria bearing on credit worthiness or insurability, as applicable, that are the basis for determining whether or not to extend credit or insurance pursuant to the offer, and any requirement for the furnishing of collateral as a condition of the extension of credit or insurance, until the expiration of the 3-year period beginning on the date on which the offer is made to the consumer.

(4) Authority of federal agencies regarding unfair or deceptive acts or practices not affected. This section is not intended to affect the authority of any Federal or State agency to enforce a prohibition against unfair or deceptive acts or practices, including the making of false or misleading statements in connection with a credit or insurance transaction that is not initiated by the consumer.

(e) Red Flag Guidelines and Regulations Required

(1) Guidelines. The Federal banking agencies, the National Credit Union Administration, and the Commission shall jointly, with respect to the entities that are subject to their respective enforcement authority under section 621–

(A) establish and maintain guidelines for use by each financial institution and each creditor regarding identity theft with respect to account holders at, or customers of, such entities, and update such guidelines as often as necessary;

(B) prescribe regulations requiring each financial institution and each creditor to establish reasonable policies and procedures for implementing the guidelines established pursuant to subparagraph (A), to identify possible risks to account holders or customers or to the safety and soundness of the institution or customers; and

(C) prescribe regulations applicable to card issuers to ensure that, if a card issuer receives notification of a change of address for an existing account, and within a short period of time (during at least the first 30 days after such notification is received) receives a request for an additional or replacement card for the same account, the card issuer may not issue the additional or replacement card, unless the card issuer, in accordance with reasonable policies and procedures—

(i) notifies the cardholder of the request at the former address of the cardholder and provides to the cardholder a means of promptly reporting incorrect address changes;

(ii) notifies the cardholder of the request by such other means of communication as the cardholder and the card issuer previously agreed to; or

(iii) uses other means of assessing the validity of the change of address, in accordance with reasonable policies and procedures established by the card issuer in accordance with the regulations prescribed under subparagraph (B).

(2) Criteria

(A) In general. In developing the guidelines required by paragraph (1)(A), the agencies described in paragraph (1) shall identify patterns, practices, and specific forms of activity that indicate the possible existence of identity theft.

(B) Inactive accounts. In developing the guidelines required by paragraph (1)(A), the agencies described in paragraph (1) shall consider including reasonable guidelines providing that when a transaction occurs with respect to a credit or deposit account that has been inactive for more than 2 years, the creditor or financial institution shall follow reasonable policies and procedures that provide for notice to be given to a consumer in a manner reasonably designed to reduce the likelihood of identity theft with respect to such account.

(3) Consistency with verification requirements. Guidelines established pursuant to paragraph (1) shall not be inconsistent with the policies and procedures required under section 5318(l) of title 31, United States Code.

(f) Prohibition on Sale or Transfer of Debt Caused by Identity Theft

(1) In general. No person shall sell, transfer for consideration, or place for collection a debt that such person has been notified under section 605B has resulted from identity theft.

(2) Applicability. The prohibitions of this subsection shall apply to all persons collecting a debt described in paragraph (1) after the date of a notification under paragraph (1).

(3) Rule of construction. Nothing in this subsection shall be construed to prohibit—

(A) the repurchase of a debt in any case in which the assignee of the debt requires such repurchase because the debt has resulted from identity theft;

(B) the securitization of a debt or the pledging of a portfolio of debt as collateral in connection with a borrowing; or

(C) the transfer of debt as a result of a merger, acquisition, purchase and assumption transaction, or transfer of substantially all of the assets of an entity.

(g) Debt collector communications concerning identity theft. If a person acting as a debt collector (as that term is defined in title VIII) on behalf of a third party that is a creditor or other user of a consumer report is notified that any information relating to a debt that the person is attempting to collect may be fraudulent or may be the result of identity theft, that person shall—

(1) notify the third party that the information may be fraudulent or may be the result of identity theft; and

(2) upon request of the consumer to whom the debt purportedly relates, provide to the consumer all information to which the consumer would otherwise be entitled if the consumer were not a victim of identity theft, but wished to dispute the debt under provisions of law applicable to that person.

(h) Duties of Users in Certain Credit Transactions

(1) In general. Subject to rules prescribed as provided in paragraph (6), if any person uses a consumer report in connection with an application for, or a grant, extension, or other provision of, credit on material terms that are materially less favorable than the most favorable terms available to a substantial proportion of consumers from or through that person, based in whole or in part on a consumer report, the person shall provide an oral, written, or electronic notice to the consumer in the form and manner required by regulations prescribed in accordance with this subsection.

(2) Timing. The notice required under paragraph (1) may be provided at the time of an application for, or a grant, extension, or other provision of, credit or the time of communication of an approval of an application for, or grant, extension, or other provision of, credit, except as provided in the regulations prescribed under paragraph (6).

(3) Exceptions. No notice shall be required from a person under this subsection if—

(A) the consumer applied for specific material terms and was granted those terms, unless those terms were initially specified by the person after the transaction was initiated by the consumer and after the person obtained a consumer report; or

(B) the person has provided or will provide a notice to the consumer under subsection (a) in connection with the transaction.

(4) Other notice not sufficient. A person that is required to provide a notice under subsection (a) cannot meet that requirement by providing a notice under this subsection.

(5) Content and delivery of notice. A notice under this subsection shall, at a minimum—

(A) include a statement informing the consumer that the terms offered to the consumer are set based on information from a consumer report;

(B) identify the consumer reporting agency furnishing the report;

(C) include a statement informing the consumer that the consumer may obtain a copy of a consumer report from that consumer reporting agency without charge; and

(D) include the contact information specified by that consumer reporting agency for obtaining such consumer reports (including a toll-free telephone number established by the agency in the case of a consumer reporting agency described in section 603(p)).

(6) Rulemaking

(A) Rules required. The Commission and the Board shall jointly prescribe rules.

(B) Content. Rules required by subparagraph (A) shall address, but are not limited to–

(i) the form, content, time, and manner of delivery of any notice under this subsection;

(ii) clarification of the meaning of terms used in this subsection, including what credit terms are material, and when credit terms are materially less favorable;

(iii) exceptions to the notice requirement under this subsection for classes of persons or transactions regarding which the agencies determine that notice would not significantly benefit consumers;

(iv) a model notice that may be used to comply with this subsection; and

(v) the timing of the notice required under paragraph (1), including the circumstances under which the notice must be provided after the terms offered to the consumer were set based on information from a consumer report.

(7) Compliance. A person shall not be liable for failure to perform the duties required by this section if, at the time of the failure, the person maintained reasonable policies and procedures to comply with this section.

(8) Enforcement

(A) No civil actions. Sections 616 and 617 shall not apply to any failure by any person to comply with this section.

(B) Administrative enforcement. This section shall be enforced exclusively under section 621 by the Federal agencies and officials identified in that section.

§ 616. CIVIL LIABILITY FOR WILLFUL NONCOMPLIANCE. [15 U.S.C. § 1681n]

(a) In general. Any person who willfully fails to comply with any requirement imposed under this title with respect to any consumer is liable to that consumer in an amount equal to the sum of:

(1) (A) any actual damages sustained by the consumer as a result of the failure or damages of not less than $100 and not more than $1,000; or

(B) in the case of liability of a natural person for obtaining a consumer report under false pretenses or knowingly without a permissible purpose, actual damages sustained by the consumer as a result of the failure or $1,000, whichever is greater;

(2) such amount of punitive damages as the court may allow; and

(3) in the case of any successful action to enforce any liability under this section, the costs of the action together with reasonable attorney's fees as determined by the court.

(b) Civil liability for knowing noncompliance. Any person who obtains a consumer report from a consumer reporting agency under false pretenses or knowingly without a permissible purpose shall be liable to the consumer reporting agency for actual damages sustained by the consumer reporting agency or $1,000, whichever is greater.

(c) Attorney's fees. Upon a finding by the court that an unsuccessful pleading, motion, or other paper filed in connection with an action under this section was filed in bad faith or for purposes of harassment, the court shall award to the prevailing party attorney's fees reasonable in relation to the work expended in responding to the pleading, motion, or other paper.

§ 617. CIVIL LIABILITY FOR NEGLIGENT NONCOMPLIANCE.
[15 U.S.C. § 1681o]

(a) In general. Any person who is negligent in failing to comply with any requirement imposed under this title with respect to any consumer is liable to that consumer in an amount equal to the sum of:

(1) any actual damages sustained by the consumer as a result of the failure; and

(2) in the case of any successful action to enforce any liability under this section, the costs of the action together with reasonable attorney's fees as determined by the court.

(b) Attorney's fees. On a finding by the court that an unsuccessful pleading, motion, or other paper filed in connection with an action under this section was filed in bad faith or for purposes of harassment, the court shall award to the prevailing party attorney's fees reasonable in relation to the work expended in responding to the pleading, motion, or other paper.

§ 618. JURISDICTION OF COURTS; LIMITATION OF ACTIONS.
[15 U.S.C. § 1681p]

An action to enforce any liability created under this title may be brought in any appropriate United States district court, without regard to the amount in controversy, or in any other court of competent jurisdiction, not later than the earlier of (1) 2 years after the date of discovery by the plaintiff of the violation that is the basis for such liability; or (2) 5 years after the date on which the violation that is the basis for such liability occurs.

§ 619. OBTAINING INFORMATION UNDER FALSE PRETENSES.
[15 U.S.C. § 1681q]

Any person who knowingly and willfully obtains information on a consumer from a consumer reporting agency under false pretenses shall be fined under title 18, United States Code, imprisoned for not more than 2 years, or both.

§ 620. UNAUTHORIZED DISCLOSURES BY OFFICERS OR EMPLOYEES.
[15 U.S.C. § 1681r]

Any officer or employee of a consumer reporting agency who knowingly and willfully provides information concerning an individual from the agency's files to a person not authorized to receive that information shall be fined under title 18, United States Code, imprisoned for not more than 2 years, or both.

§ 621. ADMINISTRATIVE ENFORCEMENT. [15 U.S.C. § 1681s]

(a) (1) Enforcement by Federal Trade Commission.

Compliance with the requirements imposed under this title shall be enforced under the Federal Trade Commission Act [15 U.S.C. §§ 41 et seq.] by the Federal Trade Commission with respect to consumer reporting agencies and all other persons subject thereto, except to the extent that enforcement of the requirements imposed under this title is specifically committed to some other government agency under subsection (b) hereof. For the purpose of the exercise by the Federal Trade Commission of its functions and powers under the Federal Trade Commission Act, a violation of any requirement or prohibition imposed under this title shall constitute an unfair or deceptive act or practice in commerce in violation of section 5(a) of the Federal Trade Commission Act [15 U.S.C. § 45(a)] and shall be subject to enforcement by the Federal Trade Commission under section 5(b) thereof [15 U.S.C. § 45(b)] with respect to any consumer reporting agency or person subject to enforcement by the Federal Trade Commission pursuant to this subsection, irrespective of whether that person is engaged in commerce or meets any other jurisdictional tests in the Federal Trade Commission Act. The Federal Trade Commission shall have such procedural, investigative, and enforcement powers, including the power to issue procedural rules in enforcing compliance with the requirements imposed under this title and to require the filing of reports, the production of documents, and the appearance of witnesses as though the applicable terms and conditions of the Federal Trade Commission Act were part of this title. Any person violating any of the provisions of this title shall be subject to the penalties and entitled to the privileges and immunities provided in the Federal Trade Commission Act as though the applicable terms and provisions thereof were part of this title.

(2) (A) In the event of a knowing violation, which constitutes a pattern or practice of violations of this title, the Commission may commence a civil action to recover a civil penalty in a district court of the United States against any person that violates this title. In such action, such person shall be liable for a civil penalty of not more than $2,500 per violation.

(B) In determining the amount of a civil penalty under subparagraph (A), the court shall take into account the degree of culpability, any history of prior such conduct, ability to pay, effect on ability to continue to do business, and such other matters as justice may require.

(3) Notwithstanding paragraph (2), a court may not impose any civil penalty on a person for a violation of section 623(a)(1) [§1681s-2]

unless the person has been enjoined from committing the violation, or ordered not to commit the violation, in an action or proceeding brought by or on behalf of the Federal Trade Commission, and has violated the injunction or order, and the court may not impose any civil penalty for any violation occurring before the date of the violation of the injunction or order.

(4) Neither the Commission nor any other agency referred to in subsection (b) may prescribe trade regulation rules or other regulations with respect to this title.

(b) Enforcement by other agencies. Compliance with the requirements imposed under this title with respect to consumer reporting agencies, persons who use consumer reports from such agencies, persons who furnish information to such agencies, and users of information that are subject to subsection (d) of section 615 [§1681m] shall be enforced under

(1) section 8 of the Federal Deposit Insurance Act [12 U.S.C. § 1818], in the case of:

> (A) national banks, and Federal branches and Federal agencies of foreign banks, by the Office of the Comptroller of the Currency;

> (B) member banks of the Federal Reserve System (other than national banks), branches and agencies of foreign banks (other than Federal branches, Federal agencies, and insured State branches of foreign banks), commercial lending companies owned or controlled by foreign banks, and organizations operating under section 25 or 25A of the Federal Reserve Act [12 U.S.C. §§ 601 et seq., §§ 611 et seq], by the Board of Governors of the Federal Reserve System; and

> (C) banks insured by the Federal Deposit Insurance Corporation (other than members of the Federal Reserve System) and insured State branches of foreign banks, by the Board of Directors of the Federal Deposit Insurance Corporation;

(2) section 8 of the Federal Deposit Insurance Act [12 U.S.C. § 1818], by the Director of the Office of Thrift Supervision, in the case of a savings association the deposits of which are insured by the Federal Deposit Insurance Corporation;

(3) the Federal Credit Union Act [12 U.S.C. §§ 1751 et seq.], by the Administrator of the National Credit Union Administration [National Credit Union Administration Board] with respect to any Federal credit union;

(4) subtitle IV of title 49 [49 U.S.C. §§ 10101 et seq.], by the Secretary of Transportation, with respect to all carriers subject to the jurisdiction of the Surface Transportation Board;

(5) the Federal Aviation Act of 1958 [49 U.S.C. Appx §§ 1301 et seq.], by the Secretary of Transportation with respect to any air carrier or foreign air carrier subject to that Act [49 U.S.C. Appx §§ 1301 et seq.]; and

(6) the Packers and Stockyards Act, 1921 [7 U.S.C. §§ 181 et seq.] (except as provided in section 406 of that Act [7 U.S.C. §§ 226 and 227]), by the Secretary of Agriculture with respect to any activities subject to that Act.

The terms used in paragraph (1) that are not defined in this title or otherwise defined in section 3(s) of the Federal Deposit Insurance Act (12 U.S.C. §1813(s)) shall have the meaning given to them in section 1(b) of the International Banking Act of 1978 (12 U.S.C. §3101).

(c) State action for violations.

(1) Authority of states. In addition to such other remedies as are provided under State law, if the chief law enforcement officer of a State, or an official or agency designated by a State, has reason to believe that any person has violated or is violating this title, the State:

(A) may bring an action to enjoin such violation in any appropriate United States district court or in any other court of competent jurisdiction;

(B) subject to paragraph (5), may bring an action on behalf of the residents of the State to recover:

(i) damages for which the person is liable to such residents under sections 616 and 617 [§§1681n and 1681o] as a result of the violation;

(ii) in the case of a violation described in any of paragraphs (1) through (3) of Section 623(c), damages for which the person would, but for section 623(c) [§1681s-2], be liable to such residents as a result of the violation; or

(iii) damages of not more than $1,000 for each willful or negligent violation; and

(C) in the case of any successful action under subparagraph (A) or (B), shall be awarded the costs of the action and reasonable attorney fees as determined by the court.

(2) Rights of federal regulators. The State shall serve prior written notice of any action under paragraph (1) upon the Federal Trade

Commission or the appropriate Federal regulator determined under subsection (b) and provide the Commission or appropriate Federal regulator with a copy of its complaint, except in any case in which such prior notice is not feasible, in which case the State shall serve such notice immediately upon instituting such action. The Federal Trade Commission or appropriate Federal regulator shall have the right:

(A) to intervene in the action;

(B) upon so intervening, to be heard on all matters arising therein;

(C) to remove the action to the appropriate United States district court; and

(D) to file petitions for appeal.

(3) Investigatory powers. For purposes of bringing any action under this subsection, nothing in this subsection shall prevent the chief law enforcement officer, or an official or agency designated by a State, from exercising the powers conferred on the chief law enforcement officer or such official by the laws of such State to conduct investigations or to administer oaths or affirmations or to compel the attendance of witnesses or the production of documentary and other evidence.

(4) Limitation on state action while federal action pending. If the Federal Trade Commission or the appropriate Federal regulator has instituted a civil action or an administrative action under section 8 of the Federal Deposit Insurance Act for a violation of this title, no State may, during the pendency of such action, bring an action under this section against any defendant named in the complaint of the Commission or the appropriate Federal regulator for any violation of this title that is alleged in that complaint.

(5) Limitations on state actions for certain violations.

(A) Violation of injunction required. A State may not bring an action against a person under paragraph (1)(B) for a violation described in any of paragraphs (1) through (3) of Section 623(c), unless:

(i) the person has been enjoined from committing the violation, in an action brought by the State under paragraph (1)(A); and

(ii) the person has violated the injunction.

(B) Limitation on damages recoverable. In an action against a person under paragraph (1)(B) for a violation described in any of paragraphs (1) through (3) of Section 623(c), a State may not recover any damages incurred before the date of the violation of an injunction on which the action is based.

(d) Enforcement under other authority. For the purpose of the exercise by any agency referred to in subsection (b) of this section of its powers under any Act referred to in that subsection, a violation of any requirement imposed under this title shall be deemed to be a violation of a requirement imposed under that Act. In addition to its powers under any provision of law specifically referred to in subsection (b) of this section, each of the agencies referred to in that subsection may exercise, for the purpose of enforcing compliance with any requirement imposed under this title any other authority conferred on it by law.

(e) Regulatory authority

(1) The Federal banking agencies referred to in paragraphs (1) and (2) of subsection (b) shall jointly prescribe such regulations as necessary to carry out the purposes of this Act with respect to any persons identified under paragraphs (1) and (2) of subsection (b), and the Board of Governors of the Federal Reserve System shall have authority to prescribe regulations consistent with such joint regulations with respect to bank holding companies and affiliates (other than depository institutions and consumer reporting agencies) of such holding companies.

(2) The Board of the National Credit Union Administration shall prescribe such regulations as necessary to carry out the purposes of this Act with respect to any persons identified under paragraph (3) of subsection (b).

(f) Coordination of Consumer Complaint Investigations

(1) In general. Each consumer reporting agency described in section 603(p) shall develop and maintain procedures for the referral to each other such agency of any consumer complaint received by the agency alleging identity theft, or requesting a fraud alert under section 605A or a block under section 605B.

(2) Model form and procedure for reporting identity theft. The Commission, in consultation with the Federal banking agencies and the National Credit Union Administration, shall develop a model form and model procedures to be used by consumers who are victims of identity theft for contacting and informing creditors and consumer reporting agencies of the fraud.

(3) Annual summary reports. Each consumer reporting agency described in section 603(p) shall submit an annual summary report to

the Commission on consumer complaints received by the agency on identity theft or fraud alerts.

(g) FTC regulation of coding of trade names. If the Commission determines that a person described in paragraph (9) of section 623(a) has not met the requirements of such paragraph, the Commission shall take action to ensure the person's compliance with such paragraph, which may include issuing model guidance or prescribing reasonable policies and procedures, as necessary to ensure that such person complies with such paragraph.

§ 622. INFORMATION ON OVERDUE CHILD SUPPORT OBLIGATIONS [15 U.S.C. §1681s-1]

Notwithstanding any other provision of this title, a consumer reporting agency shall include in any consumer report furnished by the agency in accordance with section 604 [§1681b] of this title, any information on the failure of the consumer to pay overdue support which:

(1) is provided:

(A) to the consumer reporting agency by a State or local child support enforcement agency; or

(B) to the consumer reporting agency and verified by any local, State, or Federal government agency; and

(2) antedates the report by 7 years or less.

§ 623. RESPONSIBILITIES OF FURNISHERS OF INFORMATION TO CONSUMER REPORTING AGENCIES. [15 U.S.C. § 1681s-2]

(a) Duty of furnishers of information to provide accurate information.

(1) Prohibition.

(A) Reporting information with actual knowledge of errors. A person shall not furnish any information relating to a consumer to any consumer reporting agency if the person knows or has reasonable cause to believe that the information is inaccurate.

(B) Reporting information after notice and confirmation of errors. A person shall not furnish information relating to a consumer to any consumer reporting agency if:

(i) the person has been notified by the consumer, at the address specified by the person for such notices, that specific information is inaccurate; and

(ii) the information is, in fact, inaccurate.

(C) No address requirement. A person who clearly and conspicuously specifies to the consumer an address for notices referred to in subparagraph (B) shall not be subject to subparagraph (A); however, nothing in subparagraph (B) shall require a person to specify such an address.

(D) Definition. For purposes of subparagraph (A), the term "reasonable cause to believe that the information is inaccurate" means having specific knowledge, other than solely allegations by the consumer, that would cause a reasonable person to have substantial doubts about the accuracy of the information.

(2) Duty to correct and update information. A person who:

(A) regularly and in the ordinary course of business furnishes information to one or more consumer reporting agencies about the person's transactions or experiences with any consumer; and

(B) has furnished to a consumer reporting agency information that the person determines is not complete or accurate, shall promptly notify the consumer reporting agency of that determination and provide to the agency any corrections to that information, or any additional information, that is necessary to make the information provided by the person to the agency complete and accurate, and shall not thereafter furnish to the agency any of the information that remains not complete or accurate.

(3) Duty to provide notice of dispute. If the completeness or accuracy of any information furnished by any person to any consumer reporting agency is disputed to such person by a consumer, the person may not furnish the information to any consumer reporting agency without notice that such information is disputed by the consumer.

(4) Duty to provide notice of closed accounts. A person who regularly and in the ordinary course of business furnishes information to a consumer reporting agency regarding a consumer who has a credit account with that person shall notify the agency of the voluntary closure of the account by the consumer, in information regularly furnished for the period in which the account is closed.

(5) Duty to Provide Notice of Delinquency of Accounts

(A) In general. A person who furnishes information to a consumer reporting agency regarding a delinquent account being placed for collection, charged to profit or loss, or subjected to any similar action shall, not later than 90 days after furnishing the information, notify the agency of the date of delinquency on the account, which shall be the month and year of the commencement of the delinquency on the account that immediately preceded the action.

(B) Rule of construction. For purposes of this paragraph only, and provided that the consumer does not dispute the information, a person that furnishes information on a delinquent account that is placed for collection, charged for profit or loss, or subjected to any similar action, complies with this paragraph, if—

(i) the person reports the same date of delinquency as that provided by the creditor to which the account was owed at the time at which the commencement of the delinquency occurred, if the creditor previously reported that date of delinquency to a consumer reporting agency;

(ii) the creditor did not previously report the date of delinquency to a consumer reporting agency, and the person establishes and follows reasonable procedures to obtain the date of delinquency from the creditor or another reliable source and reports that date to a consumer reporting agency as the date of delinquency; or

(iii) the creditor did not previously report the date of delinquency to a consumer reporting agency and the date of delinquency cannot be reasonably obtained as provided in clause (ii), the person establishes and follows reasonable procedures to ensure the date reported as the date of delinquency precedes the date on which the account is placed for collection, charged to profit or loss, or subjected to any similar action, and reports such date to the credit reporting agency.

(6) Duties of Furnishers Upon Notice of Identity Theft-Related Information

(A) Reasonable procedures. A person that furnishes information to any consumer reporting agency shall have in place reasonable procedures to respond to any notification that it receives from a consumer reporting agency under section 605B relating to information resulting from identity theft, to prevent that person from refurnishing such blocked information.

(B) Information alleged to result from identity theft. If a consumer submits an identity theft report to a person who furnishes information to a consumer reporting agency at the address specified by that person for receiving such reports stating that information maintained by such person that purports to relate to the consumer resulted from identity theft, the person may not furnish such information that purports to relate to the consumer to any consumer reporting agency, unless the person subsequently knows or is informed by the consumer that the information is correct.

(7) Negative Information

(A) Notice to Consumer Required

(i) In general. If any financial institution that extends credit and regularly and in the ordinary course of business furnishes information to a consumer reporting agency described in section 603(p) furnishes negative information to such an agency regarding credit extended to a customer, the financial institution shall provide a notice of such furnishing of negative information, in writing, to the customer.

(ii) Notice effective for subsequent submissions. After providing such notice, the financial institution may submit additional negative information to a consumer reporting agency described in section 603(p) with respect to the same transaction, extension of credit, account, or customer without providing additional notice to the customer.

(B) Time of Notice

(i) In general. The notice required under subparagraph (A) shall be provided to the customer prior to, or no later than 30 days after, furnishing the negative information to a consumer reporting agency described in section 603(p).

(ii) Coordination with new account disclosures. If the notice is provided to the customer prior to furnishing the negative information to a consumer reporting agency, the notice may not be included in the initial disclosures provided under section 127(a) of the Truth in Lending Act.

(C) Coordination with other disclosures- The notice required under subparagraph (A)—

(i) may be included on or with any notice of default, any billing statement, or any other materials provided to the customer; and

(ii) must be clear and conspicuous.

(D) Model Disclosure

(i) Duty of board to prepare. The Board shall prescribe a brief model disclosure a financial institution may use to comply with subparagraph (A), which shall not exceed 30 words.

(ii) Use of model not required. No provision of this paragraph shall be construed as requiring a financial institution to use any such model form prescribed by the Board.

(iii) Compliance using model. A financial institution shall be deemed to be in compliance with subparagraph (A) if the financial institution uses any such model form prescribed by the Board, or the financial institution uses any such model form and rearranges its format.

(E) Use of notice without submitting negative information. No provision of this paragraph shall be construed as requiring a financial institution that has provided a customer with a notice described in subparagraph (A) to furnish negative information about the customer to a consumer reporting agency.

(F) Safe harbor. A financial institution shall not be liable for failure to perform the duties required by this paragraph if, at the time of the failure, the financial institution maintained reasonable policies and procedures to comply with this paragraph or the financial institution reasonably believed that the institution is prohibited, by law, from contacting the consumer.

(G) Definitions. For purposes of this paragraph, the following definitions shall apply:

(i) The term "negative information" means information concerning a customer's delinquencies, late payments, insolvency, or any form of default.

(ii) The terms "customer" and "financial institution" have the same meanings as in section 509 Public Law 106-102.

(8) Ability of Consumer to Dispute Information Directly with Furnisher

(A) In general. The Federal banking agencies, the National Credit Union Administration, and the Commission shall jointly prescribe regulations that shall identify the circumstances under which a furnisher shall be required to reinvestigate a dispute concerning the accuracy of information contained in a consumer report on the consumer, based on a direct request of a consumer.

(B) Considerations. In prescribing regulations under subparagraph (A), the agencies shall weigh—

(i) the benefits to consumers with the costs on furnishers and the credit reporting system;

(ii) the impact on the overall accuracy and integrity of consumer reports of any such requirements;

(iii) whether direct contact by the consumer with the furnisher would likely result in the most expeditious resolution of any such dispute; and

(iv) the potential impact on the credit reporting process if credit repair organizations, as defined in section 403(3) [15 U.S.C. §1679a(3)], including entities that would be a credit repair organization, but for section 403(3)(B)(i), are able to circumvent the prohibition in subparagraph (G).

(C) Applicability. Subparagraphs (D) through (G) shall apply in any circumstance identified under the regulations promulgated under subparagraph (A).

(D) Submitting a notice of dispute- A consumer who seeks to dispute the accuracy of information shall provide a dispute notice directly to such person at the address specified by the person for such notices that—

(i) identifies the specific information that is being disputed;

(ii) explains the basis for the dispute; and

(iii) includes all supporting documentation required by the furnisher to substantiate the basis of the dispute.

(E) Duty of person after receiving notice of dispute. After receiving a notice of dispute from a consumer pursuant to subparagraph (D), the person that provided the information in dispute to a consumer reporting agency shall—

(i) conduct an investigation with respect to the disputed information;

(ii) review all relevant information provided by the consumer with the notice;

(iii) complete such person's investigation of the dispute and report the results of the investigation to the consumer before the expiration of the period under section 611(a)(1) within which a consumer reporting agency would be required to complete its action if the consumer had elected to dispute the information under that section; and

(iv) if the investigation finds that the information reported was inaccurate, promptly notify each consumer reporting agency to which the person furnished the inaccurate information of that determination and provide to the agency any correction to that information that is necessary to make the information provided by the person accurate.

(F) Frivolous or Irrelevant Dispute

(i) In general. This paragraph shall not apply if the person receiving a notice of a dispute from a consumer reasonably determines that the dispute is frivolous or irrelevant, including—

(I) by reason of the failure of a consumer to provide sufficient information to investigate the disputed information; or

(II) the submission by a consumer of a dispute that is substantially the same as a dispute previously submitted by or for the consumer, either directly to the person or through a consumer reporting agency under subsection (b), with respect to which the person has already performed the person's duties under this paragraph or subsection (b), as applicable.

(ii) Notice of determination. Upon making any determination under clause (i) that a dispute is frivolous or irrelevant, the person shall notify the consumer of such determination not later than 5 business days after making such determination, by mail or, if authorized by the consumer for that purpose, by any other means available to the person.

(iii) Contents of notice. A notice under clause (ii) shall include—

(I) the reasons for the determination under clause (i); and

(II) identification of any information required to investigate the disputed information, which may consist of a standardized form describing the general nature of such information.

(G) Exclusion of credit repair organizations. This paragraph shall not apply if the notice of the dispute is submitted by, is prepared on behalf of the consumer by, or is submitted on a form supplied to the consumer by, a credit repair organization, as defined in section 403(3), or an entity that would be a credit repair organization, but for section 403(3)(B)(i).

(9) Duty to provide notice of status as medical information furnisher. A person whose primary business is providing medical services, products, or devices, or the person's agent or assignee, who furnishes information to a consumer reporting agency on a consumer shall be considered a medical information furnisher for purposes of this title, and shall notify the agency of such status.

(b) Duties of furnishers of information upon notice of dispute.

(1) In general. After receiving notice pursuant to section 611(a)(2) [§1681i] of a dispute with regard to the completeness or accuracy of any information provided by a person to a consumer reporting agency, the person shall:

(A) conduct an investigation with respect to the disputed information;

(B) review all relevant information provided by the consumer reporting agency pursuant to section 611(a)(2) [§1681i];

(C) report the results of the investigation to the consumer reporting agency; and

(D) if the investigation finds that the information is incomplete or inaccurate, report those results to all other consumer reporting agencies to which the person furnished the information and that compile and maintain files on consumers on a nationwide basis.

(E) if an item of information disputed by a consumer is found to be inaccurate or incomplete or cannot be verified after any reinvestigation under paragraph (1), for purposes of reporting to a consumer reporting agency only, as appropriate, based on the results of the reinvestigation promptly–

(i) modify that item of information;

(ii) delete that item of information; or

(iii) permanently block the reporting of that item of information.

(2) Deadline. A person shall complete all investigations, reviews, and reports required under paragraph (1) regarding information provided by the person to a consumer reporting agency, before the expiration of the period under section 611(a)(1) [§1681i] within which the consumer reporting agency is required to complete actions required by that section regarding that information.

(c) Limitation on liability. Except as provided in section 621(c)(1)(B), sections 616 and 617 do not apply to any violation of—

(1) subsection (a) of this section, including any regulations issued thereunder;

(2) subsection (e) of this section, except that nothing in this paragraph shall limit, expand, or otherwise affect liability under section 616 or 617, as applicable, for violations of subsection (b) of this section; or

(3) subsection (e) of section 615.

(d) Limitation on enforcement. The provisions of law described in paragraphs (1) through (3) of subsection (c) (other than with respect to the exception described in paragraph (2) of subsection (c)) shall be enforced exclusively as provided under section 621 by the Federal agencies and officials and the State officials identified in section 621.

(e) Accuracy Guidelines and Regulations Required

(1) Guidelines. The Federal banking agencies, the National Credit Union Administration, and the Commission shall, with respect to the entities that are subject to their respective enforcement authority under section 621, and in coordination as described in paragraph (2)—

(A) establish and maintain guidelines for use by each person that furnishes information to a consumer reporting agency regarding the accuracy and integrity of the information relating to consumers that such entities furnish to consumer reporting agencies, and update such guidelines as often as necessary; and

(B) prescribe regulations requiring each person that furnishes information to a consumer reporting agency to establish reasonable policies and procedures for implementing the guidelines established pursuant to subparagraph (A).

(2) Coordination. Each agency required to prescribe regulations under paragraph (1) shall consult and coordinate with each other such agency so that, to the extent possible, the regulations prescribed by each such entity are consistent and comparable with the regulations prescribed by each other such agency.

(3) Criteria. In developing the guidelines required by paragraph (1)(A), the agencies described in paragraph (1) shall—

(A) identify patterns, practices, and specific forms of activity that can compromise the accuracy and integrity of information furnished to consumer reporting agencies;

(B) review the methods (including technological means) used to furnish information relating to consumers to consumer reporting agencies;

(C) determine whether persons that furnish information to consumer reporting agencies maintain and enforce policies to assure the accuracy and integrity of information furnished to consumer reporting agencies; and

(D) examine the policies and processes that persons that furnish information to consumer reporting agencies employ to conduct reinvestigations and correct inaccurate information relating to consumers that has been furnished to consumer reporting agencies.

§ 624. AFFILIATE SHARING [15 U.S.C. § 1681s-3]

(a) Special Rule for Solicitation for Purposes of Marketing

(1) Notice. Any person that receives from another person related to it by common ownership or affiliated by corporate control a communication of information that would be a consumer report, but for clauses (i), (ii), and (iii) of section 603(d)(2)(A), may not use the information to make a solicitation for marketing purposes to a consumer about its products or services, unless—

(A) it is clearly and conspicuously disclosed to the consumer that the information may be communicated among such persons for purposes of making such solicitations to the consumer; and

(B) the consumer is provided an opportunity and a simple method to prohibit the making of such solicitations to the consumer by such person.

(2) Consumer Choice

(A) In general. The notice required under paragraph (1) shall allow the consumer the opportunity to prohibit all solicitations referred to in such paragraph, and may allow the consumer to choose from different options when electing to prohibit the sending of such solicitations, including options regarding the types of entities and information covered, and which methods of delivering solicitations the consumer elects to prohibit.

(B) Format. Notwithstanding subparagraph (A), the notice required under paragraph (1) shall be clear, conspicuous, and concise, and any method provided under paragraph (1)(B) shall be simple. The regulations prescribed to implement this section shall provide specific guidance regarding how to comply with such standards.

(3) Duration

(A) In general. The election of a consumer pursuant to paragraph (1)(B) to prohibit the making of solicitations shall be effective for at least 5 years, beginning on the date on which the person receives the election of the consumer, unless the consumer requests that such election be revoked.

(B) Notice upon expiration of effective period. At such time as the election of a consumer pursuant to paragraph (1)(B) is no longer effective, a person may not use information that the person receives in the manner described in paragraph (1) to make any solicitation for marketing purposes to the consumer, unless the consumer receives a notice and an opportunity, using a simple method, to extend the opt-out for another period of at least 5 years, pursuant to the procedures described in paragraph (1).

(4) Scope. This section shall not apply to a person–

(A) using information to make a solicitation for marketing purposes to a consumer with whom the person has a pre-existing business relationship;

(B) using information to facilitate communications to an individual for whose benefit the person provides employee benefit or other services pursuant to a contract with an employer related to and arising out of the current employment relationship or status of the individual as a participant or beneficiary of an employee benefit plan;

(C) using information to perform services on behalf of another person related by common ownership or affiliated by corporate control, except that this subparagraph shall not be construed as permitting a person to send solicitations on behalf of another person, if such other person would not be permitted to send the solicitation on its own behalf as a result of the election of the consumer to prohibit solicitations under paragraph (1)(B);

(D) using information in response to a communication initiated by the consumer;

(E) using information in response to solicitations authorized or requested by the consumer; or

(F) if compliance with this section by that person would prevent compliance by that person with any provision of State insurance laws pertaining to unfair discrimination in any State in which the person is lawfully doing business.

(5) No retroactivity. This subsection shall not prohibit the use of information to send a solicitation to a consumer if such information was received prior to the date on which persons are required to comply with regulations implementing this subsection.

(b) Notice for other purposes permissible. A notice or other disclosure under this section may be coordinated and consolidated with any other notice required to be issued under any other provision of law by a person that is subject to this section, and a notice or other disclosure that is equivalent to the notice required by subsection (a), and that is provided by a person described in subsection (a) to a consumer together with disclosures required by any other provision of law, shall satisfy the requirements of subsection (a).

(c) User requirements. Requirements with respect to the use by a person of information received from another person related to it by common ownership or affiliated by corporate control, such as the requirements of this section, constitute requirements with respect to the exchange of information among persons affiliated by common ownership or common corporate control, within the meaning of section 625(b)(2).

(d) Definitions. For purposes of this section, the following definitions shall apply:

(1) The term "pre-existing business relationship" means a relationship between a person, or a person's licensed agent, and a consumer, based on—

(A) a financial contract between a person and a consumer which is in force;

(B) the purchase, rental, or lease by the consumer of that person's goods or services, or a financial transaction (including holding an active account or a policy in force or having another continuing relationship) between the consumer and that person during the 18-month period immediately preceding the date on which the consumer is sent a solicitation covered by this section;

(C) an inquiry or application by the consumer regarding a product or service offered by that person, during the 3-month period immediately preceding the date on which the consumer is sent a solicitation covered by this section; or

(D) any other pre-existing customer relationship defined in the regulations implementing this section.

(2) The term "solicitation" means the marketing of a product or service initiated by a person to a particular consumer that is based on an exchange of information described in subsection (a), and is intended to encourage the consumer to purchase such product or service, but does not include communications that are directed at the general public or determined not to be a solicitation by the regulations prescribed under this section.

§ 625. RELATION TO STATE LAWS [15 U.S.C. §1681t]

(a) In general. Except as provided in subsections (b) and (c), this title does not annul, alter, affect, or exempt any person subject to the provisions of this title from complying with the laws of any State with respect to the collection, distribution, or use of any information on consumers, or for the prevention or mitigation of identity theft, except to the extent that those laws are inconsistent with any provision of this title, and then only to the extent of the inconsistency.

(b) General exceptions. No requirement or prohibition may be imposed under the laws of any State:

(1) with respect to any subject matter regulated under:

(A) subsection (c) or (e) of section 604 [§1681b], relating to the prescreening of consumer reports;

(B) section 611 [§1681i], relating to the time by which a consumer reporting agency must take any action, including the provision of notification to a consumer or other person, in any procedure related to the disputed accuracy of information in a consumer's file, except that this subparagraph shall not apply to any State law in effect on the date of enactment of the Consumer Credit Reporting Reform Act of 1996;

(C) subsections (a) and (b) of section 615 [§1681m], relating to the duties of a person who takes any adverse action with respect to a consumer;

(D) section 615(d) [§1681m], relating to the duties of persons who use a consumer report of a consumer in connection with any credit or insurance transaction that is not initiated by the consumer and that consists of a firm offer of credit or insurance;

(E) section 605 [§1681c], relating to information contained in consumer reports, except that this subparagraph shall not apply to any State law in effect on the date of enactment of the Consumer Credit Reporting Reform Act of 1996;

(F) section 623 [§1681s-2], relating to the responsibilities of persons who furnish information to consumer reporting agencies, except that this paragraph shall not apply:

(i) with respect to section 54A(a) of chapter 93 of the Massachusetts Annotated Laws (as in effect on the date of enactment of the Consumer Credit Reporting Reform Act of 1996); or

(ii) with respect to section 1785.25(a) of the California Civil Code (as in effect on the date of enactment of the Consumer Credit Reporting Reform Act of 1996);

(G) section 609(e), relating to information available to victims under section 609(e);

(H) section 624, relating to the exchange and use of information to make a solicitation for marketing purposes; or

(I) section 615(h), relating to the duties of users of consumer reports to provide notice with respect to terms in certain credit transactions;

(2) with respect to the exchange of information among persons affiliated by common ownership or common corporate control, except that this paragraph shall not apply with respect to subsection (a) or (c)(1) of section 2480e of title 9, Vermont Statutes Annotated (as in effect on the date of enactment of the Consumer Credit Reporting Reform Act of 1996); or

(3) with respect to the disclosures required to be made under subsection (c), (d), (e), or (g) of section 609, or subsection (f) of section 609 relating to the disclosure of credit scores for credit granting purposes, except that this paragraph—

(A) shall not apply with respect to sections 1785.10, 1785.16, and 1785.20.2 of the California Civil Code (as in effect on the date of enactment of the Fair and Accurate Credit Transactions Act of 2003) and section 1785.15 through section 1785.15.2 of such Code (as in effect on such date);

(B) shall not apply with respect to sections 5-3-106(2) and 212-14.3-104.3 of the Colorado Revised Statutes (as in effect on the date of enactment of the Fair and Accurate Credit Transactions Act of 2003); and

(C) shall not be construed as limiting, annulling, affecting, or superseding any provision of the laws of any State regulating the use in an insurance activity, or regulating disclosures concerning such use, of a credit-based insurance score of a consumer by any person engaged in the business of insurance;

(4) with respect to the frequency of any disclosure under section 612(a), except that this paragraph shall not apply—

(A) with respect to section 12-14.3-105(1)(d) of the Colorado Revised Statutes (as in effect on the date of enactment of the Fair and Accurate Credit Transactions Act of 2003);

(B) with respect to section 10-1-393(29)(C) of the Georgia Code (as in effect on the date of enactment of the Fair and Accurate Credit Transactions Act of 2003);

(C) with respect to section 1316.2 of title 10 of the Maine Revised Statutes (as in effect on the date of enactment of the Fair and Accurate Credit Transactions Act of 2003);

(D) with respect to sections 14-1209(a)(1) and 14-1209(b)(1)(i) of the Commercial Law Article of the Code of Maryland (as in effect on the date of enactment of the Fair and Accurate Credit Transactions Act of 2003);

(E) with respect to section 59(d) and section 59(e) of chapter 93 of the General Laws of Massachusetts (as in effect on the date of enactment of the Fair and Accurate Credit Transactions Act of 2003);

(F) with respect to section 56:11-37.10(a)(1) of the New Jersey Revised Statutes (as in effect on the date of enactment of the Fair and Accurate Credit Transactions Act of 2003); or

(G) with respect to section 2480c(a)(1) of title 9 of the Vermont Statutes Annotated (as in effect on the date of enactment of the Fair and Accurate Credit Transactions Act of 2003); or

(5) with respect to the conduct required by the specific provisions of—

(A) section 605(g);

(B) section 605A;

(C) section 605B;

(D) section 609(a)(1)(A);

(E) section 612(a);

(F) subsections (e), (f), and (g) of section 615;

(G) section 621(f);

(H) section 623(a)(6); or

(I) section 628.

(c) Definition of firm offer of credit or insurance. Notwithstanding any definition of the term "firm offer of credit or insurance" (or any equivalent term) under the laws of any State, the definition of that term contained in section 603(l) [§ 1681a] shall be construed to apply in the enforcement and interpretation of the laws of any State governing consumer reports.

(d) Limitations. Subsections (b) and (c) do not affect any settlement, agreement, or consent judgment between any State Attorney General and any consumer reporting agency in effect on the date of enactment of the Consumer Credit Reporting Reform Act of 1996.

§ 626. DISCLOSURES TO FBI FOR COUNTERINTELLIGENCE PURPOSES. [15 U.S.C. §1681u]

(a) Identity of financial institutions. Notwithstanding section 604 [§1681b] or any other provision of this title, a consumer reporting agency shall furnish to the Federal Bureau of Investigation the names and addresses of all financial institutions (as that term is defined in section 1101 of the Right to Financial Privacy Act of 1978 [12 U.S.C. § 3401]) at which a consumer maintains or has maintained an account, to the extent that information is in the files of the agency, when presented with a written request for that information, signed by the Director of the Federal Bureau of Investigation, or the Director's designee, which certifies compliance with this section. The Director or the Director's designee may make such a certification only if the Director or the Director's designee has determined in writing that:

(1) such information is necessary for the conduct of an authorized foreign counterintelligence investigation; and

(2) there are specific and articulable facts giving reason to believe that the consumer:

(A) is a foreign power (as defined in section 101 of the Foreign Intelligence Surveillance Act of 1978 [50 U.S.C. § 1801]) or a person who is not a United States person (as defined in such section 101) and is an official of a foreign power; or

(B) is an agent of a foreign power and is engaging or has engaged in an act of international terrorism (as that term is defined in section 101(c) of the Foreign Intelligence Surveillance Act of 1978 [50 U.S.C. § 1801(c)]) or clandestine intelligence activities that involve or may involve a violation of criminal statutes of the United States.

(b) Identifying information. Notwithstanding the provisions of section 604 [§1681b] or any other provision of this title, a consumer reporting agency shall furnish identifying information respecting a consumer, limited to name, address, former addresses, places of employment, or former places of employment, to the Federal Bureau of Investigation when presented with a written request, signed by the Director or the Director's designee, which certifies compliance with this subsection. The Director or the Director's designee may make such a certification only if the Director or the Director's designee has determined in writing that:

(1) such information is necessary to the conduct of an authorized counterintelligence investigation; and

(2) there is information giving reason to believe that the consumer has been, or is about to be, in contact with a foreign power or an agent of a foreign power (as defined in section 101 of the Foreign Intelligence Surveillance Act of 1978 [50 U.S.C. § 1801]).

(c) Court order for disclosure of consumer reports. Notwithstanding section 604 [§1681b] or any other provision of this title, if requested in writing by the Director of the Federal Bureau of Investigation, or a designee of the Director, a court may issue an order ex parte directing a consumer reporting agency to furnish a consumer report to the Federal Bureau of Investigation, upon a showing in camera that:

(1) the consumer report is necessary for the conduct of an authorized foreign counterintelligence investigation; and

(2) there are specific and articulable facts giving reason to believe that the consumer whose consumer report is sought

(A) is an agent of a foreign power, and

(B) is engaging or has engaged in an act of international terrorism (as that term is defined in section 101(c) of the Foreign Intelligence Surveillance Act of 1978 [50 U.S.C. § 1801(c)]) or clandestine intelligence activities that involve or may involve a violation of criminal statutes of the United States. The terms of an order issued under this subsection shall not disclose that the order is issued for purposes of a counterintelligence investigation.

(d) Confidentiality. No consumer reporting agency or officer, employee, or agent of a consumer reporting agency shall disclose to any person, other than those officers, employees, or agents of a consumer reporting agency necessary to fulfill the requirement to disclose information to the Federal Bureau of Investigation under this section, that the Federal Bureau of Investigation has sought or obtained the identity of financial institutions or a consumer report respecting any consumer under subsection (a), (b), or (c), and no consumer reporting agency or officer, employee, or agent of a consumer reporting agency shall include in any consumer report any information that would indicate that the Federal Bureau of Investigation has sought or obtained such information or a consumer report.

(e) Payment of fees. The Federal Bureau of Investigation shall, subject to the availability of appropriations, pay to the consumer reporting agency assembling or providing report or information in accordance with procedures established under this section a fee for reimbursement for such costs as are reasonably necessary and which have been directly incurred in searching, reproducing, or transporting books, papers, records, or other data required or requested to be produced under this section.

(f) Limit on dissemination. The Federal Bureau of Investigation may not disseminate information obtained pursuant to this section outside of the Federal Bureau of Investigation, except to other Federal agencies as may be necessary for the approval or conduct of a foreign counterintelligence investigation, or, where the information concerns a person subject to the Uniform Code of Military Justice, to appropriate investigative authorities within the military department concerned as may be necessary for the conduct of a joint foreign counterintelligence investigation.

(g) Rules of construction. Nothing in this section shall be construed to prohibit information from being furnished by the Federal Bureau of Investigation pursuant to a subpoena or court order, in connection with a judicial or administrative proceeding to enforce the provisions of this Act. Nothing in this section shall be construed to authorize or permit the withholding of information from the Congress.

(h) Reports to Congress. On a semiannual basis, the Attorney General shall fully inform the Permanent Select Committee on Intelligence and the Committee on Banking, Finance and Urban Affairs of the House of Representatives, and the Select Committee on Intelligence and the Committee on Banking, Housing, and Urban Affairs of the Senate concerning all requests made pursuant to subsections (a), (b), and (c).

(i) Damages. Any agency or department of the United States obtaining or disclosing any consumer reports, records, or information contained therein in violation of this section is liable to the consumer to whom such consumer reports, records, or information relate in an amount equal to the sum of:

(1) $100, without regard to the volume of consumer reports, records, or information involved;

(2) any actual damages sustained by the consumer as a result of the disclosure;

(3) if the violation is found to have been willful or intentional, such punitive damages as a court may allow; and

(4) in the case of any successful action to enforce liability under this subsection, the costs of the action, together with reasonable attorney fees, as determined by the court.

(j) Disciplinary actions for violations. If a court determines that any agency or department of the United States has violated any provision of this section and the court finds that the circumstances surrounding the violation raise questions of whether or not an officer or employee of the agency or department acted willfully or intentionally with respect to the violation, the agency or department shall promptly initiate a proceeding to determine whether or not disciplinary action is warranted against the officer or employee who was responsible for the violation.

(k) Good-faith exception. Notwithstanding any other provision of this title, any consumer reporting agency or agent or employee thereof making disclosure of consumer reports or identifying information pursuant to this subsection in good-faith reliance upon a certification of the Federal Bureau of Investigation pursuant to provisions of this section shall not be liable to any person for such disclosure under this title, the constitution of any State, or any law or regulation of any State or any political subdivision of any State.

(l) Limitation of remedies. Notwithstanding any other provision of this title, the remedies and sanctions set forth in this section shall be the only judicial remedies and sanctions for violation of this section.

(m) Injunctive relief. In addition to any other remedy contained in this section, injunctive relief shall be available to require compliance with the procedures of this section. In the event of any successful action under this subsection, costs together with reasonable attorney fees, as determined by the court, may be recovered.

* * *

APPENDIX 11:
SUPREME COURT OPINION IN TRW INC. v. ANDREWS, 534 U.S. 19 (2001)

SUPREME COURT OF THE UNITED STATES
[NO. 00-1045]

TRW INC., PETITIONER v. ADELAIDE ANDREWS
ON WRIT OF CERTIORARI TO THE UNITED STATES COURT
OF APPEALS FOR THE NINTH CIRCUIT
[November 13, 2001]

JUSTICE GINSBURG delivered the opinion of the Court.

This case concerns the running of the two-year statute of limitations governing suits based on the Fair Credit Reporting Act (FCRA or Act), as added, 84 Stat.1127, and amended, 15 U.S.C.§1681 et seq. (1994 ed. and Supp.V). The time prescription appears in §1681p, which sets out a general rule and an exception. Generally, an action to enforce any liability created by the Act may be brought "within two years from the date on which the liability arises." The exception covers willful misrepresentation of "any information required under [the Act] to be disclosed to [the plaintiff]":

> when such a representation is material to a claim under the Act, suit may be brought "within two years after [the plaintiff's] discovery . . . of the misrepresentation."

Section 1681p's exception is not involved in this case; the complaint does not allege misrepresentation of information that the FCRA "require[s] . . . to be disclosed to [the plaintiff]." Plaintiff-respondent Adelaide Andrews nevertheless contends, and the Ninth Circuit held, that §1681p's generally applicable two-year limitation commenced to run on Andrews' claims only upon her discovery of defendant-petitioner TRW Inc.'s alleged violations of the Act.

We hold that a discovery rule does not govern §1681p. That section explicitly delineates the exceptional case in which discovery triggers the two-year limitation. We are not at liberty to make Congress' explicit exception the general rule as well.

I
A

Congress enacted the FCRA in 1970 to promote efficiency in the Nation's banking system and to protect consumer privacy. See 15 U.S.C.§1681(a)(1994 ed.). As relevant here, the Act seeks to accomplish those goals by requiring credit reporting agencies to maintain "reasonable procedures" designed "to assure maximum possible accuracy of the information" contained in credit reports, §1681e(b), and to "limit the furnishing of [such reports] to" certain statutorily enumerated purposes, §1681e(a); 15 U.S.C.§1681b (1994 ed. and Supp.V). The Act creates a private right of action allowing injured consumers to recover "any actual damages" caused by negligent violations and both actual and punitive damages for willful noncompliance. See 15 U.S.C.§§1681n, 1681o (1994 ed.).

B

The facts of this case are for the most part undisputed. On June 17, 1993, Adelaide Andrews visited a radiologist's office in Santa Monica, California. She filled out a new patient form listing certain basic information, including her name, birth date, and Social Security number. Andrews handed the form to the office receptionist, one Andrea Andrews (the Impostor), who copied the information and thereafter moved to Las Vegas, Nevada. Once there, the Impostor attempted on numerous occasions to open credit accounts using Andrews' Social Security number and her own last name and address.

On four of those occasions, the company from which the Impostor sought credit requested a report from TRW. Each time, TRW's computers registered a match between Andrews' Social Security number, last name, and first initial and therefore responded by furnishing her file. TRW thus disclosed Andrews' credit history at the Impostor's request to a bank on July 25, 1994; to a cable television company on September 27, 1994; to a department store on October 28, 1994; and to another credit provider on January 3, 1995. All recipients but the cable company rejected the Impostor's applications for credit.

Andrews did not learn of these disclosures until May 31, 1995, when she sought to refinance her home mortgage and in the process received a copy of her credit report reflecting the Impostor's activity. Andrews concedes that TRW promptly corrected her file upon learning of its mistake. She alleges, however, that the blemishes on her report not only caused her inconvenience and emotional distress; they also forced her to abandon her refinancing efforts and settle for an alternative line of credit on less favorable terms.

On October 21, 1996, almost 17 months after she discovered the Impostor's fraudulent conduct and more than two years after TRW's first two disclosures, Andrews filed suit in the United States District Court for the Central District of California. Her complaint stated two categories of FCRA claims against TRW, only the first of which is relevant here. Those claims alleged that TRW's four disclosures of her information in response to the Impostor's credit applications were improper because TRW failed to verify, predisclosure, that Adelaide Andrews of Santa Monica initiated the requests or was otherwise involved in the underlying transactions. Andrews asserted that by processing requests that matched her profile on Social Security number, last name, and first initial but did not correspond on other key identifiers, notably birth date, address, and first name, TRW had facilitated the Impostor's identity theft. According to Andrews, TRW's verification failure constituted a willful violation of §1681e(a), which requires credit reporting agencies to maintain "reasonable procedures" to avoid improper disclosures. She sought injunctive relief, punitive damages, and compensation for the "expenditure of time and money, commercial impairment, inconvenience, embarrassment, humiliation and emotional distress" that TRW had allegedly inflicted upon her.

TRW moved for partial summary judgment, arguing, inter alia, that the FCRA's statute of limitations had expired on Andrews' claims based on the July 25 and September 27, 1994, disclosures because both occurred more than two years before she brought suit. Andrews countered that her claims as to all four disclosures were timely because the limitations period did not commence until May 31, 1995, the date she learned of TRW's alleged wrongdoing. The District Court, agreeing with TRW that §1681p does not incorporate a general discovery rule, held that relief stemming from the July and September 1994 disclosures was time barred. Andrews v. Trans Union Corp., 7 F.Supp.2d 1056, 1066–1067 (CD Cal.1998).

The Court of Appeals for the Ninth Circuit reversed this ruling, applying what it considered to be the "general federal rule . . . that a federal statute of limitations begins to run when a party knows or has reason to know that she was injured." 225 F.3d 1063, 1066 (2000). The court rejected the District Court's conclusion that the text of §1681p, and in particular the limited exception set forth in that section, precluded judicial attribution of such a rule to the FCRA. "[U]nless Congress has expressly legislated otherwise," the Ninth Circuit declared, "the equitable doctrine of discovery is read into every federal statute of limitations." Id., at 1067. Finding no such express directive, the Court of Appeals held that "none of [Andrews'] injuries were stale when suit was brought." Id., at 1066. Accordingly, the court reinstated Andrews' improper disclosure claims and remanded them for trial.

In holding that §1681p incorporates a general discovery rule, the Ninth Circuit parted company with four other Circuits; those courts have concluded that a discovery exception other than the one Congress expressed may not be read into the Act. See Clark v. State Farm Fire & Casualty Ins. Co., 54 F.3d 669 (CA10 1995); Rylewicz v. Beaton Servs., Ltd., 888 F.2d 1175 (CA7 1989); Houghton v. Insurance Crime Prevention Institute, 795 F.2d 322 (CA3 1986); Clay v. Equifax, Inc., 762 F.2d 952 (CA11 1985). We granted certiorari to resolve this conflict, 532 U.S.902 (2001), and now reverse.

II

The Court of Appeals rested its decision on the premise that all federal statutes of limitations, regardless of context, incorporate a general discovery rule "unless Congress has expressly legislated otherwise." 225 F.3d, at 1067. To the extent such a presumption exists, a matter this case does not oblige us to decide, the Ninth Circuit conspicuously overstated its scope and force.

The Appeals Court principally relied on our decision in Holmberg v. Armbrecht, 327 U.S.392 (1946). See 225 F.3d, at 1067. In that case, we instructed with particularity that "where a plaintiff has been injured by fraud and remains in ignorance of it without any fault or want of diligence or care on his part, the bar of the statute does not begin to run until the fraud is discovered." Holmberg, 327 U.S., at 397. Holmberg thus stands for the proposition that equity tolls the statute of limitations in cases of fraud or concealment; it does not establish a general presumption applicable across all contexts. The only other cases in which we have recognized a prevailing discovery rule, moreover, were decided in two contexts, latent disease and medical malpractice, "where the cry for [such a] rule is loudest," Rotella v. Wood, 528 U.S.549, 555 (2000). See United States v. Kubrick, 444 U.S.111 (1979); Urie v. Thompson, 337 U.S.163 (1949).

We have also observed that lower federal courts "generally apply a discovery accrual rule when a statute is silent on the issue." Rotella, 528 U.S., at 555; see also Klehr v. A.O. Smith Corp., 521 U.S. 179, 191 (1997)(citing Connors v. Hallmark & Son Coal Co., 935 F.2d 336, 342 (CADC 1991), for the proposition that "federal courts generally apply

[a] discovery accrual rule when [the] statute does not call for a different rule"). But we have not adopted that position as our own. And, beyond doubt, we have never endorsed the Ninth Circuit's view that Congress can convey its refusal to adopt a discovery rule only by explicit command, rather than by implication from the structure or text of the particular statute.

The Ninth Circuit thus erred in holding that a generally applied discovery rule controls this case. The FCRA does not govern an area of the law that cries out for application of a discovery rule, nor is the statute "silent on the issue" of when the statute of limitations begins to run. Section 1681p addresses that precise question; the provision reads:

> "An action to enforce any liability created under [the Act] may be brought . . . within two years from the date on which the liability arises, except that where a defendant has materially and willfully misrepresented any information required under [the Act] to be disclosed to an individual and the information so misrepresented is material to the establishment of the defendant's liability to that individual under [the Act], the action may be brought at any time within two years after discovery by the individual of the misrepresentation."

We conclude that the text and structure of §1681p evince Congress' intent to preclude judicial implication of a discovery rule.

"Where Congress explicitly enumerates certain exceptions to a general prohibition, additional exceptions are not to be implied, in the absence of evidence of a contrary legislative intent." Andrus v. Glover Constr. Co., 446 U.S. 608, 616 –617 (1980). Congress provided in the FCRA that the two-year statute of limitations runs from "the date on which the liability arises," subject to a single exception for cases involving a defendant's willful misrepresentation of material information. The most natural reading of §1681p is that Congress implicitly excluded a general discovery rule by explicitly including a more limited one. See Leatherman v. Tarrant County Narcotics Intelligence and Coordination Unit, 507 U.S.163, 168 (1993) ("Expressio unius est exclusio alterius."). We would distort §1681p's text by converting the exception into the rule. Cf. United States v. Brockamp, 519 U.S. 347, 352 (1997)("explicit listing of exceptions" to running of limitations period considered indicative of Congress' intent to preclude "courts [from] read[ing] other unmentioned, open-ended, 'equitable' exceptions into the statute").

At least equally telling, incorporating a general discovery rule into §1681p would not merely supplement the explicit exception contrary to Congress' apparent intent; it would in practical effect render that exception entirely superfluous in all but the most unusual circumstances. A consumer will generally not discover the tortious conduct alleged here—the improper disclosure of her credit history to a potential user—until she requests her file from a credit reporting agency. If the agency responds by concealing the offending disclosure, both a generally applicable discovery rule and the misrepresentation exception would operate to toll the statute of limitations until the concealment is revealed. Once triggered, the statute of limitations would run under either for two years from the discovery date. In this paradigmatic setting, then, the misrepresentation exception would have no work to do.

Both Andrews and the Government, appearing as *amicus* in her support, attempt to generate some role for the express exception independent of that filled by a general discovery rule. They conceive of the exception as a codification of the judge-made doctrine of equitable estoppel, which, they argue, operates only *after* the discovery rule has triggered the limitations period, preventing a defendant from benefiting from its misrepresentation by tolling that period until the concealment is uncovered.

To illustrate this supposed separate application, Andrews and the Government frame the following scenario: A credit reporting agency injures a consumer by disclosing her file for an improper purpose. The consumer has no reason to suspect the violation until a year later, when she applies for and is denied credit as a result of the agency's wrongdoing. At that point, the Government asserts, "the consumer would presumably be put on inquiry notice of the violation, and the discovery rule would start the running of the normal limitation period." Brief for United States et al.as Amici Curiae 22 (emphasis omitted); see Tr. of Oral Arg.35–36 (argument in accord by Andrews' counsel). Some days or months later, the consumer follows up on her suspicions by requesting a copy of her credit report, to which the agency responds by concealing the initial improper disclosure. According to Andrews and the Government, the misrepresentation exception would then operate to toll the already-commenced limitations period until the agency reveals its wrongdoing.

We reject this argument for several reasons. As an initial matter, we are not persuaded by this effort to distinguish the practical function of a discovery rule and the express exception, because we doubt that the supporting scenario is likely to occur outside the realm of theory. The fatal weakness in the narrative is its assumption that a consumer would be charged with constructive notice of an improper disclosure upon denial of a credit application. If the consumer habitually paid her bills on time, the denial might well lead her to suspect a prior credit agency error. But the credit denial would place her on "inquiry notice," and the discovery rule would trigger the limitations period at that point, only if a reasonable person in her position would have learned of the injury in the exercise of due diligence. See Stone v. Williams, 970 F.2d 1043, 1049 (CA2 1992)("The duty of inquiry having arisen, plaintiff is charged with whatever knowledge an inquiry would have revealed."); 2 C. Corman, Limitation of Actions §11.1.6, p.164 (1991)("It is obviously unreasonable to charge the plaintiff with failure to search for the missing element of the cause of action if such element would not have been revealed by such search.").

In the usual circumstance, the plaintiff will gain knowledge of her injury from the credit reporting agency. The scenario put forth by Andrews and the Government, however, requires the assumption that, even if the consumer exercised reasonable diligence by requesting her credit report without delay, she would not in fact learn of the disclosure because the credit reporting agency would conceal it. The uncovering of that concealment would remain the triggering event for both the discovery rule and the express exception. In this scenario, as in the paradigmatic one, the misrepresentation exception would be superfluous.

In any event, both Andrews and the Government concede that the independent function one could attribute to the express exception would arise only in "rare and egregious case[s]." Brief for Respondent 32–33; see Brief for United States et al. as Amici Curiae 24 (implied discovery rule would apply in "vast majority" of cases)). The result is that a rule nowhere contained in the text of §1681p would do the bulk of that provision's work, while a proviso accounting for more than half of that text would lie dormant in all but the most unlikely situations.

It is "a cardinal principle of statutory construction" that "a statute ought, upon the whole, to be so construed that, if it can be prevented, no clause, sentence, or word shall be superfluous, void, or insignificant." Duncan v. Walker, 533 U.S.___, ___(2001)(slip op., at 6); see United States v. Menasche, 348 U.S. 528, 538 –539 (1955)("It is our duty 'to give effect, if possible, to every clause and word of a statute.'" (Quoting Montclair v. Ramsdell, 107 U.S. 147, 152 (1883))). "[W]ere we to adopt [Andrews'] construction of the statute," the express exception would be rendered "insignificant, if not wholly superfluous." Duncan, 533 U.S., at 174. We are "reluctant to treat statutory terms as surplusage in any setting," ibid. (internal alteration and quotation marks omitted), and we decline to do so here.

Andrews advances two additional arguments in defense of the decision below, neither of which we find convincing. She contends, first, that the words "date on which the liability arises"—the phrase Congress used to frame the general rule in §1681p—"literally expres[s]" a discovery rule because liability does not "arise" until it "present[s] itself" or comes to the attention of the potential plaintiff. Brief for Respondent 13. The dictionary definition of the word "arise" does not compel such a reading; to the contrary, it can be used to support either party's position. See Webster's Third New International Dictionary 117 (1966) (arise defined as "to come into being"; "to come about"; or "to become apparent in such a way as to demand attention"); Black's Law Dictionary 138 (rev.4th ed.1968)("to come into being or notice"). And TRW offers a strong argument that we have in fact construed that word to imply the result Andrews seeks to avoid. See Brief for Petitioner 16–20 (citing, *inter alia*, McMahon v. United States, 342 U.S.25 (1951)(statute of limitations triggered on date "cause of action arises" incorporates injury-occurrence rule)). On balance, we conclude, the phrase "liability arises" is not particularly instructive, much less dispositive of this case.

Similarly unhelpful, in our view, is Andrews' reliance on the legislative history of §1681p. She observes that early versions of that provision, introduced in both the House and Senate, keyed the start of the limitations period to "the date of the occurrence of the violation." S.823, 91st Cong., 1st Sess., §618 (1969); H.R.16340, 91st Cong., 2d. Sess., §27 (1970); H.R.14765, 91st Cong., 1st Sess., §617 (1969). From the disappearance of that language in the final version of §1681p, Andrews infers a congressional intent to reject the rule that the deleted words would have plainly established.

As TRW notes, however, Congress also heard testimony urging it to enact a statute of limitations that runs from "the date on which the violation is discovered" but declined to do so. Hearings before the Subcommittee on Consumer Affairs of the House Committee on Banking and Currency, 91st Cong., 2d Sess., 188 (1970). In addition, the very change to §1681p's language on which Andrews relies could be read to refute her position. The misrepresentation exception was added at the same time Congress changed the language "date of the occurrence of the violation" to "liability arises." Compare S.823, 91st Cong., 1st Sess., §618 (1969); H.R.16340, 91st Cong., 2d. Sess., §27 (1970); H.R.14765, 91st Cong., 1st Sess., §617 (1969), with H.R. Rep. No. 91–1587, p.22 (1970). We doubt that Congress, when it inserted a carefully worded exception to the main rule, intended simultaneously to create a general discovery rule that would render that exception superfluous. In sum, the evidence of the early incarnations of §1681p, like the "liability arises" language on which Congress ultimately settled, fails to convince us that Congress intended sub silentio to adopt a general discovery rule in addition to the limited one it expressly provided.

III

In this Court, Andrews for the first time presents an alternative argument based on the "liability arises" language of §1681p. Brief for Respondent 22–25. She contends that even if §1681p does not incorporate a discovery rule, "liability" under the FCRA does not necessarily "arise" when a violation of the Act occurs. Noting that the FCRA's substantive provisions tie "liability" to the presence of "actual damages," §§1681n, 1681o, and that "arise " means at least "to come into existence," Andrews concludes that "liability arises" only when actual damages materialize. Not until then, she maintains, will all the essential elements of a claim coalesce: "duty, breach, causation, and injury." Brief for Respondent 23; see Hyde v. Hibernia Nat. Bank, 861 F.2d 446, 449 (CA5 1988) ("The requirement that a consumer sustain some injury in order to establish a cause of action suggests that the statute should be triggered when the agency issues an erroneous report to an institution with which the consumer is dealing.").

Accordingly, Andrews asserts, her claims are timely: The disputed "liability" for actual damages did not "arise" until May 1995, when she suffered the emotional distress, missed opportunities, and inconvenience cataloged in her complaint; prior to that time, "she had no FCRA claim to bring," Brief for Respondent 24 ((emphasis omitted). Cf. Bay Area Laundry and Dry Cleaning Pension Trust Fund v. Ferbar Corp. of Cal., 522 U.S. 192, 200–201 (1997) (rejecting construction of statute under which limitations period would begin running before cause of action existed in favor of "standard rule" that the period does not commence earlier than the date "the plaintiff can file suit and obtain relief").

We do not reach this issue because it was not raised or briefed below. See Reply Brief for Petitioner 18–19. We note, however, that the Ninth Circuit has not embraced Andrews' alternative argument, see 225 F.3d, at 1066 ("Liability under the [Act] arises when a consumer reporting agency fails to comply with §1681e."), and the Government does not join her in advancing it here.

Further, we doubt that the argument, even if valid, would aid Andrews in this case. Her claims alleged willful violations of §1681e(a) and are thus governed by §1681n. At the time of the events in question, that provision stated: "Any consumer reporting agency . . . which willfully fails to comply with any requirement imposed under [the Act] with respect to any consumer is liable to that consumer in an amount equal to the sum of . . . any actual damages" and "such amount of punitive damages as the court may allow." 15 U.S.C. §1681n (1994 ed.). Punitive damages, which Andrews sought in this case, could presumably be awarded at the moment of TRW's alleged wrongdoing, even if "actual damages" did not accrue at that time. On Andrews' theory, then, at least some of the liability she sought to enforce arose when the violations occurred, and the limitations period therefore began to run at that point.

For the reasons stated, the judgment of the Court of Appeals for the Ninth Circuit is reversed, and the case is remanded for further proceedings consistent with this opinion. It is so ordered.

APPENDIX 12
THE FAIR CREDIT BILLING ACT (15 U.S.C. §1601)

TITLE III—FAIR CREDIT BILLING

§ 301. Short Title

This title may be cited as the "Fair Credit Billing Act".

§ 302. Declaration of purpose

The last sentence of section 102 of the Truth in Lending Act (15 U.S.C. 1601) is amended by striking out the period and inserting in lieu thereof a comma and the following: "and to protect the consumer against inaccurate and unfair credit billing and credit card practices."

§ 303. Definitions of creditor and open-end credit plan.

The first sentence of section 103(f) of the Truth in Lending Act (15 U.S.C. 1602(f)) is amended to read as follows: "The term, 'creditor' refers only to creditors who regularly extend, or arrange for the extension of, credit which is payable by agreement in more than four installments or for which the payment of a finance charge is or may be required, whether in connection with loans, sales of property or services, or otherwise." For the purposes of the requirements imposed under Chapter 4 and sections 127(a) (6), 127(a) (7), 127(a)(8), 127(b) (1), 127(b) (2), 127(b) (3), 127(b) (9), an 127(b) (11) of Chapter 2 of this Title, the term, 'creditor' shall also include card issuers whether or not the amount due is payable by agreement in more than four installments or the payment of a finance charge is or may be required, and the Board shall, by regulation, apply these requirements to such card issuers, to the extent appropriate, even though the requirements are by their terms applicable only to creditors offering open-end credit plans.

§ 304. Disclosure of fair credit billing rights.

(a) Section 127(a) of the Truth in Lending Act (15 U.S.C. 1637(a)) is amended by adding at the end thereof a new paragraph as follows:

"(8) A statement, in a form prescribed by regulations of the Board of the protection provided by sections 161 and 170 to an obligor and the creditor's responsibilities under sections 162 and 170. With respect to each of two billing cycles per year, at semiannual intervals, the creditor shall transmit such statement to each obligor to whom the creditor is required to transmit a statement pursuant to sections 127(b) for such billing cycle."

(b) Section 127(c) of such Act (15 U.S.C. 1637(c)) is amended to read:

"(c) In the case of any existing account under an open end consumer credit plan having an outstanding balance of more than $1 at or after the close of the creditor's first full billing cycle under the plan after the effective date of subsection (a) or any amendments thereto, the items described in subsection (a), to the extent applicable and not previously disclosed, shall be disclosed in a notice mailed or delivered to the obligor not later than the time of mailing the next statement required by subsection (b)."

§ 305. Disclosure of billing contact.

Section 127(b) of the Truth in Lending Act (15 U.S.C. 1637(b)) is amended by adding at the end thereof a new paragraph as follows:

"(11) The address to be used by the creditor for the purpose of receiving billing inquiries from the obligor."

§ 306. Billing practices.

The Truth in Lending Act (15 U.S.C. 1601-1665) is amended by adding at the end thereof a new chapter as follows:

"Chapter 4—CREDIT BILLING

§ 161. Correction of billing errors.

(a) If a creditor, within sixty days after having transmitted to an obligor a statement of the obligor's account in connection with an extension of consumer credit, receives at the address disclosed under section 127(b)(11) a written notice (other than notice on a payment stub or other payment medium supplied by the creditor if the creditor so stipulates with the disclosure required under section 127(a)(8)) from the obligor in which the obligor:

(1) sets forth or otherwise enables the creditor to identify the name and account number (if any) of the obligor,

(2) indicates the obligor's belief that the statement contains a billing error and the amount of such billing error, and

(3) sets forth the reasons for the obligor's belief (to the extent applicable) that the statement contains a billing error, the creditor shall, unless the obligor has, after giving such written notice and before the expiration of the time limits herein specified, agreed that the statement was correct:

(A) not later than thirty days after the receipt of the notice, send a written acknowledgment thereof to the obligor, unless the action required in subparagraph (B) is taken within such thirty-day period, and

(B) not later than two complete billing cycles of the creditor (in no event later than ninety days) after the receipt of the notice and prior to taking any action to collect the amount, or any part thereof, indicated by the obligor under paragraph (2) either:

(i) make appropriate corrections in the account of the obligor, including the crediting of any finance charges on amounts erroneously billed, and transmit to the obligor a notification of such corrections and the creditor's explanation of any cage in the amount indicated by the obligor under paragraph (2) and, if any such change is made and the obligor so requests, copies of documentary evidence of the obligor's indebtedness; or

(ii) send a written explanation or clarification to the obligor, after having conducted an investigation, setting forth to the extent applicable the reasons why the creditor believes the account of the obligor was correctly shown in the statement and, upon request of the obligor, provide copies of documentary evidence of the obligor's indebtedness. In the case of a billing error where the obligor alleges that the creditor's billing statement reflects goods not delivered to the obligor or his designee in accordance with the agreement made at the time of the transaction, a creditor may not construe such amount to be correctly shown unless he determines that such goods were actually delivered, mailed, or otherwise sent to the obligor an provides the obligor with a statement of such determination.

After complying with the provisions of this subsection with respect to an alleged billing error, a creditor has no further responsibility under this section if the obligor continues to make substantially the same allegation with respect to such error.

(b) For the purpose of this section, a 'billing error' consists of any of the following:

(1) A reflection on a statement of an extension of credit which was not made to the obligor or, if made, was not in the amount reflected on such statement.

(2) A reflection on a statement of an extension of credit for which the obligor requests additional clarification including documentary evidence thereof.

(3) A reflection on a statement of goods or services not accepted by the obligor or his designee or not delivered to the obligor or his designee in accordance with the agreement made at the time of a transaction.

(4) The creditor's failure to reflect properly on a statement a payment made by the obligor or a credit issued to the obligor.

(5) A computation error or similar error of an accounting nature of the creditor on a statement.

(6) Any other error described in regulations of the Board.

(c) For the purposes of this section, 'action to collect the amount, or any part thereof, indicated by an obligor under paragraph (2)' does not include the sending of statements of account to the obligor following written notice from the obligor as specified under subsection (a) if:

(1) the obligor's account is not restricted or closed because of the failure of the obligor to pay the amount indicated under paragraph (2) of subsection (a) and

(2) the creditor indicates the payment of such amount is not required pending the creditor's compliance with this section.

Nothing in this section shall be construed to prohibit any action by a creditor to collect any amount which has not been indicated by the obligor to contain a billing error.

(d) Pursuant to regulations of the Board, a creditor operating an open end consumer credit plan may not, prior to the sending of the written explanation or clarification required under paragraph (B) (ii), restrict or close an account with respect to which the obligor has indicated pursuant to subsection (a) that he believes such account to contain a billing error solely because of the obligor's failure to pay the amount indicated to be in error. Nothing in this subsection shall be deemed to prohibit a creditor from applying against the credit limit on the obligor's account the amount indicated to be in error.

(e) Any creditor who fails to comply with the requirements of this section or section 162 forfeits any right to collect from the obligor the amount indicated by the obligor under paragraph (2) of subsection (a) of this section, and any finance charges thereon, except that the amount required to be forfeited under this subsection may not exceed $50.

§ 162. Regulation of credit reports.

(a) After receiving a notice from an obligor as provided in section 161(a), a creditor or his agent may not directly or indirectly threaten to report to any person adversely on the obligor's credit rating or credit standing because of the obligor's failure to pay the amount indicated by the obligor under section 161(a) (2) and such amount may not be reported as delinquent to any third party until the creditor has met the requirements of section 161 and has allowed the obligor the same number of days (not less than ten) thereafter to make payment as is provided under the credit agreement with the obligor for the payment of undisputed amounts.

(b) If a creditor receives a further written notice from an obligor that an amount is still in dispute within the time allowed for payment under subsection (a) of this section, a creditor may not report to any third party that the amount of the obligor is delinquent because the obligor has failed to pay an amount which he has indicated under section 161(a) (2), unless the creditor also reports that the amount is in dispute and, at the same time, notifies the obligor of the name and address of each party to whom the creditor is reporting information concerning the delinquency.

(c) A creditor shall report any subsequent resolution of any delinquencies reported pursuant to subsection (b) to the parties to whom such delinquencies were initially reported.

§ 163. Length of billing period

(a) If an open end consumer credit plan provides a time period within which an obligor may repay any portion of the credit extended without incurring an additional finance charge, such additional finance charge may not be imposed with respect to such portion of the credit extended for the billing cycle of which such period is a part unless a statement which includes the amount upon which the finance charge for that period is based was mailed at least fourteen days prior to the date specified in the statement by which payment must be made in order to avoid imposition of that finance charge.

(b) Subsection (a) does not apply in any case where a creditor has been prevented, delayed, or hindered in making timely mailing or delivery of such periodic statement within the time period specified in such subsection because of an act of God, war, natural disaster, strike, or other excusable or justifiable cause, as determined under regulations of the Board.

§ 164. Prompt crediting of payments.

Payments received from an obligor under an open end consumer credit plan by the creditor shall be posted promptly to the obligor's account as specified in regulations of the Board. Such regulations shall prevent a finance charge from being imposed on any obligor if the creditor has received the obligor's payment in readily identifiable form in the amount, manner, location, and time indicated by the creditor to avoid the imposition thereof.

§ 165. Crediting excess payments.

Whenever an obligor transmits funds to a creditor in excess of the total balance due on an open end consumer credit account, the creditor shall promptly (1) upon request of the obligor refund the amount of the overpayment, or (2) credit such amount to the obligor's account.

§ 166. Prompt notification of returns.

With respect to any sales transaction where a credit card has been used to obtain credit, where the seller is a person other than the card issuer, and where the seller accepts or allows a return of the goods or forgiveness of a debit for services which were the subject of such sale, the seller shall promptly transmit to the credit card issuer, a credit statement with respect thereto and the credit card issuer shall credit the account of the obligor for the amount of the transaction.

§ 167. Use of cash discounts.

(a) With respect to credit card which may be used for extensions of credit in sales transactions in which the seller is a person other than the card issuer, the card issuer may not, by contract or otherwise, prohibit any such seller from offering a discount to a cardholder to induce the cardholder to pay by cash, check, or similar means rather than use a credit card.

(b) With respect to any sales transaction, any discount not in excess of 5 per centum offered by the seller for the purpose of inducing payment by cash, check, or other means not involving the use of a credit card shall not constitute a finance charge as determined under section 106, if such discount is offered to all prospective buyers and its availability is disclosed to all prospective buyers clearly and conspicuously in accordance with regulations of the Board.

§ 168. Prohibition of tie-in services

Notwithstanding any agreement to the contrary, a card issuer may not require a seller, as a condition to participating in a credit card plan, to open an account with or procure any other service from the card issuer or its subsidiary or agent.

§ 169. Prohibition of offsets.

(a) A card issuer may not take any action to offset a cardholder's indebtedness arising in connection with a consumer credit transaction under the relevant credit card plan against funds of the cardholder held on deposit with the card issuer unless:

> (1) such action was previously authorized in writing by the cardholder in accordance with a credit plan whereby the cardholder agrees periodically to pay debts incurred in his open end credit account by permitting the card issuer periodically to deduct all or a portion of such debt from the cardholder's deposit account, and

> (2) such action with respect to any outstanding disputed amount not be taken by the card issuer upon request of the cardholder.

In the case of any credit card account in existence on the effective date of this section, the previous written authorization referred to in clause (1) shall not be required until the date (after such effective date) when such account is renewed, but in no case later than one year after such effective date. Such written authorization shall be deemed to exist if the card issuer has previously notified the cardholder that the use of his credit card account will subject any funds, which the card issuer holds in deposit accounts of such cardholder to offset against any amounts due and payable on his credit card account which have not been paid in accordance with the terms of the agreement between the card issuer and the cardholder.

(b) This section does not alter or affect the right under State law of a card issuer to attach or otherwise levy upon funds of a cardholder held on deposit with the card issuer if that remedy is constitutionally available to creditors generally.

§ 170. Rights of credit card customers.

(a) Subject to the limitation contained in subsection (b), a card issuer who has issued a credit card to a cardholder pursuant to an open end consumer credit plan shall be subject to all claims (other than tort claims) and defenses arising out of any transaction in which the credit card is used as a method of payment or extension of credit if:

> (1) the obligor has made a good faith attempt to obtain satisfactory resolution of a disagreement or problem relative to the transaction from the person honoring the credit card;

> (2) the amount of the initial transaction exceeds $50; and

> (3) the place where the initial transaction occurred was in the same State as the mailing address previously provided by the cardholder or was within 100 miles from such address, except that the limitations set forth in clauses (2) and (3) with respect to an obligor's right to assert claims and defenses against a card issuer shall not be applicable to any transaction in which the person honoring the credit card:

(A) is the same person as the card issuer,

(B) is controlled by the card issuer,

(C) is under direct or indirect common control with the card issuer,

(D) is a franchised dealer in the card issuer's products or services, or

(E) has obtained the order for such transaction through a mail solicitation made by or participated in by the card issuer in which the cardholder is solicited to enter into such transaction by using the credit card issued by the card issuer.

(b) The amount of claims or defenses asserted by the cardholder may not exceed the amount of credit outstanding with respect to such transaction at the time the cardholder first notifies the card issuer or the person honoring the credit card of such claim or defense. For the purpose of determining the amount of credit outstanding in the preceding sentence, payments and credits to the cardholder's account are deemed to have been applied, in the order indicated, to the payment of:

(1) late charges in the order of their entry to the account;

(2) finance charges in order of their entry to the account; and

(3) debits to the account other than those set forth above, in the order in which each debit entry to the account was made.

§ 171. Relation to State laws

(a) This chapter does not annul, alter, or affect, or exempt any person subject to the provisions of this chapter from complying with, the laws of any State with respect to credit billing practices, except to the extent that those laws are inconsistent with any provision of this chapter, and then only to the extent of the inconsistency. The Board is authorized to determine whether such inconsistencies exist. The Board may not determine that any State law is inconsistent with any provision of this chapter if the Board determines that such law gives greater protection to the consumer.

(b) The Board shall by regulation exempt from the requirements of this chapter any class of credit transactions within any State if it determines that under the law of that State that class of transactions is subject to requirements substantially similar to those imposed under this chapter or that such law gives greater protection to the consumer, and that there is adequate provision for enforcement."

§ 307. CONFORMING AMENDMENTS.

(a) The table of chapter of the Truth in Lending Act is amended by adding immediately under item 3 the following:

"4. CREDIT BILLING . . . . .161"

(b) Section 111(d) of such Act (15 U.S.C. 1610(d)) is amended by striking out "and 130" and inserting in lieu thereof a comma and the following: "130, and 166"

(c) Section 121(a) of such Act (15 U.S.C. 1631(a)) is amended:

(1) by striking out "and upon whom a finance charge is or may be imposed"; and

(2) by inserting "or chapter 4" immediately after "this chapter".

(d) Section 121(b) of such Act (15 U.S.C. 1631(b)) is amended by inserting "or chapter 4" immediately after "this chapter".

(e) Section 122(a) of such Act (15 U.S.C. 1632(a)) is amended by inserting "or chapter 4" immediately after "this chapter".

(f) Section 122(b) of such Act (15 U.S.C. 1632(b)) is amended by inserting "or chapter 4" immediately after "this chapter".

§ 308. EFFECTIVE DATE.

This title takes effect upon the expiration of one year after the date of its enactment.

APPENDIX 13:
FAIR DEBT COLLECTION PRACTICES ACT

[15 U.S.C]

SECTION 1692. CONGRESSIONAL FINDINGS AND DECLARATION OF PURPOSE

(a) Abusive practices.

There is abundant evidence of the use of abusive, deceptive, and unfair debt collection practices by many debt collectors. Abusive debt collection practices contribute to the number of personal bankruptcies, to marital instability, to the loss of jobs, and to invasions of individual privacy.

(b) Inadequacy of laws.

Existing laws and procedures for redressing these injuries are inadequate to protect consumers.

(c) Available non-abusive collection methods.

Means other than misrepresentation or other abusive debt collection practices are available for the effective collection of debts.

(d) Interstate commerce.

Abusive debt collection practices are carried on to a substantial extent in interstate commerce and through means and instrumentalities of such commerce. Even where abusive debt collection practices are purely intrastate in character, they nevertheless directly affect interstate commerce.

(e) Purposes.

It is the purpose of this title to eliminate abusive debt collection practices by debt collectors, to insure that those debt collectors who refrain from using abusive debt collection practices are not competitively disadvantaged, and to promote consistent State action to protect consumers against debt collection abuses.

SECTION 1692a. DEFINITIONS

As used in this title:

(1) The term "Commission" means the Federal Trade Commission.

(2) The term "communication" means the conveying of information regarding a debt directly or indirectly to any person through any medium.

(3) The term "consumer" means any natural person obligated or allegedly obligated to pay any debt.

(4) The term "creditor" means any person who offers or extends credit creating a debt or to whom a debt is owed, but such term does not include any person to the extent that he receives an assignment or transfer of a debt in default solely for the purpose of facilitating collection of such debt for another.

(5) The term "debt" means any obligation or alleged obligation of a consumer to pay money arising out of a transaction in which the money, property, insurance, or services which are the subject of the transaction are primarily for personal, family, or household purposes, whether or not such obligation has been reduced to judgment.

(6) The term "debt collector" means any person who uses any instrumentality of interstate commerce or the mails in any business the principal purpose of which is the collection of any debts, or who regularly collects or attempts to collect, directly or indirectly, debts owed or due or asserted to be owed or due another. Notwithstanding the exclusion provided by clause (F) of the last sentence of this paragraph, the term includes any creditor who, in the process of collecting his own debts, uses any name other than his own which would indicate that a third person is collecting or attempting to collect such debts. For the purpose of section 808(6) [15 USCS @ 1692f(6)], such term also includes any person who uses any instrumentality of interstate commerce or the mails in any business the principal purpose of which is the enforcement of security interests. The term does not include:

(A) any officer or employee of a creditor while, in the name of the creditor, collecting debts for such creditor;

(B) any person while acting as a debt collector for another person, both of whom are related by common ownership or affiliated by corporate control, if the person acting as a debt collector does so only for persons to whom it is so related or affiliated and if the principal business of such person is not the collection of debts;

(C) any officer or employee of the United States or any State to the extent that collecting or attempting to collect any debt is in the performance of his official duties;

(D) any person while serving or attempting to serve legal process on any other person in connection with the judicial enforcement of any debt;

(E) any nonprofit organization which, at the request of consumers, performs bona fide consumer credit counseling and assists consumers in the liquidation of their debts by receiving payments from such consumers and distributing such amounts to creditors; and

(F) any person collecting or attempting to collect any debt owed or due or asserted to be owed or due another to the extent such activity (i) is incidental to a bona fide fiduciary obligation or a bona fide escrow arrangement; (ii) concerns a debt which was originated by such person; (iii) concerns a debt which was not in default at the time it was obtained by such person; or (iv) concerns a debt obtained by such person as a secured party in a commercial credit transaction involving the creditor.

(G) [Redesignated]

(7) The term "location information" means a consumer's place of abode and his telephone number at such place, or his place of employment.

(8) The term "State" means any State, territory, or possession of the United States, the District of Columbia, the Commonwealth of Puerto Rico, or any political subdivision of any of the foregoing.

SECTION 1692b. ACQUISITION OF LOCATION INFORMATION.

Any debt collector communicating with any person other than the consumer for the purpose of acquiring location information about the consumer shall:

(1) identify himself, state that he is confirming or correcting location information concerning the consumer, and, only if expressly requested, identify his employer;

(2) not state that such consumer owes any debt;

(3) not communicate with any such person more than once unless requested to do so by such person or unless the debt collector reasonably believes that the earlier response of such person is erroneous or incomplete and that such person now has correct or complete location information;

(4) not communicate by postcard;

(5) not use any language or symbol on any envelope or in the contents of any communication effected by the mails or telegram that indicates that the debt collector is in the debt collection business or that the communication relates to the collection of a debt; and

(6) after the debt collector knows the consumer is represented by an attorney with regard to the subject debt and has knowledge of, or can readily ascertain, such attorney's name and address, not communicate with any person other than that attorney, unless the attorney fails to respond within a reasonable period of time to communication from the debt collector.

SECTION 1692c. COMMUNICATION IN CONNECTION WITH DEBT COLLECTION

(a) Communication with the consumer generally.

Without the prior consent of the consumer given directly to the debt collector or the express permission of a court of competent jurisdiction, a debt collector may not communicate with a consumer in connection with the collection of any debt:

(1) at any unusual time or place or a time or place known or which should be known to be inconvenient to the consumer. In the absence of knowledge of circumstances to the contrary, a debt collector shall assume that the convenient time for communicating with a consumer is after 8 o'clock antimeridian and before 9 o'clock postmeridian, local time at the consumer's location;

(2) if the debt collector knows the consumer is represented by an attorney with respect to such debt and has knowledge of, or can readily ascertain, such attorney's name and address, unless the attorney fails to respond within a reasonable period of time to a communication from the debt collector or unless the attorney consents to direct communication with the consumer; or

(3) at the consumer's place of employment if the debt collector knows or has reason to know that the consumer's employer prohibits the consumer from receiving such communication.

(b) Communication with third parties.

Except as provided 15 USCS §1692b, without the prior consent of the consumer given directly to the debt collector, or the express permission of a court of competent jurisdiction, or as reasonably necessary to effectuate a postjudgment judicial remedy, a debt collector may not communicate, in connection with the collection of any debt, with any person other than the consumer, his attorney, a consumer reporting agency if otherwise permitted by law, the creditor, the attorney of the creditor, or the attorney of the debt collector.

(c) Ceasing communication.

If a consumer notifies a debt collector in writing that the consumer refuses to pay a debt or that the consumer wishes the debt collector to cease further communication with the consumer, the debt collector shall not communicate further with the consumer with respect to such debt, except:

(1) to advise the consumer that the debt collector's further efforts are being terminated;

(2) to notify the consumer that the debt collector or creditor may invoke specified remedies which are ordinarily invoked by such debt collector or creditor; or

(3) where applicable, to notify the consumer that the debt collector or creditor intends to invoke a specified remedy. If such notice from the consumer is made by mail, notification shall be complete upon receipt.

(d) "Consumer" defined.

For the purpose of this section, the term "consumer" includes the consumer's spouse, parent (if the consumer is a minor), guardian, executor, or administrator.

SECTION 1692d. HARASSMENT OR ABUSE

A debt collector may not engage in any conduct the natural consequence of which is to harass, oppress, or abuse any person in connection with the collection of a debt. Without limiting the general application of the foregoing, the following conduct is a violation of this section:

(1) The use or threat of use of violence or other criminal means to harm the physical person, reputation, or property of any person.

(2) The use of obscene or profane language or language the natural consequence of which is to abuse the hearer or reader.

(3) The publication of a list of consumers who allegedly refuse to pay debts, except to a consumer reporting agency or to persons meeting the requirements of section 1681a(f) or 1681b(3)] of this title.

(4) The advertisement for sale of any debt to coerce payment of the debt.

(5) Causing a telephone to ring or engaging any person in telephone conversation repeatedly or continuously with intent to annoy, abuse or harass any person at the called number.

SECTION 1692e. FALSE OR MISLEADING REPRESENTATIONS

A debt collector may not use any false, deceptive, or misleading representation or means in connection with the collection of any debt. Without limiting the general application of the foregoing, the following conduct is a violation of this section:

(1) The false representation or implication that the debt collector is vouched for, bonded by, or affiliated with the United States or any State, including the use of any badge, uniform, or facsimile thereof.

(2) The false representation of:

(A) the character, amount, or legal status of any debt; or

(B) any services rendered or compensation which may be lawfully received by any debt collector for the collection of a debt.

(3) The false representation or implication that any individual is an attorney or that any communication is from an attorney.

(4) The representation or implication that nonpayment of any debt will result in the arrest or imprisonment of any person or the seizure, garnishment, attachment, or sale of any property or wages of any person unless such action is lawful and the debt collector or creditor intends to take such action.

(5) The threat to take any action that cannot legally be taken or that is not intended to be taken.

(6) The false representation or implication that a sale, referral, or other transfer of any interest in a debt shall cause the consumer to:

(A) lose any claim or defense to payment of the debt; or

(B) become subject to any practice prohibited by this title.

(7) The false representation or implication that the consumer committed any crime or other conduct in order to disgrace the consumer.

(8) Communicating or threatening to communicate to any person credit information which is known or which should be known to be false, including the failure to communicate that a disputed debt is disputed.

(9) The use or distribution of any written communication which simulates or is falsely represented to be a document authorized, issued, or approved by any court, official, or agency of the United States or

any State, or which creates a false impression as to its source, authorization, or approval.

(10) The use of any false representation or deceptive means to collect or attempt to collect any debt or to obtain information concerning a consumer.

(11) Except as otherwise provided for communications to acquire location information under section 1692b], the failure to disclose clearly in all communications made to collect a debt or to obtain information about a consumer, that the debt collector is attempting to collect a debt and that any information obtained will be used for that purpose.

(12) The false representation or implication that accounts have been turned over to innocent purchasers for value.

(13) The false representation or implication that documents are legal process.

(14) The use of any business, company, or organization name other than the true name of the debt collector's business, company, or organization.

(15) The false representation or implication that documents are not legal process forms or do not require action by the consumer.

(16) The false representation or implication that a debt collector operates or is employed by a consumer reporting agency as defined by section 1681a(f)] of this title.

SECTION 1692f. UNFAIR PRACTICES

A debt collector may not use unfair or unconscionable means to collect or attempt to collect any debt. Without limiting the general application of the foregoing, the following conduct is a violation of this section:

(1) The collection of any amount (including any interest, fee, charge, or expense incidental to the principal obligation) unless such amount is expressly authorized by the agreement creating the debt or permitted by law.

(2) The acceptance by a debt collector from any person of a check or other payment instrument postdated by more than five days unless such person is notified in writing of the debt collector's intent to deposit such check or instrument not more than ten nor less than three business days prior to such deposit.

(3) The solicitation by a debt collector of any postdated check or other postdated payment instrument for the purpose of threatening or instituting criminal prosecution.

(4) Depositing or threatening to deposit any postdated check or other postdated payment instrument prior to the date on such check or instrument.

(5) Causing charges to be made to any person for communications by concealment of the true purpose of the communication. Such charges include, but are not limited to, collect telephone calls and telegram fees.

(6) Taking or threatening to take any nonjudicial action to effect dispossession or disablement of property if:

(A) there is no present right to possession of the property claimed as collateral through an enforceable security interest;

(B) there is no present intention to take possession of the property; or

(C) the property is exempt by law from such dispossession or disablement.

(7) Communicating with a consumer regarding a debt by postcard.

(8) Using any language or symbol, other than the debt collector's address, on any envelope when communicating with a consumer by use of the mails or by telegram, except that a debt collector may use his business name if such name does not indicate that he is in the debt collection business.

SECTION 1692g. VALIDATION OF DEBTS

(a) Notice of debt; contents.

Within five days after the initial communication with a consumer in connection with the collection of any debt, a debt collector shall, unless the following information is contained in the initial communication or the consumer has paid the debt, send the consumer a written notice containing:

(1) the amount of the debt;

(2) the name of the creditor to whom the debt is owed;

(3) a statement that unless the consumer, within thirty days after receipt of the notice, disputes the validity of the debt, or any portion thereof, the debt will be assumed to be valid by the debt collector;

(4) a statement that if the consumer notifies the debt collector in writing within the thirty-day period that the debt, or any portion thereof, is disputed, the debt collector will obtain verification of the debt or a copy of a judgment against the consumer and a copy of such

verification or judgment will be mailed to the consumer by the debt collector; and

(5) a statement that, upon the consumer's written request within the thirty-day period, the debt collector will provide the consumer with the name and address of the original creditor, if different from the current creditor.

(b) Disputed debts.

If the consumer notifies the debt collector in writing within the thirty-day period described in subsection (a) that the debt, or any portion thereof, is disputed, or that the consumer requests the name and address of the original creditor, the debt collector shall cease collection of the debt, or any disputed portion thereof, until the debt collector obtains verification of the debt or a copy of a judgment, or the name and address of the original creditor, and a copy of such verification or judgment, or name and address of the original creditor, is mailed to the consumer by the debt collector.

(c) Admission of liability.

The failure of a consumer to dispute the validity of a debt under this section may not be construed by any court as an admission of liability by the consumer.

SECTION 1692h. MULTIPLE DEBTS

If any consumer owes multiple debts and makes any single payment to any debt collector with respect to such debts, such debt collector may not apply such payment to any debt which is disputed by the consumer and, where applicable, shall apply such payment in accordance with the consumer's directions.

SECTION 1692i. LEGAL ACTIONS BY DEBT COLLECTORS

(a) Venue.

Any debt collector who brings any legal action on a debt against any consumer shall:

(1) in the case of an action to enforce an interest in real property securing the consumer's obligation, bring such action only in a judicial district or similar legal entity in which such real property is located; or

(2) in the case of an action not described in paragraph (1), bring such action only in the judicial district or similar legal entity:

(A) in which such consumer signed the contract sued upon; or

(B) in which such consumer resides at the commencement of the action.

(b) Authorization of actions.

Nothing in this title shall be construed to authorize the bringing of legal actions by debt collectors.

SECTION 1692j. FURNISHING CERTAIN DECEPTIVE FORMS

(a) It is unlawful to design, compile, and furnish any form knowing that such form would be used to create the false belief in a consumer that a person other than the creditor of such consumer is participating in the collection of or in an attempt to collect a debt such consumer allegedly owes such creditor, when in fact such person is not so participating.

(b) Any person who violates this section shall be liable to the same extent and in the same manner as a debt collector is liable under section 1692k of this title for failure to comply with a provision of this subchapter.

SECTION 1692k. CIVIL LIABILITY

(a) Amount of damages.

Except as otherwise provided by this section, any debt collector who fails to comply with any provision of this title with respect to any person is liable to such person in an amount equal to the sum of:

(1) any actual damage sustained by such person as a result of such failure;

(2)(A) in the case of any action by an individual, such additional damages as the court may allow, but not exceeding $1,000; or

(2)(B) in the case of a class action, (i) such amount for each named plaintiff as could be recovered under subparagraph (A), and (ii) such amount as the court may allow for all other class members, without regard to a minimum individual recovery, not to exceed the lesser of $500,000 or 1 per centum of the net worth of the debt collector; and

(3) in the case of any successful action to enforce the foregoing liability, the costs of the action, together with a reasonable attorney's fee as determined by the court. On a finding by the court that an action under this section was brought in bad faith and for the purpose of harassment, the court may award to defendant attorney's fees reasonable in relation to the work expended and costs.

(b) Factors considered by court.

In determining the amount of liability in any action under subsection (a), the court shall consider, among other relevant factors:

(1) in any individual action under subsection (a)(2)(A), the frequency and persistence of noncompliance by the debt collector, the nature of such noncompliance, and the extent to which such noncompliance was intentional; or

(2) in any class action under subsection (a)(2)(B), the frequency and persistence of noncompliance by the debt collector, the nature of such noncompliance, the resources of the debt collector, the number of persons adversely affected, and the extent to which the debt collector's noncompliance was intentional.

(c) Intent.

A debt collector may not be held liable in any action brought under this title if the debt collector shows by a preponderance of evidence that the violation was not intentional and resulted from a bona fide error the maintenance of procedures reasonably adapted to avoid any such error.

(d) Jurisdiction.

An action to enforce any liability created by this title may be brought in any appropriate United States district court without regard to the amount in controversy, or in any other court of competent jurisdiction, within one year from the date on which the violation occurs.

(e) Advisory opinions of Commission.

No provision of this section imposing any liability shall apply to any act done or omitted in good faith in conformity with any advisory opinion of the Commission, notwithstanding that after such act or omission has occurred, such opinion is amended, rescinded, or determined by judicial or other authority to be invalid for any reason.

SECTION 1692l. ADMINISTRATIVE ENFORCEMENT

(a) Federal Trade Commission.

Compliance with this title shall be enforced by the Commission, except to the extent that enforcement of the requirements imposed under this title is specifically committed to another agency under subsection (b). For purpose of the exercise by the Commission of its functions and powers under the Federal Trade Commission Act, a violation of this title shall be deemed an unfair or deceptive act or practice in violation of that Act. All of the functions and powers of the Commission under the Federal Trade Commission Act are available to the Commission to enforce compliance by any person with this title, irrespective of whether that person is engaged in commerce or meets any other jurisdictional tests in the Federal Trade Commission Act, including the power to enforce the provisions of this title in the same manner as if the violation had been a violation of a Federal Trade Commission trade regulation rule.

(b) Applicable provisions of law.

Compliance with any requirements imposed under this title shall be enforced under:

(1) section 8 of the Federal Deposit Insurance Act, in the case of:

(A) national banks, and Federal branches and Federal agencies of foreign banks, by the Office of the Comptroller of the Currency;

(B) member banks of the Federal Reserve System (other than national banks), branches and agencies of foreign banks (other than Federal branches, Federal agencies, and insured State branches of foreign banks), commercial lending companies owned or controlled by foreign banks, and organizations operating under section 25 or 25(a) [25A] of the Federal Reserve Act, by the Board of Governors of the Federal Reserve System; and

(C) banks insured by the Federal Deposit Insurance Corporation (other than members of the Federal Reserve System) and insured State branches of foreign banks, by the Board of Directors of the Federal Deposit Insurance Corporation;

(2) section 8 of the Federal Deposit Insurance Act, by the Director of the Office of Thrift Supervision, in the case of a savings association the deposits of which are insured by the Federal Deposit Insurance Corporation;

(3) the Federal Credit Union Act, by the Administrator of the National Credit Union Administration [National Credit Union Administration Board] with respect to any Federal credit union;

(4) the Acts to regulate commerce, by the Secretary of Transportation, with respect to all carriers subject to the jurisdiction of the Surface Transportation Board;

(5) the Federal Aviation Act of 1958, by the Secretary of Transportation with respect to any air carrier or any foreign air carrier subject to that Act; and

(6) the Packers and Stockyards Act (except as provided in section 406 of that Act, by the Secretary of Agriculture with respect to any activities subject to that Act.

(c) Agency powers.

For the purpose of the exercise by any agency referred to in subsection (b) of its powers under any Act referred to in that subsection, a violation of any requirement imposed under this title shall be deemed to be a violation of a requirement imposed under that Act. In addition to its powers under any provision of law specifically referred to in subsection (b), each of the agencies referred to in that subsection may exercise, for the purpose of enforcing compliance with any requirement imposed under this title any other authority conferred on it by law, except as provided in subsection (d).

(d) Rules and regulations.

Neither the Commission nor any other agency referred to in subsection (b) may promulgate trade regulation rules or other regulations with respect to the collection of debts by debt collectors as defined in this title.

SECTION 1692m. REPORTS TO CONGRESS BY THE COMMISSION

(a) Not later than one year after the effective date of this subchapter and at one-year intervals thereafter, the Commission shall make reports to the Congress concerning the administration of its functions under this subchapter, including such recommendations as the Commission deems necessary or appropriate. In addition, each report of the Commission shall include its assessment of the extent to which compliance with this subchapter is being achieved and a summary of the enforcement actions taken by the commission under section 1692l of this title.

(b) In the exercise of its functions under this subchapter, the Commission may obtain upon request the views of any other Federal agency which exercises enforcement functions under section 1692l of this title.

SECTION 1692n. RELATION TO STATE LAWS

This subchapter does not annul, alter, or affect, or exempt any person subject to the provisions of this subchapter from complying with the laws of any State with respect to debt collection practices, except to the extent that those laws are inconsistent with any provision of this subchapter, and then only to the extent of the inconsistency. For purposes of this section, a State law is not inconsistent with this subchapter if the protection such law affords any consumer is greater than the protection provided by this subchapter.

SECTION 1692o. EXEMPTION FOR STATE REGULATION

The Commission shall by regulation exempt from the requirements of this subchapter any class of debt collection practices within any State if the Commission determines that under the law of that State that class of debt collection practices is subject to requirements substantially similar to those imposed by this subchapter, and that there is adequate provision for enforcement.

APPENDIX 14:
ELECTRONIC FUNDS TRANSFER ACT

[15 U.S.C]

SEC. 1693. CONGRESSIONAL FINDINGS AND DECLARATION OF PURPOSE.

(a) Rights and liabilities undefined.

The Congress finds that the use of electronic systems to transfer funds provides the potential for substantial benefits to consumers. However, due to the unique characteristics of such systems, the application of existing consumer protection legislation is unclear, leaving the rights and liabilities of consumers, financial institutions, and intermediaries in electronic fund transfers undefined.

(b) Purposes.

It is the purpose of this subchapter to provide a basic framework establishing the rights, liabilities, and responsibilities of participants in electronic fund transfer systems. The primary objective of this subchapter, however, is the provision of individual consumer rights.

SEC. 1693a. DEFINITIONS.

As used in this subchapter—

(1) the term "accepted card or other means of access" means a card, code, or other means of access to a consumer's account for the purpose of initiating electronic fund transfers when the person to whom such card or other means of access was issued has requested and received or has signed or has used, or authorized another to use, such card or other means of access for the purpose of transferring money between accounts or obtaining money, property, labor, or services;

(2) the term "account" means a demand deposit, savings deposit, or other asset account (other than an occasional or incidental credit balance in an open end credit plan as defined in section 1602(i) of this title), as described in regulations of the Board, established primarily for personal, family, or household purposes, but such term

does not include an account held by a financial institution pursuant to a bona fide trust agreement;

(3) the term "Board" means the Board of Governors of the Federal Reserve System;

(4) the term "business day" means any day on which the offices of the consumer's financial institution involved in an electronic fund transfer are open to the public for carrying on substantially all of its business functions;

(5) the term "consumer" means a natural person;

(6) the term "electronic fund transfer" means any transfer of funds, other than a transaction originated by check, draft, or similar paper instrument, which is initiated through an electronic terminal, telephonic instrument, or computer or magnetic tape so as to order, instruct, or authorize a financial institution to debit or credit an account. Such term includes, but is not limited to, point-of-sale transfers, automated teller machine transactions, direct deposits or withdrawals of funds, and transfers initiated by telephone. Such term does not include—

(A) any check guarantee or authorization service which does not directly result in a debit or credit to a consumer's account:

(B) any transfer of funds, other than those processed by automated clearinghouse, made by a financial institution on behalf of a consumer by means of a service that transfers funds held at either Federal Reserve banks or other depository institutions and which is not designed primarily to transfer funds on behalf of a consumer;

(C) any transaction the primary purpose of which is the purchase or sale of securities or commodities through a broker-dealer registered with or regulated by the Securities and Exchange Commission;

(D) any automatic transfer from a savings account to a demand deposit account pursuant to an agreement between a consumer and a financial institution for the purpose of covering an overdraft or maintaining an agreed upon minimum balance in the consumer's demand deposit account; or

(E) any transfer of funds which is initiated by a telephone conversation between a consumer and an officer or employee of a financial institution which is not pursuant to a prearranged plan and under which periodic or recurring transfers are not contemplated; as determined under regulations of the Board;

(7) the term "electronic terminal" means an electronic device, other than a telephone operated by a consumer, through which a consumer may initiate an electronic fund transfer. Such term includes, but is not limited to, point-of-sale terminals, automated teller machines, and cash dispensing machines;

(8) the term "financial institution" means a State or National bank, a State or Federal savings and loan association, a mutual savings bank, a State or Federal credit union, or any other person who, directly or indirectly, holds an account belonging to a consumer;

(9) the term "preauthorized electronic fund transfer" means an electronic fund transfer authorized in advance to recur at substantially regular intervals;

(10) the term "State" means any State, territory, or possession of the United States, the District of Columbia, the Commonwealth of Puerto Rico, or any political subdivision of any of the foregoing; and

(11) the term "unauthorized electronic fund transfer" means an electronic fund transfer from a consumer's account initiated by a person other than the consumer without actual authority to initiate such transfer and from which the consumer receives no benefit, but the term does not include any electronic fund transfer (A) initiated by a person other than the consumer who was furnished with the card, code, or other means of access to such consumer's account by such consumer, unless the consumer has notified the financial institution involved that transfers by such other person are no longer authorized, (B) initiated with fraudulent intent by the consumer or any person acting in concert with the consumer, or (C) which constitutes an error committed by a financial institution.

SEC. 1693b. REGULATIONS.

* * *

(d) Applicability to service providers other than certain financial institutions.

(1) In general.

If electronic fund transfer services are made available to consumers by a person other than a financial institution holding a consumer's account, the Board shall by regulation assure that the disclosures, protections, responsibilities, and remedies created by this subchapter are made applicable to such persons and services.

(2) State and local government electronic benefit transfer systems.

(A) "Electronic benefit transfer system" defined.

In this paragraph, the term "electronic benefit transfer system"—

(i) means a system under which a government agency distributes needs-tested benefits by establishing accounts that may be accessed by recipients electronically, such as through automated teller machines or point-of-sale terminals; and

(ii) does not include employment-related payments, including salaries and pension, retirement, or unemployment benefits established by a Federal, State, or local government agency.

(B) Exemption generally.

The disclosures, protections, responsibilities, and remedies established under this subchapter, and any regulation prescribed or order issued by the Board in accordance with this subchapter, shall not apply to any electronic benefit transfer system established under State or local law or administered by a State or local government.

(C) Exception for direct deposit into recipient's account.

Subparagraph (B) shall not apply with respect to any electronic funds transfer under an electronic benefit transfer system for a deposit directly into a consumer account held by the recipient of the benefit.

(D) Rule of construction.

No provision of this paragraph—

(i) affects or alters the protections otherwise applicable with respect to benefits established by any other provision of Federal, State, or local law; or

(ii) otherwise supersedes the application of any State or local law.

(3) Fee disclosures at automated teller machines.

(A) In general.

The regulations prescribed under paragraph (1) shall require any automated teller machine operator who imposes a fee on any consumer for providing host transfer services to such consumer to provide notice in accordance with subparagraph (B) to the consumer (at the time the service is provided) of—

(i) the fact that a fee is imposed by such operator for providing the service; and

(ii) the amount of any such fee.

(B) Notice requirements.

(i) On the machine.

The notice required under clause (i) of subparagraph (A) with respect to any fee described in such subparagraph shall be posted in a prominent and conspicuous location on or at the automated teller machine at which the electronic fund transfer is initiated by the consumer.

(ii) On the screen.

The notice required under clauses (i) and (ii) of subparagraph (A) with respect to any fee described in such subparagraph shall appear on the screen of the automated teller machine, or on a paper notice issued from such machine, after the transaction is initiated and before the consumer is irrevocably committed to completing the transaction, except that during the period beginning on November 12, 1999, and ending on December 31, 2004, this clause shall not apply to any automated teller machine that lacks the technical capability to disclose the notice on the screen or to issue a paper notice after the transaction is initiated and before the consumer is irrevocably committed to completing the transaction.

(C) Prohibition on fees not properly disclosed and explicitly assumed by consumer.

No fee may be imposed by any automated teller machine operator in connection with any electronic fund transfer initiated by a consumer for which a notice is required under subparagraph (A), unless—

(i) the consumer receives such notice in accordance with subparagraph (B); and

(ii) the consumer elects to continue in the manner necessary to effect the transaction after receiving such notice.

(D) Definitions.

For purposes of this paragraph, the following definitions shall apply:

(i) Automated teller machine operator.

The term "automated teller machine operator" means any person who—

(I) operates an automated teller machine at which consumers initiate electronic fund transfers; and

(II) is not the financial institution that holds the account of such consumer from which the transfer is made.

(ii) Electronic fund transfer.

The term "electronic fund transfer" includes a transaction that involves a balance inquiry initiated by a consumer in the same manner as an electronic fund transfer, whether or not the consumer initiates a transfer of funds in the course of the transaction.

(iii) Host transfer services.

The term "host transfer services" means any electronic fund transfer made by an automated teller machine operator in connection with a transaction initiated by a consumer at an automated teller machine operated by such operator.

SEC. 1693c. TERMS AND CONDITIONS OF TRANSFERS.

(a) Disclosures; time; form; contents.

The terms and conditions of electronic fund transfers involving a consumer's account shall be disclosed at the time the consumer contracts for an electronic fund transfer service, in accordance with regulations of the Board. Such disclosures shall be in readily understandable language and shall include, to the extent applicable—

(1) the consumer's liability for unauthorized electronic fund transfers and, at the financial institution's option, notice of the advisability of prompt reporting of any loss, theft, or unauthorized use of a card, code, or other means of access;

(2) the telephone number and address of the person or office to be notified in the event the consumer believes than [1] an unauthorized electronic fund transfer has been or may be effected;

(3) the type and nature of electronic fund transfers which the consumer may initiate, including any limitations on the frequency or dollar amount of such transfers, except that the details of such limitations need not be disclosed if their confidentiality is necessary to

maintain the security of an electronic fund transfer system, as determined by the Board;

(4) any charges for electronic fund transfers or for the right to make such transfers;

(5) the consumer's right to stop payment of a preauthorized electronic fund transfer and the procedure to initiate such a stop payment order;

(6) the consumer's right to receive documentation of electronic fund transfers under section 1693d of this title;

(7) a summary, in a form prescribed by regulations of the Board, of the error resolution provisions of section 1693f of this title and the consumer's rights thereunder. The financial institution shall thereafter transmit such summary at least once per calendar year;

(8) the financial institution's liability to the consumer under section 1693h of this title;

(9) under what circumstances the financial institution will in the ordinary course of business disclose information concerning the consumer's account to third persons; and

(10) a notice to the consumer that a fee may be imposed by—

(A) an automated teller machine operator (as defined in section 1693b(d)(3)(D)(i) of this title) if the consumer initiates a transfer from an automated teller machine that is not operated by the person issuing the card or other means of access; and

(B) any national, regional, or local network utilized to effect the transaction.

(b) Notification of changes to consumer.

A financial institution shall notify a consumer in writing at least twenty-one days prior to the effective date of any change in any term or condition of the consumer's account required to be disclosed under subsection (a) of this section if such change would result in greater cost or liability for such consumer or decreased access to the consumer's account. A financial institution may, however, implement a change in the terms or conditions of an account without prior notice when such change is immediately necessary to maintain or restore the security of an electronic fund transfer system or a consumer's account. Subject to subsection (a)(3) of this section, the Board shall require subsequent notification if such a change is made permanent.

(c) Time for disclosures respecting accounts accessible prior to effective date of this subchapter.

For any account of a consumer made accessible to electronic fund transfers prior to the effective date of this subchapter, the information required to be disclosed to the consumer under subsection (a) of this section shall be disclosed not later than the earlier of—

(1) the first periodic statement required by section 1693d(c) of this title after the effective date of this subchapter; or

(2) thirty days after the effective date of this subchapter.

SEC. 1693d. DOCUMENTATION OF TRANSFERS.

(a) Availability of written documentation to consumer; contents.

For each electronic fund transfer initiated by a consumer from an electronic terminal, the financial institution holding such consumer's account shall, directly or indirectly, at the time the transfer is initiated, make available to the consumer written documentation of such transfer. The documentation shall clearly set forth to the extent applicable—

(1) the amount involved and date the transfer is initiated;

(2) the type of transfer;

(3) the identity of the consumer's account with the financial institution from which or to which funds are transferred;

(4) the identity of any third party to whom or from whom funds are transferred; and

(5) the location or identification of the electronic terminal involved.

(b) Notice of credit to consumer.

For a consumer's account which is scheduled to be credited by a preauthorized electronic fund transfer from the same payor at least once in each successive sixty-day period, except where the payor provides positive notice of the transfer to the consumer, the financial institution shall elect to provide promptly either positive notice to the consumer when the credit is made as scheduled, or negative notice to the consumer when the credit is not made as scheduled, in accordance with regulations of the Board. The means of notice elected shall be disclosed to the consumer in accordance with section 1693c of this title.

(c) Periodic statement; contents.

A financial institution shall provide each consumer with a periodic statement for each account of such consumer that may be accessed by means of an electronic fund transfer. Except as provided in subsections (d) and (e) of this section, such statement shall be provided at least monthly for each monthly or shorter cycle in which an electronic fund transfer affecting the account has occurred, or every three months, whichever is more frequent. The statement, which may include information regarding transactions other than electronic fund transfers, shall clearly set forth—

(1) with regard to each electronic fund transfer during the period, the information described in subsection (a) of this section, which may be provided on an accompanying document;

(2) the amount of any fee or charge assessed by the financial institution during the period for electronic fund transfers or for account maintenance;

(3) the balances in the consumer's account at the beginning of the period and at the close of the period; and

(4) the address and telephone number to be used by the financial institution for the purpose of receiving any statement inquiry or notice of account error from the consumer. Such address and telephone number shall be preceded by the caption "Direct Inquiries To:" or other similar language indicating that the address and number are to be used for such inquiries or notices.

(d) Consumer passbook accounts.

In the case of a consumer's passbook account which may not be accessed by electronic fund transfers other than preauthorized electronic fund transfers crediting the account, a financial institution may, in lieu of complying with the requirements of subsection (c) of this section, upon presentation of the passbook provide the consumer in writing with the amount and date of each such transfer involving the account since the passbook was last presented.

(e) Accounts other than passbook accounts.

In the case of a consumer's account, other than a passbook account, which may not be accessed by electronic fund transfers other than preauthorized electronic fund transfers crediting the account, the financial institution may provide a periodic statement on a quarterly basis which otherwise complies with the requirements of subsection (c) of this section.

(f) Documentation as evidence.

In any action involving a consumer, any documentation required by this section to be given to the consumer which indicates that an electronic fund transfer was made to another person shall be admissible as evidence of such transfer and shall constitute prima facie proof that such transfer was made.

SEC. 1693e. PREAUTHORIZED TRANSFERS.

(a) A preauthorized electronic fund transfer from a consumer's account may be authorized by the consumer only in writing, and a copy of such authorization shall be provided to the consumer when made. A consumer may stop payment of a preauthorized electronic fund transfer by notifying the financial institution orally or in writing at any time up to three business days preceding the scheduled date of such transfer. The financial institution may require written confirmation to be provided to it within fourteen days of an oral notification if, when the oral notification is made, the consumer is advised of such requirement and the address to which such confirmation should be sent.

(b) In the case of preauthorized transfers from a consumer's account to the same person which may vary in amount, the financial institution or designated payee shall, prior to each transfer, provide reasonable advance notice to the consumer, in accordance with regulations of the Board, of the amount to be transferred and the scheduled date of the transfer.

SEC. 1693f. ERROR RESOLUTION.

(a) Notification to financial institution of error.

If a financial institution, within sixty days after having transmitted to a consumer documentation pursuant to section 1693d(a), (c), or (d) of this title or notification pursuant to section 1693d(b) of this title, receives oral or written notice in which the consumer—

(1) sets forth or otherwise enables the financial institution to identify the name and account number of the consumer;

(2) indicates the consumer's belief that the documentation, or, in the case of notification pursuant to section 1693d(b) of this title, the consumer's account, contains an error and the amount of such error; and

(3) sets forth the reasons for the consumer's belief (where applicable) that an error has occurred, the financial institution shall investigate the alleged error, determine whether an error has occurred, and report or mail the results of such investigation and determination to the consumer within ten business days. The financial institution may require written confirmation to be provided to it within ten business days of an oral notification of error if, when the oral notification is made, the consumer is advised of such requirement and the address to which such confirmation should be sent. A financial institu-

tion which requires written confirmation in accordance with the previous sentence need not provisionally recredit a consumer's account in accordance with subsection (c) of this section, nor shall the financial institution be liable under subsection (e) of this section if the written confirmation is not received within the ten-day period referred to in the previous sentence.

(b) Correction of error; interest.

If the financial institution determines that an error did occur, it shall promptly, but in no event more than one business day after such determination, correct the error, subject to section 1693g of this title, including the crediting of interest where applicable.

(c) Provisional recredit of consumer's account.

If a financial institution receives notice of an error in the manner and within the time period specified in subsection (a) of this section, it may, in lieu of the requirements of subsections (a) and (b) of this section, within ten business days after receiving such notice provisionally recredit the consumer's account for the amount alleged to be in error, subject to section 1693g of this title, including interest where applicable, pending the conclusion of its investigation and its determination of whether an error has occurred. Such investigation shall be concluded not later than forty-five days after receipt of notice of the error. During the pendency of the investigation, the consumer shall have full use of the funds provisionally recredited.

(d) Absence of error; finding; explanation.

If the financial institution determines after its investigation pursuant to subsection (a) or (c) of this section that an error did not occur, it shall deliver or mail to the consumer an explanation of its findings within 3 business days after the conclusion of its investigation, and upon request of the consumer promptly deliver or mail to the consumer reproductions of all documents which the financial institution relied on to conclude that such error did not occur. The financial institution shall include notice of the right to request reproductions with the explanation of its findings.

(e) Treble damages.

If in any action under section 1693m of this title, the court finds that—

(1) the financial institution did not provisionally recredit a consumer's account within the ten-day period specified in subsection (c) of this section, and the financial institution (A) did not make a good faith investigation of the alleged error, or (B) did not have a reason-

able basis for believing that the consumer's account was not in error; or

(2) the financial institution knowingly and willfully concluded that the consumer's account was not in error when such conclusion could not reasonably have been drawn from the evidence available to the financial institution at the time of its investigation, then the consumer shall be entitled to treble damages determined under section 1693m(a)(1) of this title.

(f) Acts constituting error.

For the purpose of this section, an error consists of—

(1) an unauthorized electronic fund transfer;

(2) an incorrect electronic fund transfer from or to the consumer's account;

(3) the omission from a periodic statement of an electronic fund transfer affecting the consumer's account which should have been included;

(4) a computational error by the financial institution;

(5) the consumer's receipt of an incorrect amount of money from an electronic terminal;

(6) a consumer's request for additional information or clarification concerning an electronic fund transfer or any documentation required by this subchapter; or

(7) any other error described in regulations of the Board.

SEC. 1693g. CONSUMER LIABILITY.

(a) Unauthorized electronic fund transfers; limit.

A consumer shall be liable for any unauthorized electronic fund transfer involving the account of such consumer only if the card or other means of access utilized for such transfer was an accepted card or other means [1] of access and if the issuer of such card, code, or other means of access has provided a means whereby the user of such card, code, or other means of access can be identified as the person authorized to use it, such as by signature, photograph, or fingerprint or by electronic or mechanical confirmation. In no event, however, shall a consumer's liability for an unauthorized transfer exceed the lesser of—

(1) $50; or

(2) the amount of money or value of property or services obtained in such unauthorized electronic fund transfer prior to the time the fi-

nancial institution is notified of, or otherwise becomes aware of, circumstances which lead to the reasonable belief that an unauthorized electronic fund transfer involving the consumer's account has been or may be effected. Notice under this paragraph is sufficient when such steps have been taken as may be reasonably required in the ordinary course of business to provide the financial institution with the pertinent information, whether or not any particular officer, employee, or agent of the financial institution does in fact receive such information. Notwithstanding the foregoing, reimbursement need not be made to the consumer for losses the financial institution establishes would not have occurred but for the failure of the consumer to report within sixty days of transmittal of the statement (or in extenuating circumstances such as extended travel or hospitalization, within a reasonable time under the circumstances) any unauthorized electronic fund transfer or account error which appears on the periodic statement provided to the consumer under section 1693d of this title. In addition, reimbursement need not be made to the consumer for losses which the financial institution establishes would not have occurred but for the failure of the consumer to report any loss or theft of a card or other means of access within two business days after the consumer learns of the loss or theft (or in extenuating circumstances such as extended travel or hospitalization, within a longer period which is reasonable under the circumstances), but the consumer's liability under this subsection in any such case may not exceed a total of $500, or the amount of unauthorized electronic fund transfers which occur following the close of two business days (or such longer period) after the consumer learns of the loss or theft but prior to notice to the financial institution under this subsection, whichever is less.

(b) Burden of proof.

In any action which involves a consumer's liability for an unauthorized electronic fund transfer, the burden of proof is upon the financial institution to show that the electronic fund transfer was authorized or, if the electronic fund transfer was unauthorized, then the burden of proof is upon the financial institution to establish that the conditions of liability set forth in subsection (a) of this section have been met, and, if the transfer was initiated after the effective date of section 1693c of this title, that the disclosures required to be made to the consumer under section 1693c(a)(1) and (2) of this title were in fact made in accordance with such section.

(c) Determination of limitation on liability.

In the event of a transaction which involves both an unauthorized electronic fund transfer and an extension of credit as defined in section 1602(e) of this title pursuant to an agreement between the consumer and the financial institution to extend such credit to the consumer in the event the consumer's account is overdrawn, the limitation on the consumer's liability for such transaction shall be determined solely in accordance with this section.

(d) Restriction on liability.

Nothing in this section imposes liability upon a consumer for an unauthorized electronic fund transfer in excess of his liability for such a transfer under other applicable law or under any agreement with the consumer's financial institution.

(e) Scope of liability.

Except as provided in this section, a consumer incurs no liability from an unauthorized electronic fund transfer.

SEC. 1693h. LIABILITY OF FINANCIAL INSTITUTIONS.

(a) Action or failure to act proximately causing damages.

Subject to subsections (b) and (c) of this section, a financial institution shall be liable to a consumer for all damages proximately caused by—

(1) the financial institution's failure to make an electronic fund transfer, in accordance with the terms and conditions of an account, in the correct amount or in a timely manner when properly instructed to do so by the consumer, except where—

(A) the consumer's account has insufficient funds;

(B) the funds are subject to legal process or other encumbrance restricting such transfer;

(C) such transfer would exceed an established credit limit;

(D) an electronic terminal has insufficient cash to complete the transaction; or

(E) as otherwise provided in regulations of the Board;

(2) the financial institution's failure to make an electronic fund transfer due to insufficient funds when the financal institution failed to credit, in accordance with the terms and conditions of an account, a deposit of funds to the consumer's account which would have provided sufficient funds to make the transfer, and preauthorized transfer from a consumer's account when instructed to do so in accordance with the terms and conditions of the account.

(b) Acts of God and technical malfunctions.

A financial institution shall not be liable under subsection (a)(1) or (2) of this section if the financial institution shows by a preponderance of the evidence that its action or failure to act resulted from—

(1) an act of God or other circumstance beyond its control, that it exercised reasonable care to prevent such an occurrence, and that it exercised such diligence as the circumstances required; or

(2) a technical malfunction which was known to the consumer at the time he attempted to initiate an electronic fund transfer or, in the case of a preauthorized transfer, at the

(c) Intent

In the case of a failure described in subsection (a) of this section which was not intentional and which resulted from a bona fide error, notwithstanding the maintenance of procedures reasonably adapted to avoid any such error, the financial institution shall be liable for actual damages proved.

(d) Exception for damaged notices.

If the notice required to be posted pursuant to section 1693b(d)(3)(B)(i) of this title by an automated teller machine operator has been posted by such operator in compliance with such section and the notice is subsequently removed, damaged, or altered by any person other than the operator of the automated teller machine, the operator shall have no liability under this section for failure to comply with section 1693b(d)(3)(B)(i) of this title.

SEC. 1693i. ISSUANCE OF CARDS OR OTHER MEANS OF ACCESS.

(a) Prohibition; proper issuance.

No person may issue to a consumer any card, code, or other means of access to such consumer's account for the purpose of initiating an electronic fund transfer other than—

(1) in response to a request or application therefor; or

(2) as a renewal of, or in substitution for, an accepted card, code, or other means of access, whether issued by the initial issuer or a successor.

(b) Exceptions.

Notwithstanding the provisions of subsection (a) of this section, a person may distribute to a consumer on an unsolicited basis a card, code, or other means of access for use in initiating an electronic fund transfer from such consumer's account, if—

(1) such card, code, or other means of access is not validated;

(2) such distribution is accompanied by a complete disclosure, in accordance with section 1693c of this title, of the consumer's rights and liabilities which will apply if such card, code, or other means of access is validated;

(3) such distribution is accompanied by a clear explanation, in accordance with regulations of the Board, that such card, code, or other means of access is not validated and how the consumer may dispose of such code, card, or other means of access if validation is not desired; and

(4) such card, code, or other means of access is validated only in response to a request or application from the consumer, upon verification of the consumer's identity.

(c) Validation.

For the purpose of subsection (b) of this section, a card, code, or other means of access is validated when it may be used to initiate an electronic fund transfer.

SEC. 1693j. SUSPENSION OF OBLIGATIONS.

If a system malfunction prevents the effectuation of an electronic fund transfer initiated by a consumer to another person, and such other person has agreed to accept payment by such means, the consumer's obligation to the other person shall be suspended until the malfunction is corrected and the electronic fund transfer may be completed, unless such other person has subsequently, by written request, demanded payment by means other than an electronic fund transfer.

SEC. 1693k. COMPULSORY USE OF ELECTRONIC FUND TRANSFERS.

No person may—

(1) condition the extension of credit to a consumer on such consumer's repayment by means of preauthorized electronic fund transfers; or

(2) require a consumer to establish an account for receipt of electronic fund transfers with a particular financial institution as a condition of employment or receipt of a government benefit.

SEC. 1693l. WAIVER OF RIGHTS.

No writing or other agreement between a consumer and any other person may contain any provision which constitutes a waiver of any right conferred or cause of action created by this subchapter. Nothing in this section prohibits, however, any writing or other agreement which grants to a consumer a more extensive right or remedy or greater protection than contained in this subchapter or a waiver given in settlement of a dispute or action.

SEC. 1693m. CIVIL LIABILITY.

(a) Individual or class action for damages; amount of award.

Except as otherwise provided by this section and section 1693h of this title, any person who fails to comply with any provision of this subchapter with respect to any consumer, except for an error resolved in accordance with section 1693f of this title, is liable to such consumer in an amount equal to the sum of—

(1) any actual damage sustained by such consumer as a result of such failure;

(2)(A) in the case of an individual action, an amount not less than $100 nor greater than $1,000; or

(2)(B) in the case of a class action, such amount as the court may allow, except that (i) as to each member of the class no minimum recovery shall be applicable, and (ii) the total recovery under this subparagraph in any class action or series of class actions arising out of the same failure to comply by the same person shall not be more than the lesser of $500,000 or 1 per centum of the net worth of the defendant; and

(3) in the case of any successful action to enforce the foregoing liability, the costs of the action, together with a reasonable attorney's fee as determined by the court.

(b) Factors determining amount of award.

In determining the amount of liability in any action under subsection (a) of this section, the court shall consider, among other relevant factors—

(1) in any individual action under subsection (a)(2)(A) of this section, the frequency and persistence of noncompliance, the nature of such noncompliance, and the extent to which the noncompliance was intentional; or

(2) in any class action under subsection (a)(2)(B) of this section, the frequency and persistence of noncompliance, the nature of such noncompliance, the resources of the defendant, the number of persons adversely affected, and the extent to which the noncompliance was intentional.

(c) Unintentional violations; bona fide error.

Except as provided in section 1693h of this title, a person may not be held liable in any action brought under this section for a violation of this subchapter if the person shows by a preponderance of evidence that the violation was not intentional and resulted from a bona fide error notwithstanding the maintenance of procedures reasonably adapted to avoid any such error.

(d) Good faith compliance with rule, regulation, or interpretation of Board or approval of duly authorized official or employee of Federal Reserve System.

No provision of this section or section 1693n of this title imposing any liability shall apply to—

(1) any act done or omitted in good faith in conformity with any rule, regulation, or interpretation thereof by the Board or in conformity with any interpretation or approval by an official or employee of the Federal Reserve System duly authorized by the Board to issue such interpretations or approvals under such procedures as the Board may prescribe therefor; or

(2) any failure to make disclosure in proper form if a financial institution utilized an appropriate model clause issued by the Board, notwithstanding that after such act, omission, or failure has occurred, such rule, regulation, approval, or model clause is amended, rescinded, or determined by judicial or other authority to be invalid for any reason.

(e) Notification to consumer prior to action; adjustment of consumer's account.

A person has no liability under this section for any failure to comply with any requirement under this subchapter if, prior to the institution of an action under this section, the person notifies the consumer concerned of the failure, complies with the requirements of this subchapter, and makes an appropriate adjustment to the consumer's account and pays actual damages or, where applicable, damages in accordance with section 1693h of this title.

(f) Action in bad faith or for harassment; attorney's fees.

On a finding by the court that an unsuccessful action under this section was brought in bad faith or for purposes of harassment, the court shall award to the defendant attorney's fees reasonable in relation to the work expended and costs.

(g) Jurisdiction of courts; time for maintenance of action.

Without regard to the amount in controversy, any action under this section may be brought in any United States district court, or in any other court of competent jurisdiction, within one year from the date of the occurrence of the violation.

SEC. 1693n. CRIMINAL LIABILITY.

(a) Violations respecting giving of false or inaccurate information, failure to provide information, and failure to comply with provisions of this subchapter.

Whoever knowingly and willfully—

(1) gives false or inaccurate information or fails to provide information which he is required to disclose by this subchapter or any regulation issued thereunder; or

(2) otherwise fails to comply with any provision of this subchapter; shall be fined not more than $5,000 or imprisoned not more than one year, or both.

(b) Violations affecting interstate or foreign commerce.

Whoever—

(1) knowingly, in a transaction affecting interstate or foreign commerce, uses or attempts or conspires to use any counterfeit, fictitious, altered, forged, lost, stolen, or fraudulently obtained debit instrument to obtain money, goods, services, or anything else of value which within any one-year period has a value aggregating $1,000 or more; or

(2) with unlawful or fraudulent intent, transports or attempts or conspires to transport in interstate or foreign commerce a counterfeit, fictitious, altered, forged, lost, stolen, or fraudulently obtained debit instrument knowing the same to be counterfeit, fictitious, altered, forged, lost, stolen, or fraudulently obtained; or

(3) with unlawful or fraudulent intent, uses any instrumentality of interstate or foreign commerce to sell or transport a counterfeit, fictitious, altered, forged, lost, stolen, or fraudulently obtained debit instrument knowing the same to be counterfeit, fictitious, altered, forged, lost, stolen, or fraudulently obtained; or

(4) knowingly receives, conceals, uses, or transports money, goods, services, or anything else of value (except tickets for interstate or foreign transportation) which (A) within any one-year period has a value aggregating $1,000 or more, (B) has moved in or is part of, or which constitutes interstate or foreign commerce, and (C) has been

obtained with a counterfeit, fictitious, altered, forged, lost, stolen, or fraudulently obtained debit instrument; or

(5) knowingly receives, conceals, uses, sells, or transports in interstate or foreign commerce one or more tickets for interstate or foreign transportation, which (A) within any one-year period have a value aggregating $500 or more, and (B) have been purchased or obtained with one or more counterfeit, fictitious, altered, forged, lost, stolen, or fraudulently obtained debit instrument; or

(6) in a transaction affecting interstate or foreign commerce, furnishes money, property, services, or anything else of value, which within any one-year period has a value aggregating $1,000 or more, through the use of any counterfeit, fictitious, altered, forged, lost, stolen, or fraudulently obtained debit instrument knowing the same to be counterfeit, fictitious, altered, forged, lost, stolen, or fraudulently obtained—shall be fined not more than $10,000 or imprisoned not more than ten years, or both.

(c) "Debit instrument" defined.

As used in this section, the term "debit instrument" means a card, code, or other device, other than a check, draft, or similar paper instrument, by the use of which a person may initiate an electronic fund transfer.

SEC. 1693q. RELATION TO STATE LAWS.

This subchapter does not annul, alter, or affect the laws of any State relating to electronic fund transfers, except to the extent that those laws are inconsistent with the provisions of this subchapter, and then only to the extent of the inconsistency. A State law is not inconsistent with this subchapter if the protection such law affords any consumer is greater than the protection afforded by this subchapter.

APPENDIX 15:
STATE IDENTITY THEFT LEGISLATION

ALABAMA [2001 AL. PUB. ACT 312]

Identity theft.

(a) A person commits the crime of identity theft if, without the authorization, consent, or permission of the victim, and with the intent to defraud for his or her own benefit or the benefit of a third person, he or she does any of the following:

(1) Obtains, records, or accesses identifying information that would assist in accessing financial resources, obtaining identification documents, or obtaining benefits of the victim.

(2) Obtains goods or services through the use of identifying information of the victim.

(3) Obtains identification documents in the victim's name.

(b) Identity theft in which there is a financial loss of greater than two hundred fifty dollars ($250) or the defendant has previously been convicted of identity theft constitutes identity theft in the first degree. Identity theft in the first degree is a Class C felony.

(c) Identity theft in which the defendant has not previously been convicted of identity theft and there is no financial loss or the financial loss is two hundred fifty dollars ($250) or less constitutes identity theft in the second degree. Identity theft in the second degree is a Class A misdemeanor.

(d) This section shall not apply when a person obtains the identity of another person to misrepresent his age for the sole purpose of obtaining alcoholic beverages, tobacco, or another privilege denied to minors.

ALASKA [ALASKA STAT. § 11.46.180]

Theft by deception.

(a) A person commits theft by deception if, with intent to deprive another of property or to appropriate property of another to oneself or a third person, the person obtains the property of another by deception.

(b) In a prosecution based on theft by deception, if the state seeks to prove that the defendant used deception by promising performance which the defendant did not intend to perform or knew would not be performed, that intent or knowledge may not be established solely by or inferred solely from the fact that the promise was not performed.

(c) As used in this section, "deception" has the meaning ascribed to it in AS 11.81.900 but does not include falsity as to matters having no pecuniary significance or "puffing" by statements unlikely to deceive reasonable persons in the group addressed.

ARIZONA [ARIZ. REV. STAT. § 13-2008]

Taking identity of another person; classification

A. A person commits taking the identity of another person if the person knowingly takes, uses, sells or transfers any personal identifying information of another person, without the consent of that other person, with the intent to obtain, use, sell or transfer the other person's identity for any unlawful purpose or to cause loss to a person.

B. A peace officer in any jurisdiction in which an element of the offense is committed or a result of the offense occurs may take a report.

C. If a defendant is alleged to have committed multiple violations of this section within the same county, the prosecutor may file a complaint charging all of the violations and any related charges under other sections that have not been previously filed in the justice of the peace precinct in which the greatest number of violations are alleged to have occurred.

D. Taking the identity of another person is class 4 felony.

ARKANSAS [ARK. CODE AN. § 5-37-227]

Financial identity fraud.

(a)(1) A person commits financial identity fraud if, with the intent to unlawfully appropriate financial resources of another person to his or her own use or to the use of a third party, and without the authorization of that person, he or she:

(A) Obtains or records identifying information that would assist in accessing the financial resources of the other person; or

(B) Accesses or attempts to access the financial resources of the other person through the use of the identifying information, as defined in subdivision (a)(2) of this section.

(a)(2) "Identifying information", as used in this section, includes, but is not limited to:

(A) Social Security numbers;

(B) Driver's license numbers;

(C) Checking account numbers;

(D) Savings account numbers;

(E) Credit card numbers;

(F) Debit card numbers;

(G) Personal identification numbers;

(H) Electronic identification numbers;

(I) Digital signatures; or

(J) Any other numbers or information that can be used to access a person's financial resources.

(b) The provisions of this section do not apply to any person who obtains another person's driver's license or other form of identification for the sole purpose of misrepresenting his or her age.

(c) Financial identity fraud is a Class D felony.

(d)(1) A violation of this section shall constitute an unfair or deceptive act or practice as defined by the Deceptive Trade Practices Act, § 4-88-101 et seq.

(d)(2) All remedies, penalties, and authority granted to the Attorney General or other persons under the Deceptive Trade Practices Act, § 4-88-101 et seq., shall be available to the Attorney General or other persons for the enforcement of this section.

CALIFORNIA [CAL. PENAL CODE §§ 530.5; 5-530.6; 5-530.7]

PENAL CODE

Section 530.5

(a) Every person who willfully obtains personal identifying information, as defined in subdivision (b), of another person, and uses that information for any unlawful purpose, including to obtain, or attempt to obtain, credit, goods, services, or medical information in the name of the other person without the consent of that person, is guilty of a public offense, and upon conviction therefor, shall be punished either by imprisonment in a county jail not to exceed one year, a fine not to exceed one thousand dollars ($1,000), or both that imprisonment and fine, or by imprisonment in the state prison, a fine not to exceed ten thousand dollars ($10,000), or both that imprisonment and fine.

(b) "Personal identifying information," as used in this section, means the name, address, telephone number, driver's license number, social security number, place of employment, employee identification number, mother's maiden name, demand deposit account number, savings account number, or credit card number of an individual person.

(c) In any case in which a person willfully obtains personal identifying information of another person without the authorization of that person, and uses that information to commit a crime in addition to a violation of subdivision (a), and is convicted of that crime, the court records shall reflect that the person whose identity was falsely used to commit the crime did not commit the crime.

Section 530.6

(a) A person who has learned or reasonably suspects that his or her personal identifying information has been unlawfully used by another, as described in subdivision (a) of Section 530.5, may initiate a law enforcement investigation by contacting the local law enforcement agency that has jurisdiction over his or her actual residence, which shall take a police report of the matter, provide the complainant with a copy of that report, and begin an investigation of the facts or, if the suspected crime was committed in a different jurisdiction, refer the matter to the law enforcement agency where the suspected crime was committed for an investigation of the facts.

(b) A person who reasonably believes that he or she is the victim of identity theft may petition a court for an expedited judicial determination of his or her factual innocence, where the perpetrator of the identity theft was arrested for or convicted of a crime under the victim's identity, or where the victim's identity has been mistakenly associated with a record of criminal conviction. Any judicial determination of factual innocence made pursuant to this section may be heard and determined upon declarations, affidavits, police reports, or other material, relevant, and reliable information submitted by the parties. Where the court determines that the petition is meritorious and that there is no reasonable cause to believe that the petitioner committed the offense for which the perpetrator of the identity theft was arrested or convicted, the court shall find the petitioner factually innocent of that offense. If the petitioner is found factually innocent, the court shall issue an order certifying this determination. The Judicial Council of California shall develop a form for use in issuing an order pursuant to these provisions. A court issuing a determination of factual innocence pursuant to this section may at any time vacate that determination if the petition, or any information submitted in support of the petition, is found to contain any material misrepresentation or fraud.

Section 530.7

(a) In order for a victim of identity theft to be included in the data base established pursuant to subdivision (c), he or she shall submit to the Department of Justice a court order obtained pursuant to any provision of law, a full set of fingerprints, and any other information prescribed by the department.

(b) Upon receiving information pursuant to subdivision (a), the Department of Justice shall verify the identity of the victim against any driver's license or other identification record maintained by the Department of Motor Vehicles.

(c) The Department of Justice shall establish and maintain a database of individuals who have been victims of identity theft. The department shall provide a victim of identity theft or his or her authorized representative access to the database in order to establish that the individual has been a victim of identity theft. Access to the database shall be limited to criminal justice agencies, victims of identity theft, and individuals and agencies authorized by the victims.

(d) The Department of Justice shall establish and maintain a toll-free telephone number to provide access to information under subdivision (c).

(e) This section shall be operative September 1, 2001.

COLORADO [COLO. REV. STAT. §§ 18-5-102; 18-5-113]

Section 18-5-102—Forgery.

(1) A person commits forgery, if, with intent to defraud, such person falsely makes, completes, alters, or utters a written instrument which

is or purports to be, or which is calculated to become or to represent if completed:

(a) Part of an issue of money, stamps, securities, or other valuable instruments issued by a government or government agency; or

(b) Part of an issue of stock, bonds, or other instruments representing interests in or claims against a corporate or other organization or its property; or

(c) A deed, will, codicil, contract, assignment, commercial instrument, promissory note, check, or other instrument which does or may evidence, create, transfer, terminate, or otherwise affect a legal right, interest, obligation, or status; or

(d) A public record or an instrument filed or required by law to be filed or legally fileable in or with a public office or public servant; or

(e) A written instrument officially issued or created by a public office, public servant, or government agency; or

(f) Part of an issue of tokens, transfers, certificates, or other articles manufactured and designed for use in transportation fees upon public conveyances, or as symbols of value usable in place of money for the purchase of property or services available to the public for compensation; or

(g) Part of an issue of lottery tickets or shares designed for use in the lottery held pursuant to part 2 of article 35 of title 24, C.R.S.; or

(h) A document-making implement that may be used or is used in the production of a false identification document or in the production of another document-making implement to produce false identification documents.

(2) Forgery is a class 5 felony.

Section 18-5-113—Criminal impersonation.

(1) A person commits criminal impersonation if he knowingly assumes a false or fictitious identity or capacity, and in such identity or capacity he:

(a) Marries, or pretends to marry, or to sustain the marriage relation toward another without the connivance of the latter; or

(b) Becomes bail or surety for a party in an action or proceeding, civil or criminal, before a court or officer authorized to take the bail or surety; or

(c) Confesses a judgment, or subscribes, verifies, publishes, acknowledges, or proves a written instrument which by law may be recorded, with the intent that the same may be delivered as true; or

(d) Does an act which if done by the person falsely impersonated, might subject such person to an action or special proceeding, civil or criminal, or to liability, charge, forfeiture, or penalty; or

(e) Does any other act with intent to unlawfully gain a benefit for himself or another or to injure or defraud another.

(2) Criminal impersonation is a class 6 felony.

CONNECTICUT [1999 GEN. STAT. § 53]

Identity Theft

(a) A person is guilty of identity theft when such person intentionally obtains personal identifying information of another person without the authorization of such other person and uses that information for any unlawful purpose including, but not limited to, obtaining, or attempting to obtain, credit, goods, services or medical information in the name of such other person without the consent of such other person. As used in this section, "personal identifying information" means a motor vehicle operator's license number, Social Security number, employee identification number, mother's maiden name, demand deposit number, savings account number or credit card number.

(b) The victim of an identity theft may report the theft to the police department of their residence. The police department of the victim's residence shall receive the complaint and coordinate, if necessary, with any other police department the investigation of the identity theft and crimes committed or attempted as a result of the identity theft. Any subsequent prosecution of the identity theft and crimes committed or attempted, within the state, as a result of the identity theft may be prosecuted in the judicial district of the victim's residence.

(c) Identity theft is a Class D felony.

DELAWARE [DEL. CODE AN. TIT. 11 § 854]

Identity theft; class E felony; class D felony.

(a) A person commits identity theft when the person knowingly or recklessly obtains, produces, possesses, uses, sells, gives or transfers personal identifying information belonging or pertaining to another person without the consent of the other person and with intent to use the information to commit or facilitate any crime set forth in this title.

(b) A person commits identity theft when the person knowingly or recklessly obtains, produces, possesses, uses, sells, gives or transfers personal identifying information belonging or pertaining to another person without the consent of the other person, thereby knowingly or recklessly facilitating the use of the information by a third person to commit or facilitate any crime set forth in this title.

(c) For the purposes of this section, "personal identifying information" includes name, address, birth date, Social Security number, driver's license number, telephone number, financial services account number, savings account number, checking account number, credit card number, debit card number, identification document or false identification document, electronic identification number, educational record, health care record, financial record, credit record, employment record, e-mail address, computer system password, mother's maiden name or similar personal number, record or information.

(d) Identity theft is a class E felony, unless the victim is 62 years of age or older, in which case identity theft is a class D felony.

(e) When a person is convicted of or pleads guilty to identity theft, the sentencing judge shall order full restitution for monetary loss, including documented loss of wages and reasonable attorney fees, suffered by the victim.

(f) Prosecution under this section does not preclude prosecution or sentencing under any other section of this Code.

FLORIDA [FLA. STAT. AN. § 817.568]

Criminal use of personal identification information.

(1) As used in this section, the term:

(a) "Access device" means any card, plate, code, account number, electronic serial number, mobile identification number, personal identification number, or other telecommunications service, equipment, or instrument identifier, or other means of account access that can be used, alone or in conjunction with another access device, to obtain money, goods, services, or any other thing of value, or that can be used to initiate a transfer of funds, other than a transfer originated solely by paper instrument.

(b) "Authorization" means empowerment, permission, or competence to act.

(c) "Harass" means to engage in conduct directed at a specific person that is intended to cause substantial emotional distress to such person and serves no legitimate purpose. "Harass" does not mean to use personal identification information for accepted commercial purposes. The term does not include constitutionally protected conduct such as organized protests or the use of personal identification information for accepted commercial purposes.

(d) "Individual" means a single human being and does not mean a firm, association of individuals, corporation, partnership, joint venture, sole proprietorship, or any other entity.

(e) "Person" means a "person" as defined in s. 1.01(3).

(f) "Personal identification information" means any name or number that may be used, alone or in conjunction with any other information, to identify a specific individual, including any:

1. Name, social security number, date of birth, official state-issued or United States-issued driver's license or identification number, alien registration number, government passport number, employer or taxpayer identification number, or Medicaid or food stamp account number;

2. Unique biometric data, such as fingerprint, voice print, retina or iris image, or other unique physical representation;

3. Unique electronic identification number, address, or routing code; or

4. Telecommunication identifying information or access device.

(2)(a) Any person who willfully and without authorization fraudulently uses, or possesses with intent to fraudulently use, personal identification information concerning an individual without first obtaining that individual's consent, commits the offense of fraudulent use of personal identification information, which is a felony of the third degree, punishable as provided in s. 775.082, s. 775.083, or s. 775.084.

(2)(b) Any person who willfully and without authorization fraudulently uses personal identification information concerning an individual without first obtaining that individual's consent commits a felony of the second degree, punishable as provided in s. 775.082, s. 775.083, or s. 775.084, if the pecuniary benefit, the value of the services received, the payment sought to be avoided, or the amount of the injury or fraud perpetrated is $75,000 or more.

(3) Any person who willfully and without authorization possesses, uses, or attempts to use personal identification information concerning an individual without first obtaining that individual's consent, and who does so for the purpose of harassing that individual, commits the offense of harassment by use of personal identification information,

which is a misdemeanor of the first degree, punishable as provided in s. 775.082 or s. 775.083.

(4) If an offense prohibited under this section was facilitated or furthered by the use of a public record, as defined in s. 119.011, the offense is reclassified to the next higher degree as follows:

(a) A misdemeanor of the first degree is reclassified as a felony of the third degree.

(b) A felony of the third degree is reclassified as a felony of the second degree.

(c) A felony of the second degree is reclassified as a felony of the first degree.

GEORGIA [GA. CODE AN. §§ 16-9-121; 16-9-127]

Section 16-9-121

A person commits the offense of financial identity fraud when without the authorization or permission of another person and with the intent unlawfully to appropriate financial resources of that other person to his or her own use or to the use of a third party he or she:

(1) Obtains or records identifying information which would assist in accessing the financial resources of the other

(2) Accesses or attempts to access the financial resources of the other person through the use of identifying information. Such identifying information shall include but not be limited to:

(A) Social security numbers;

(B) Driver's license numbers;

(C) Checking account numbers;

(D) Savings account numbers;

(E) Credit card numbers;

(F) Debit card numbers;

(G) Personal identification numbers;

(H) Electronic identification numbers;

(I) Digital signatures; or

(J) Any other numbers or information which can be used to access a person's financial resources.

Section 16-9-127

The prohibitions set forth in Code Section 16-9-121 shall not apply to:

(1) The lawful obtaining of credit information in the course of a bona fide consumer or commercial transaction;

(2) The lawful, good faith exercise of a security interest or a right to offset by a creditor or a financial institution; or

(3) The lawful, good faith compliance by any party when required by any warrant, levy, garnishment, attachment, court order, or other judicial or administrative order, decree, or directive.

HAWAII [HAW. REV. STAT. § 708]

Identity theft in the first degree.

(1) A person commits the offense of identity theft in the first degree if that person makes or causes to be made, either directly or indirectly, a transmission of any personal information of another by any oral statement, any written statement, or any statement conveyed by any electronic means, with the intent to:

(a) Facilitate the commission of a murder in any degree, a class A felony, kidnapping, unlawful imprisonment in any degree, extortion in any degree, any offense under chapter 134, criminal property damage in the first or second degree, escape in any degree, any offense under part VI of chapter 710, any offense under section 711-1103, or any offense under chapter 842; or

(b) Commit the offense of theft in the first degree from the person whose personal information is used, or from any other person or entity.

(2) Identity theft in the first degree is a class A felony.

Identity theft in the second degree.

(1) A person commits the offense of identity theft in the second degree if that person makes or causes to be made, either directly or indirectly, a transmission of any personal information of another by any oral statement, any written statement, or any statement conveyed by any electronic means, with the intent to commit the offense of theft in the second degree from the person whose personal information is used, or from any other person or entity.

(2) Identity theft in the second degree is a class B felony.

Identity theft in the third degree.

(1) A person commits the offense of identity theft in the third degree if that person makes or causes to be made, either directly or indirectly, a transmission of any personal information of another by any oral statement, any written statement, or any statement conveyed by any electronic means, with the intent to commit the offense of theft in the third or fourth degree from the person whose personal information is used, or from any other person or entity.

(2) Identity theft in the third degree is a class C felony.

IDAHO [IDAHO CODE 18-3126]

Misappropriation of Personal Identifying Information.

It is unlawful for any person to obtain or record personal identifying information of another person without the authorization of that person, with the intent that the information be used to obtain, or attempt to obtain, credit, money, goods or services in the name of the other person without the consent of that person.

ILLINOIS [720 ILL. COMP. STAT. 5/16G-15; 5/16G-20]

Section 5/16G-15. Financial identity theft.

(a) A person commits the offense of financial identity theft when he or she knowingly uses any personal identifying information or personal identification document of another person to fraudulently obtain credit, money, goods, services, or other property in the name of the other person.

(b) Knowledge shall be determined by an evaluation of all circumstances surrounding the use of the other person's identifying information or document.

(c) When a charge of financial identity theft of credit, money, goods, services, or other property exceeding a specified value is brought the value of the credit, money, goods, services, or other property is an element of the offense to be resolved by the trier of fact as either exceeding or not exceeding the specified value.

(d) Sentence.

(1) Financial identity theft of credit, money, goods,services, or other property not exceeding $300 in value is a Class A misdemeanor. A person who has been previously convicted of financial identity theft of less than $300 who is convicted of a second or subsequent offense of financial identity theft of less than $300 is guilty of a Class 4 felony. A person who has been convicted of financial identity theft of

less than $300 who has been previously convicted of any type of theft, robbery, armed robbery, burglary, residential burglary, possession of burglary tools, home invasion, home repair fraud, aggravated home repair fraud, or financial exploitation of an elderly or disabled person is guilty of a Class 4 felony. When a person has any such prior conviction, the information or indictment charging that person shall state the prior conviction so as to give notice of the State's intention to treat the charge as a felony. The fact of the prior conviction is not an element of the offense and may not be disclosed to the jury during trial unless otherwise permitted by issues properly raised during the trial.

(2) Financial identity theft of credit, money, goods, services, or other property exceeding $300 and not exceeding $2,000 in value is a Class 4 felony.

(3) Financial identity theft of credit, money, goods, services, or other property exceeding $2,000 and not exceeding $10,000 in value is a Class 3 felony.

(4) Financial identity theft of credit, money, goods, services, or other property exceeding $10,000 and not exceeding $100,000 in value is a Class 2 felony.

(5) Financial identity theft of credit, money, goods, services, or other property exceeding $100,000 in value is a Class 1 felony. (Source: P.A. 91-517, eff. 8-13-99.)

Section 16G-20. Aggravated financial identity theft.

(a) A person commits the offense of aggravated financial identity theft when he or she commits the offense of financial identity theft as set forth in subsection (a) of Section 16G-15 against a person 60 years of age or older or a disabled person as defined in Section 16-1.3 of this Code.

(b) Knowledge shall be determined by an evaluation of all circumstances surrounding the use of the other person's identifying information or document.

(c) When a charge of aggravated financial identity theft of credit, money, goods, services, or other property exceeding a specified value is brought the value of the credit, money, goods, services, or other property is an element of the offense to be resolved by the trier of fact as either exceeding or not exceeding the specified value.

(d) A defense to aggravated financial identity theft does not exist merely because the accused reasonably believed the victim to be a person less than 60 years of age.

(e) Sentence.

(1) Aggravated financial identity theft of credit, money, goods, services, or other property not exceeding $300 in value is a Class 4 felony.

(2) Aggravated financial identity theft of credit, money, goods, services, or other property exceeding $300 and not exceeding $10,000 in value is a Class 3 felony.

(3) Aggravated financial identity theft of credit, money, goods, services, or other property exceeding $10,000 in value and not exceeding $100,000 in value is a Class 2 felony.

(4) Aggravated financial identity theft of credit, money, goods, services, or other property exceeding $100,000 in value is a Class 1 felony.

(5) A person who has been previously convicted of aggravated financial identity theft regardless of the value of the property involved who is convicted of a second or subsequent offense of aggravated financial identity theft regardless of the value of the property involved is guilty of a Class X felony.

INDIANA [IND. CODE AN. § 35-43-5-4]

A person who:

(1) with intent to defraud, obtains property by:

(A) using a credit card, knowing that the credit card was unlawfully obtained or retained;

(B) using a credit card, knowing that the credit card is forged, revoked, or expired;

(C) using, without consent, a credit card that was issued to another person;

(D) representing, without the consent of the credit card holder, that the person is the authorized holder of the credit card; or

(E) representing that the person is the authorized holder of a credit card when the card has not in fact been issued;

(2) being authorized by an issuer to furnish property upon presentation of a credit card, fails to furnish the property and, with intent to defraud the issuer or the credit card holder, represents in writing to the issuer that the person has furnished the property;

(3) being authorized by an issuer to furnish property upon presentation of a credit card, furnishes, with intent to defraud the issuer or

the credit card holder, property upon presentation of a credit card, knowing that the credit card was unlawfully obtained or retained or that the credit card is forged, revoked, or expired;

(4) not being the issuer, knowingly or intentionally sells a credit card;

(5) not being the issuer, receives a credit card, knowing that the credit card was unlawfully obtained or retained or that the credit card is forged, revoked, or expired;

(6) with intent to defraud, receives a credit card as security for debt;

(7) receives property, knowing that the property was obtained in violation of subdivision (1) of this section;

(8) with intent to defraud the person's creditor or purchaser, conceals, encumbers, or transfers property;

(9) with intent to defraud, damages property;

(10) knowingly and with intent to defraud, makes, utters, presents, or causes to be presented to an insurer or an insurance claimant, a claim statement that contains false, incomplete, or misleading information concerning the claim; or

(11) knowingly or intentionally:

(A) sells;

(B) rents;

(C) transports; or

(D) possesses a recording for commercial gain or personal financial gain that does not conspicuously display the true name and address of the manufacturer of the recording.

IOWA [IOWA CODE § 715A.8]

Identity theft.

1. For purposes of this section, "identification information" means the name, address, date of birth, telephone number, driver's license number, nonoperator's identification number, social security number, place of employment, employee identification number, parent's legal surname prior to marriage, demand deposit account number, savings or checking account number, or credit card number of a person.

2. A person commits the offense of identity theft if the person with the intent to obtain a benefit fraudulently obtains identification information of another person and uses or attempts to use that information to

obtain credit, property, or services without the authorization of that other person.

3. If the value of the credit, property, or services exceeds one thousand dollars, the person commits a class "D" felony. If the value of the credit, property, or services does not exceed one thousand dollars, the person commits an aggravated misdemeanor.

4. A violation of this section is an unlawful practice under section 714.16.

KANSAS [KAN. STAT. AN. §21-4018]

Identity theft.

(a) Identity theft is knowingly and with intent to defraud for economic benefit, obtaining, possessing, transferring, using or attempting to obtain, possess, transfer or use, one or more identification documents or personal identification number of another person other than that issued lawfully for the use of the possessor.

(b) "Identification documents" means the definition as provided in K.S.A. 21-3830, and amendments thereto.

(c) Identity theft is a severity level 7, person felony.

(d) This section shall be part of and supplemental to the Kansas criminal code.

KENTUCKY [KY. REV. STAT. AN. § 514.160]

Theft of identity.

(1) A person is guilty of the theft of the identity of another when, without the other's consent, he or she knowingly possesses or uses any identifying information of the other person, such as one's name, Social Security number, birth date, personal identification number or code, which is kept in documents, photo or electrical copies, computer storage, or any other form of document retrieval and storage, and the theft is committed with the intent to represent that he or she is the other person for the purpose of:

(a) Depriving the other person of property;

(b) Obtaining benefits or property to which he or she would otherwise not be entitled;

(c) Making financial or credit transactions using the other person's identity;

(d) Avoiding detection; or

(e) Commercial or political benefit.

(2) Theft of identity is a Class D felony.

(3) This section shall not apply when a person obtains the identity of another to misrepresent his or her age for the purpose of obtaining alcoholic beverages, tobacco, or another privilege denied to minors.

(4) This section does not apply to credit or debit card fraud under KRS 434.550 to 434.730.

(5) Where the offense consists of theft by obtaining or trafficking in the personal identity of another person, the venue of the prosecution may be in either the county where the offense was committed or the county where the other person resides.

(6) A person found guilty of violating any provisions of this section shall forfeit any lawful claim to the identifying information, property, or other realized benefit of the other person as a result of such violation.

LOUISIANA [LA. REV. STAT. AN. § 14.67.16]

IDENTITY THEFT

A. As used in this Section the following terms have the following meanings:

(1) "Personal identifying information" shall include but not be limited to an individual's:

(a) Social security number.

(b) Driver's license number.

(c) Checking account number.

(d) Savings account number.

(e) Credit card number.

(f) Debit card number.

(g) Electronic identification number.

(h) Digital signatures.

(i) Birth certificate.

(j) Date of birth.

(k) Mother's maiden name.

(l) Armed forces identification number.

B. Identity theft is the intentional use or attempted use with fraudulent intent by any person of any personal identifying information of another person to obtain, whether contemporaneously or not, credit, money, goods, services, or anything else of value without the authorization or consent of the other person.

C.(1) Whoever commits the crime of identity theft when credit, money, goods, services, or anything else of value is obtained which amounts to a value of one thousand dollars or more, shall be imprisoned, with or without hard labor, for not more than ten years, or may be fined not more than ten thousand dollars, or both.

C.(2) Whoever commits the crime of identity theft when credit, money, goods, services, or anything else of value is obtained which amounts to a value of five hundred dollars or more, but less than one thousand dollars, shall be imprisoned, with or without hard labor, for not more than five years, or may be fined not more than five thousand dollars, or both.

C.(3) Whoever commits the crime of identity theft when credit, money, goods, services, or anything else of value is obtained which amounts to a value of three hundred dollars or more, but less than five hundred dollars, shall be imprisoned, with or without hard labor, for not more than three years, or may be fined not more than three thousand dollars, or both.

C.(4) Whoever commits the crime of identity theft when credit, money, goods, services, or anything else of value is obtained which amounts to a value less than three hundred dollars, shall be imprisoned for not more than six months, or may be fined not more than five hundred dollars, or both. If the offender in such cases has been convicted under this Section two or more times previously, upon any subsequent conviction he shall be imprisoned, for not more than three years, with or without hard labor, or may be fined not more than three thousand dollars, or both.

D. When there has been a theft by a number of distinct acts of the offender, the aggregate of the amount of the theft shall determine the grade of the offense.

E. In addition to the foregoing penalties, a person convicted under this Section may be ordered to make full restitution to the victim and any other person who has suffered a financial loss as a result of the offense. If a person ordered to make restitution pursuant to this Section is found to be indigent and therefore unable to make restitution in full at the time of conviction, the court shall order a periodic payment plan consistent with the person's financial ability.

F. The provisions of this Section shall not apply to any person who obtains another's driver's license or other form of identification for the sole purpose of misrepresenting his age.

MAINE [ME. REV. STAT. AN. TIT. 17-A § 354-1; 2A]

Theft by deception.

1. A person is guilty of theft if he obtains or exercises control over property of another as a result of deception and with an intention to deprive him thereof.

2. For purposes of this section, deception occurs when a person intentionally:

A. Creates or reinforces an impression that is false and that the person does not believe to be true, including false impressions as to identity, law, value, knowledge, opinion, intention or other state of mind; except that an intention not to perform a promise, or knowledge that a promise will not be performed, may not be inferred from the fact alone that the promise was not performed.

MARYLAND [MD. CODE AN. ART. 27 § 231]

(a) In this section, "personal identifying information" means the name, address, telephone number, driver's license number, Social Security number, place of employment, employee identification number, mother's maiden name, bank or other financial institution account number, date of birth, personal identification number, or credit card number of an

(b) A person may not knowingly, willfully, and with fraudulent intent obtain or aid another person in obtaining personal identifying information of an individual, without the consent of that individual, for the purpose of using that information or selling or transferring that information to obtain any benefit, credit, goods, services, or other item of value in the name of that individual.

(c) A person may not knowingly and willfully assume the identity of another:

(1) With fraudulent intent to obtain any benefit, credit, goods, services, or other item of value;

(2) With fraudulent intent to avoid the payment of a debt or other legal obligation; or

(3) To avoid prosecution for a crime.

(d) A person who violates this section is guilty of a misdemeanor and on conviction is subject to a fine not exceeding $5,000 or imprisonment in the penitentiary not exceeding 1 year or both.

(e) In addition to the restitution provided under Title 11, Subtitle 6 of the Criminal Procedure Article, a court may order a person who pleads guilty or nolo contendere or is found guilty under this section to make restitution to the victim for reasonable costs incurred, including reasonable attorney's fees:

(1) For clearing the victim's credit history or credit rating; and

(2) In connection with any civil or administrative proceeding to satisfy a debt, lien, judgment, or other obligation of the victim that arose as a result of the violation of this section.

(f) A sentence under this section may be imposed separate from and consecutive to or concurrent with a sentence for any offense based on the act or acts establishing the violation of this section.

MASSACHUSETTS [MASS. GEN. LAWS CH. 268 § 37E]

(a) For purposes of this section, the following words shall have the following meanings:

"Harass"—willfully and maliciously engage in an act directed at a specific person or persons, which act seriously alarms or annoys such person or persons and would cause a reasonable person to suffer substantial emotional distress.

"Personal identifying information"—any name or number that may be used, alone or in conjunction with any other information, to assume the identity of an individual, including any name, address, telephone number, driver's license number, social security number, place of employment, employee identification number, mother's maiden name, demand deposit account number, savings account number, credit card number or computer password identification.

"Pose"—to falsely represent oneself, directly or indirectly, as another person or persons.

"Victim"—any person who has suffered financial loss or any entity that provided money, credit, goods, services or anything of value and has suffered financial loss as a direct result of the commission or attempted commission of a violation of this section.

(b) Whoever, with intent to defraud, poses as another person without the express authorization of that person and uses such person's personal identifying information to obtain or to attempt to obtain money, credit, goods, services, anything of value, any identification card or other evidence of such person's identity, or to harass another shall be guilty of identity fraud and shall be punished by a fine of not more than $5,000 or imprisonment in a house of correction for not more than two and one-half years, or by both such fine and imprisonment.

(c) Whoever, with intent to defraud, obtains personal identifying information about another person without the express authorization of such person, with the intent to pose as such person or who obtains personal identifying information about a person without the express authorization of such person in order to assist another to pose as such person in order to obtain money, credit, goods, services, anything of value, any identification card or other evidence of such person's identity, or to harass another shall be guilty of the crime of identity fraud and shall be punished by a fine of not more than $5,000 or imprisonment in a house of correction for not more than two and one-half years, or by both such fine and imprisonment.

(d) A person found guilty of violating any provisions of this section shall, in addition to any other punishment, be ordered to make restitution for financial loss sustained by a victim as a result of such violation. Financial loss may include any costs incurred by such victim in correcting the credit history of such victim or any costs incurred in connection with any civil or administrative proceeding to satisfy any debt or other obligation of such victim, including lost wages and attorney's fees.

MICHIGAN [MICH. COMP. LAWS § 750.285]

Obtaining personal identity information of another with intent to unlawfully use information; violation as felony; nonapplicability to discovery process; definitions.

(1) A person shall not obtain or attempt to obtain personal identity information of another person with the intent to unlawfully use that information for any of the following purposes without that person's authorization:

(a) To obtain financial credit.

(b) To purchase or otherwise obtain or lease any real or personal property.

(c) To obtain employment.

(d) To obtain access to medical records or information contained in medical records.

(e) To commit any illegal act.

(2) A person who violates this section is guilty of a felony punishable by imprisonment for not more than 5 years or a fine of not more than $10,000.00, or both.

(3) This section does not prohibit the person from being charged with, convicted of, or sentenced for any other violation of law committed by that person using information obtained in violation of this section.

(4) This section does not apply to a person who obtains or attempts to obtain personal identity information of another person pursuant to the discovery process of a civil action, an administrative proceeding, or an arbitration proceeding.

(5) As used in this section:

(a) "Financial transaction device" means that term as defined in section 157m.

(b) "Medical records" includes, but is not limited to, medical and mental health histories, reports, summaries, diagnoses and prognoses, treatment and medication information, notes, entries, and x-rays and other imaging records.

(c) "Personal identity information" means any of the following information of another person:

(i) A social security number.

(ii) A driver license number or state personal identification card number.

(iii) Employment information.

(iv) Information regarding any financial account held by another person including, but not limited to, any of the following:

(A) A savings or checking account number.

(B) A financial transaction device account number.

(C) A stock or other security certificate or account number.

(D) A personal information number for an account described in sub-subparagraphs (A) to (C).

MINNESOTA [MINN. STAT. AN. §609.527]

IDENTITY THEFT

Subdivision 1. Definitions.

(a) As used in this section, the following terms have the meanings given them in this subdivision.

(b) "Direct victim" means any person or entity described in section 611A.01, paragraph (b), whose identity has been transferred, used, or possessed in violation of this section.

(c) "Identity" means any name, number, or data transmission that may be used, alone or in conjunction with any other information, to identify a specific individual, including any of the following:

(1) a name, social security number, date of birth, official government-issued driver's license or identification number, go identification number;

(2) unique electronic identification number, address, account number, or routing code; or

(3) telecommunication identification information or access device.

(d) "Indirect victim" means any person or entity described in section 611A.01, paragraph (b), other than a direct victim.

(e) "Loss" means value obtained, as defined in section 609.52, subdivision 1, clause (3), and expenses incurred by a direct or indirect victim as a result of a violation of this section.

(f) "Unlawful activity" means:

(1) any felony violation of the laws of this state or any felony violation of a similar law of another state or the United States; and

(2) any nonfelony violation of the laws of this state involving theft, theft by swindle, forgery, fraud, or giving false information to a public official, or any nonfelony violation of a similar law of another state or the United States.

Subdivision. 2. Crime.

A person who transfers, possesses, or uses an identity that is not the person's own, with the intent to commit, aid, or abet any unlawful activity is guilty of identity theft and may be punished as provided in subdivision

Subdivision. 3. Penalties.

A person who violates subdivision 2 may be sentenced as follows:

(1) if the offense involves a single direct victim and the total, combined loss to the direct victim and any indirect victims is $250 or less, the person may be sentenced as provided in section 609.52, subdivision 3, clause (5);

(2) if the offense involves a single direct victim and the total, combined loss to the direct victim and any indirect victims is more than

$250 but not more than $500, the person may be sentenced as provided in section 609.52, subdivision 3, clause (4);

(3) if the offense involves two or three direct victims or the total, combined loss to the direct and indirect victims is more than $500 but not more than $2,500, the person may be sentenced as provided in section 609.52, subdivision 3, clause (3); and

(4) if the offense involves four or more direct victims, or if the total, combined loss to the direct and indirect victims is more than $2,500, the person may be sentenced as provided in section 609.52, subdivision 3, clause (2).

Subdivision. 4. Restitution.

A direct or indirect victim of an identity theft crime shall be considered a victim for all purposes, including any rights that accrue under chapter 611A and rights to court-ordered restitution.

MISSISSIPPI [MISS. CODE AN. § 97-19-85]

Fraudulent use of identity, social security number or other identifying information to obtain thing of value.

(1) Any person who shall make or cause to be made any false statement or representation as to his or another person's identity, social security account number or other identifying information for the purpose of fraudulently obtaining or with the intent to obtain goods, services or any thing of value, shall be guilty of a misdemeanor and upon conviction thereof shall be fined not more than Five Thousand Dollars ($5,000.00) or imprisoned for a term not to exceed one (1) year, or both.

(2) A person is guilty of fraud under subsection (1) who:

(a) Shall furnish false information wilfully, knowingly and with intent to deceive anyone as to his true identity or the true identity of another person;

(b) Wilfully, knowingly, and with intent to deceive, uses a social security account number to establish and maintain business or other records; or

(c) With intent to deceive, falsely represents a number to be the social security account number assigned to him or another person, when in fact the number is not the social security account number assigned to him or such other person; or

(d) Knowingly alters a social security card, buys or sells a social security card or counterfeit or altered social security card, counterfeits a social security card, or possesses a social security card or counterfeit social security card with intent to sell or alter it.

MISSOURI [MO. REV. STAT. § 570; 223]

Identity theft—penalty—restitution.

1. A person commits the crime of identity theft if he knowingly and with the intent to deceive or defraud obtains, possesses, transfers, uses, or attempts to obtain, transfer or use, one or more means of identification not lawfully issued for his use.

2. Identity theft is punishable by up to six months in jail for the first offense; up to one year in jail for the second offense; and one to five years imprisonment for the third or subsequent offense.

3. In addition to the provisions of subsection 2 of this section, the court may order that the defendant make restitution to any victim of the offense. Restitution may include payment for any costs, including attorney fees, incurred by the victim:

(1) In clearing the credit history or credit rating of the victim; and

(2) In connection with any civil or administrative proceeding to satisfy any debt, lien, or other obligation of the victim arising from the actions of the defendant.

MONTANA [H.B. 331, 2001 LEG.]

Section 1.Theft of identity.

(1) A person commits the offense of theft of identity if the person purposely or knowingly obtains personal identifying information of another person and uses that information for any unlawful purpose, including to obtain or attempt to obtain credit, goods, services, financial information, or medical information in the name of the other person without the consent of the other person.

(2)(a) A person convicted of the offense of theft of identity if no economic benefit was gained or was attempted to be gained or if an economic benefit of less than $1,000 was gained or attempted to be gained shall be fined an amount not to exceed $1,000, imprisoned in the county jail for a term not to exceed 6 months, or both.

(2)(b) A person convicted of the offense of theft of identity if an economic benefit of $1,000 or more was gained or attempted to be gained shall be fined an amount not to exceed $10,000, imprisoned in a state prison for a term not to exceed 10 years, or both.

(3) As used in this section, "personal identifying information" includes but is not limited to the name, date of birth, address, telephone number, driver's license number, social security number or other federal government identification number, place of employment, employee identification number, mother's maiden name, financial institution account number, credit card number, or similar identifying information relating to a person.

(4) If restitution is ordered, the court may include, as part of its determination of an amount owed, payment for any costs incurred by the victim, including attorney fees and any costs incurred in clearing the credit history or credit rating of the victim or in connection with any civil or administrative proceeding to satisfy any debt, lien, or other obligation of the victim arising as a result of the actions of the defendant.

NEVADA [NEV. REV. STAT. §205.463-465]

Obtaining and using personal identifying information of another person to harm person or for unlawful purpose.

1. Except as otherwise provided in subsection 2, a person who knowingly:

(a) Obtains any personal identifying information of another person; and

(b) Uses the personal identifying information to harm that other person or for any unlawful purpose, including, without limitation, to obtain credit, a good, a service or anything of value in the name of that person, is guilty of a category B felony and shall be punished by imprisonment in the state prison for a minimum term of not less than 1 year and a maximum term of not more than 20 years, and may be further punished by a fine of not more than $100,000.

2. A person who knowingly:

(a) Obtains any personal identifying information of another person; and

(b) Uses the personal identifying information to avoid or delay being prosecuted for an unlawful act, is guilty of a category E felony and shall be punished as provided in NRS 193.130.

3. In addition to any other penalty, the court shall order a person convicted of violating subsection 1 to pay restitution, including, without limitation, any attorney's fees and costs incurred to:

(a) Repair the credit history or rating of the person whose personal identifying information he obtained and used in violation of subsection 1; and

(b) Satisfy a debt, lien or other obligation incurred by the person whose personal identifying information he obtained and used in violation of subsection 1.

4. As used in this section, "personal identifying information" has the meaning ascribed to it in NRS 205.465.

NEW HAMPSHIRE [N.H. REV. STAT. AN. § 638.26]

Identity Fraud.

I. A person is guilty of identity fraud when the person:

(a) Poses as another person with the purpose to defraud in order to obtain money, credit, goods, services, or anything else of value;

(b) Obtains or records personal identifying information about another person without the express authorization of such person, with the intent to pose as such person;

(c) Obtains or records personal identifying information about a person without the express authorization of such person in order to assist another to pose as such person; or

(d) Poses as another person, without the express authorization of such person, with the purpose of obtaining confidential information about such person that is not available to the general public.

II. (a) Identity fraud is:

(1) A class A felony if the value of the property or services obtained exceeds $1,000.

(2) A class B felony in all other cases.

II. (b) The value may be determined according to the provisions of RSA 637:2, V.

III. A person found guilty of violating any provisions of this section shall, in addition to the penalty under paragraph II, be ordered to make restitution for economic loss sustained by a victim as a result of such violation.

NEW JERSEY [N.J. STAT. AN. § 2C:21-17]

Impersonation; theft of identity; disorderly persons offense, crime.

a. A person is guilty of an offense when he:

(1) Impersonates another or assumes a false identity and does an act in such assumed character or false identity for purpose of obtaining

a pecuniary benefit for himself or another or to injure or defraud another;

(2) Pretends to be a representative of some person or organization and does an act in such pretended capacity for the purpose of obtaining a benefit for himself or another or to injure or defraud another;

(3) Impersonates another, assumes a false identity or makes a false or misleading statement regarding the identity of any person, in an oral or written application for services, for the purpose of obtaining services; or

(4) Obtains any personal identifying information pertaining to another person and uses that information, or assists another person in using the information, in order to assume the identity of or represent themselves as another person, without that person's authorization and with the purpose to fraudulently obtain or attempt to obtain a pecuniary benefit or services, or avoid the payment of debt or other legal obligation or avoid prosecution for a crime by using the name of the other person.

As used in this paragraph: "personal identifying information" means, but is not limited to, the name, address, telephone number, social security number, place of employment, employee identification number, demand deposit account number, savings account number, credit card number or mother's maiden name of an individual person.

b. A person is guilty of an offense if, in the course of making an oral or written application for services, he impersonates another, assumes a false identity or makes a false or misleading statement with the purpose of avoiding payment for prior services. Purpose to avoid payment for prior services may be presumed upon proof that the person has not made full payment for prior services and has impersonated another, assumed a false identity or made a false or misleading statement regarding the identity of any person in the course of making oral or written application for services.

c. (1) A person who violates subsection a. or b. of this section is guilty of a crime of the second degree if the pecuniary benefit, the value of the services received, the payment sought to be avoided or the injury or fraud perpetrated on another is $75,000 or more. If the pecuniary benefit, the value of the services received, the payment sought to be avoided or the injury or fraud perpetrated on another is at least $500 but is less than $75,000, the offender is guilty of a crime of the third degree. If the pecuniary benefit, the value of the services received, the payment sought to be avoided or the injury or fraud perpetrated on another is at least $200 but is less than $500, the offender is guilty of a crime of the fourth degree.

c. (2) If the pecuniary benefit, the value of the services received, the payment sought to be avoided or the injury or fraud perpetrated on another is less than $200,or if the benefit or services received or the injury or fraud perpetrated on another has no pecuniary value, or if the person was unsuccessful in an attempt to receive a benefit or services or to injure or perpetrate a fraud on another, then the person is guilty of a disorderly persons offense.

d. A violation of R.S.39:3-37 for using the personal information of another to obtain a driver's license or register a motor vehicle or a violation of R.S.33:1-81 or section 6 of P.L.1968. c.313 (C.33:1-81.7) for using the personal information of another to illegally purchase an alcoholic beverage shall not constitute an offense under this section if the actor received only that benefit or service and did not perpetrate or attempt to perpetrate any additional injury or fraud on another.

NEW MEXICO [H.B. 317, 2001 LEG. 45TH SESS.]

Theft of Identity.

A. Theft of identity consists of willfully obtaining, recording or transferring personal identifying information of another person without the authorization or consent of that person and with the intent to defraud that person or another.

B. As used in this section, "personal identifying information" means information that alone or in conjunction with other information identifies a person, including the person's name, address, telephone number, driver's license number, social security number, place of employment, maiden name of the person's mother, demand deposit account number, checking or savings account number, credit card or debit card number, personal identification number, passwords or any other numbers or information that can be used to access a person's financial resources.

C. Whoever commits theft of identity is guilty of a misdemeanor.

D. Prosecution pursuant to this section shall not prevent prosecution pursuant to any other provision of the law when the conduct also constitutes a violation of that other provision.

E. In a prosecution brought pursuant to this section, the theft of identity shall be considered to have been committed in the county where the person whose identifying information was appropriated resided at the time of the offense, or in which any part of the offense took place, regardless of whether the defendant was ever actually present in the county.

F. A person found guilty of theft of identity shall, in addition to any other punishment, be ordered to make restitution for any financial loss sustained by a person injured as the direct result of the theft of identity. In addition to out-of-pocket costs, restitution may include payment for costs, including attorney fees, incurred by that person in clearing his credit history or credit rating or costs incurred in connection with a civil or administrative proceeding to satisfy a debt, lien, judgment or other obligation of that person arising as a result of the theft of identity.

G. The sentencing court shall issue written findings of fact and may issue orders as are necessary to correct a public record that contains false information as a result of the theft of identity.

NORTH CAROLINA [N.C. GEN. STAT. § 14-113.20]

Financial identity fraud.

(a)A person who knowingly obtains, possesses, or uses personal identifying information of another person without the consent of that other person, with the intent to fraudulently represent that the person is the other person for the purposes of making financial or credit transactions in the other person's name or for the purpose of avoiding legal consequences is guilty of a felony punishable as provided in G.S. 14-113.22(a).

(b) The term "identifying information" as used in this section includes the following:

(1) Social security numbers.

(2) Drivers license numbers.

(3) Checking account numbers.

(4) Savings account numbers.

(5) Credit card numbers.

(6) Debit card numbers.

(7) Personal Identification (PIN) Code as defined in G.S. 14-113.8(6).

(8) Electronic identification numbers.

(9) Digital signatures.

(10) Any other numbers or information that can be used to access a person's financial resources.

(c) It shall not be a violation under this section for a person to do any of the following:

(1) Lawfully obtain credit information in the course of a bona fide consumer or commercial transaction.

(2) Lawfully exercise, in good faith, a security interest or a right of offset by a creditor or financial institution.

(3) Lawfully comply, in good faith, with any warrant, court order, levy, garnishment, attachment, or other judicial or administrative order, decree, or directive, when any party is required to do so.

NORTH DAKOTA [N.D. CENT. CODES § 12.1-23-11]

Unauthorized use of personal identifying information—Penalty.

1. As used in this section, "personal identifying information" means any of the following information:

a. An individual's name;

b. An individual's address;

c. An individual's telephone number;

d. The distinguishing operator's license number assigned to an individual by the department of transportation under section 39-04-14;

e. An individual's social security number;

f. An individual's employer or place of employment;

g. An identification number assigned to the individual by the individual's employer;

h. The maiden name of the individual's mother; or

i. The identifying number of a depository account in a financial institution.

2. A person is guilty of a class C felony if the person uses or attempts to use any personal identifying information of an individual to obtain credit, money, goods, services, or anything else of value without the authorization or consent of the individual and by representing that person is the individual or is acting with the authorization or consent of the individual.

OHIO [OHIO REV. CODE AN. § 2913.49]

(A) As used in this section, "Personal Identifying Information" includes, but is not limited to, the following: the name, address, telephone number, driver's license, driver's license number, commercial driver's license, commercial driver's license number, state identification card, state identification card number, social security card, social security card number, place of employment, employee identification number, mother's maiden name, demand deposit account number, savings account number, money market account number, mutual fund account number, other financial account number, personal identification number, password or credit card number of a living or dead individual.

(B) No person shall obtain, possess, or use any personal identifying information of any living or dead individual with the intent to fraudulently obtain credit, property, or services or avoid the payment of a debt or any other legal obligation.

(C) No person shall create, obtain, possess, or use the personal identifying information of any living or dead individual with the intent to aid or abet another person in violating Division (B) of this section.

OKLAHOMA [OKLA. STAT. TIT. 21 § 1533.1]

It is unlawful for any person to willfully and with fraudulent intent obtain the name, address, social security number, date of birth, or any other personal identifying information of another person, living or dead, with intent to use, sell, or allow any other person to use or sell such personal identifying information to obtain or attempt to obtain credit, goods, property, or service in the name of the other person without the consent of that person. It is unlawful for any person to use with fraudulent intent the personal identity of another person, living or dead, or any information relating to the personal identity of another person, living or dead, to obtain or attempt to obtain credit or anything of value. Any person convicted of violating any provision of this section shall be guilty of identity theft. Identity theft is a felony offense.

OREGON [OR. REV. STAT. § 165.800]

Identity theft.

(1) A person commits the crime of identity theft if the person, with the intent to deceive or to defraud, obtains, possesses, transfers, creates, utters or converts to the person's own use the personal identification of another person.

(2) Identity theft is a Class C felony.

(3) It is an affirmative defense to violating subsection (1) of this section that the person charged with the offense:

(a) Was under 21 years of age at the time of committing the offense and the person used the personal identification of another person solely for the purpose of purchasing alcohol;

(b) Was under 18 years of age at the time of committing the offense and the person used the personal identification of another person solely for the purpose of purchasing tobacco products; or

(c) Used the personal identification of another person solely for the purpose of misrepresenting the person's age to gain access to a:

(A) Place the access to which is restricted based on age; or

(B) Benefit based on age.

(4) As used in this section:

(a) "Another person" means a real or imaginary person.

(b) "Personal identification" includes, but is not limited to, any written document or electronic data that does, or purports to, provide information concerning:

(A) A person's name, address or telephone number;

(B) A person's driving privileges;

(C) A person's Social Security number or tax identification number;

(D) A person's citizenship status or alien identification number;

(E) A person's employment status, employer or place of employment;

(F) The identification number assigned to a person by a person's employer;

(G) The maiden name of a person or a person's mother;

(H) The identifying number of a person's depository account at a financial institution, as defined in ORS 706.008, or a credit card account;

(I) A person's signature or a copy of a person's signature;

(J) A person's electronic mail name, electronic mail signature, electronic mail address or electronic mail account;

(K) A person's photograph;

(L) A person's date of birth; and

(M) A person's personal identification number.

PENNSYLVANIA [18 PA. CONS. STAT § 4120]

Identity theft.

(a) Offense Defined.—A person commits the offense of identity theft of another person if he possesses or uses identifying information of another person without the consent of that other person to further any unlawful purpose.

(b) Separate Offenses.—Each time a person possesses or uses identifying information in violation of subsection (a) constitutes a separate offense under this section.

(c) Grading.—The offenses shall be graded as follows:

1. A first offense under this section is a misdemeanor of the first degree, and a second and or subsequent offense under this section is a felony of the third degree.

2. When a person commits an offense under subsection (a) and the victim of the offense is 60 years of age or older, the grading of the offense shall be one grade higher than specified in paragraph (1).

(d) Concurrent Jurisdiction to Prosecute.—In addition to the authority conferred upon the attorney general by the act of October 15, 1980 (P.L.950, No.164), known as the Commonwealth Attorneys Act, the Attorney General shall have the authority to investigate and to institute criminal proceedings for any violation of this section or any series of such violations involving more than one county of this commonwealth or another state. No person charged with a violation of this section by the attorney general shall have standing to challenge the authority of the attorney general to investigate or prosecute the case, and, if any such challenge is made, the challenge shall be dismissed and no relief shall be made available in the courts of this Commonwealth to the person making the challenge.

(e) Use of Police Reports.—A report to a law enforcement agency by a person stating that the person's identifying information has been lost or stolen or that the person's identifying information has been used without the person's consent shall be prima facie evidence that the identifying information was possessed or used without the person's consent.

(f) Definitions.—As used in this section, the following words and phrases shall have the meaning given to them in this subsection:

"Document"—Any writing, including, but not limited to, birth certificate, social security card, driver's license, nondriver government-issued identification card, baptismal certificate, access device card, employee identification card, school identification card or other identifying information recorded by any other method, including, but not limited to, information stored on any computer, computer disc, computer printout, computer system, or part thereof, or by any other mechanical or electronic means.

"Identifying information"—Any document, photographic, pictorial or computer image of another person, or any fact used to establish identity, including, but not limited to, a name, birth date, social security number, driver'S license number, nondriver governmental identification number, telephone number, checking account number, savings account number, student identification number or employee or payroll number.

RHODE ISLAND [R.I. GEN. LAWS. § 11-49.1-1; 11-49.1-2; 11-49.1-3; 11-49.1-4]

Section 11-49.1-1. Short title.

This chapter shall be known and may be cited as the "Impersonation and Identity Fraud Act."

Section 11-49.1-2. Definitions.

As used in this chapter:

(1) "Document-making implement" means any implement, impression, electronic device, or computer hardware or software that is specifically configured or primarily used for making an identification document, a false identification document, or another document-making implement;

(2) "Identification document" means a document made or card issued by or under the authority of the United States government, a state, political subdivision of a state, a foreign government, political subdivision of a foreign government, or an international governmental or an international quasi-governmental organization which, when completed with information concerning a particular individual, is of a type intended or commonly accepted for the purpose of identification of individuals;

(3) "Means of identification" means any name or number that may be used, alone or in conjunction with any other information, to identify a specific individual, including any:

(i) Name, social security number, date of birth, official state or government issued driver's license or identification number, alien registration number, government passport number, employer, or taxpayer identification number;

(ii) Unique biometric data, such as fingerprint, voice print, retina or iris image, or other unique physical representation;

(iii) Unique electronic identification number, address, or routing code; or

(iv) Telecommunication identifying information or access device as defined in 18 U.S.C. § 1029(e).

(4) "Produce" means to manufacture, alter, authenticate, or assemble an identification document; and

(5) "State" includes any state of the United States, the District of Columbia, the Commonwealth of Puerto Rico, and any other commonwealth, possession, or territory of the United States.

Section 11-49.1-3 Identity fraud.

(a) Any person who:

(1) knowingly and without lawful authority produces an identification document or a false identification document;

(2) knowingly transfers an identification document or a false identification document knowing that the document was stolen or produced without lawful authority;

(3) knowingly possesses with intent to use unlawfully or transfer unlawfully five (5) or more identification documents (other than those issued lawfully for the use of the possessor) or false identification documents;

(4) knowingly possesses an identification document (other than one issued lawfully for the use of the possessor) or a false identification document, with the intent the document be used to defraud the United States, the state of Rhode Island, any political subdivision of them, or any public or private entity;

(5) knowingly transfers or possesses a document-making implement with the intent the document-making implement will be used in the production of a false identification document or another document-making implement which will be so used;

(6) knowingly possesses a false identification document that is or appears to be a genuine identification document of the United States, the state of Rhode Island, any political subdivision of them, or any public or private entity, which is stolen or produced without lawful authority knowing that the document was stolen or produced without lawful authority; or

(7) knowingly transfers or uses with intent to defraud, without lawful authority, a means of identification of another person with the intent to commit, or to aid or abet, any unlawful activity that constitutes a violation of federal, state or local law; is guilty of a felony and is subject to the penalties set forth in § 11-49.1-4.

(b) The provisions of this section do not apply to any person who has not reached his or her twenty-first (21st) birthday who misrepresents or misstates his or her age through the presentation of any document in order to enter any premises licensed for the retail sale of alcoholic beverages for the purpose of purchasing or having served or delivered to him or her alcoholic beverages, or attempting to purchase or have another person purchase for him or her any alcoholic beverage, pursuant to § 3-8-6.

Section 11-49.1-4.Penalties.

(a) Every person who violates the provisions of § 11-49.1-3 shall be imprisoned for not more than three (3) years and may be fined not more than five thousand dollars ($5,000) or both for a first conviction.

(b) Every person who violates the provisions of § 11-49.1-3 may be imprisoned for not less than three (3) years nor more than five (5) years and shall be fined not more than ten thousand dollars ($10,000) or both for a second conviction.

(c) Every person who violates the provisions of § 11-49.1-3 shall be imprisoned for not less than five (5) years nor more than ten (10) years and shall be fined not less than fifteen thousand dollars ($15,000) or both for a third or subsequent conviction.

SOUTH CAROLINA [S.D. CODIFIED LAWS § 16-13-510]

Personal Financial Security Act

(A) It is unlawful for a person to commit the offense of financial identity fraud.

(B) A person is guilty of financial identity fraud when he, without the authorization or permission of another person and with the intent of unlawfully appropriating the financial resources of that person to his own use or the use of a third party:

(1) obtains or records identifying information which would assist in accessing the financial records of the other person; or

(2) accesses or attempts to access the financial resources of the other person through the use of identifying information as defined in subsection (C).

(C) Identifying information includes, but is not limited to:

(1) social security numbers;

(2) driver's license numbers;

(3) checking account numbers;

(4) savings account numbers;

(5) credit card numbers;

(6) debit card numbers;

(7) personal identification numbers;

(8) electronic identification numbers;

(9) digital signatures; or

(10) other numbers or information which may be used to access a person's financial resources.

(D) A person who violates the provisions of this section is guilty of a felony and, upon conviction, must be fined in the discretion of the court or imprisoned not more than ten years, or both. The court may order restitution to the victim pursuant to the provisions of Section 17-25-322.

SOUTH DAKOTA [S.D. CODIFIED LAWS § 22-30A-3.1]
Identity theft defined — Violation as misdemeanor.

A person commits the offense of identity theft if the person without the authorization or permission of another person and with the intent to deceive or defraud:

(1) Obtains, possesses, transfers, uses, attempts to obtain, or records identifying information not lawfully issued for that person's use; or

(2) Accesses or attempts to access the financial resources of that person through the use of identifying information.

A violation of this section is a Class 1 misdemeanor.

TENNESSEE [TENN. CODE AN. § 39-14-150]
Identity theft.

(a) A person commits identity theft who knowingly transfers or uses, without lawful authority, a means of identification of another person with the intent to commit, or otherwise promote, carry on, or facilitate any unlawful activity.

(b) As used in this section, "means of identification" means any name or number that may be used, alone or in conjunction with any other information, to identify a specific individual, including:

(1) Name, social security number, date of birth, official state or government issued driver license or identification number, alien registration number, passport number, employer or taxpayer identification number;

(2) Unique biometric data, such as fingerprint, voice print, retina or iris image, or other unique physical representation;

(3) Unique electronic identification number, address, routing code or other personal identifying data which enables an individual to obtain merchandise or service or to otherwise financially encumber the legitimate possessor of the identifying data; or

(4) Telecommunication identifying information or access device.

(c) A violation of this section is a Class D felony.

TEXAS [TEX. PENAL CODE § 32.51]

Fraudulent Use or Possession of Identifying Information

In this section:

(1) "Identifying information" means information that alone or in conjunction with other information identifies an individual, including an individual's:

(A) name, social security number, date of birth, and government-issued identification number;

(B) unique biometric data, including the individual's fingerprint, voice print, and retina or iris image;

(C) unique electronic identification number, address, and routing code; and

(D) telecommunication identifying information or access device.

(2) "Telecommunication access device" means a card, plate, code, account number, personal identification number, electronic serial number, mobile identification number, or other telecommunications service, equipment, or instrument identifier or means of account access that alone or in conjunction with another telecommunication access device may be used to:

(A) obtain money, goods, services, or other thing of value; or

(B) initiate a transfer of funds other than a transfer originated solely by paper instrument.

(b) A person commits an offense if the person obtains, possesses, transfers, or uses identifying information of another person without the other person's consent and with intent to harm or defraud another.

(c) An offense under this section is a state jail felony.

(d) If a court orders a defendant convicted of an offense under this section to make restitution to the victim of the offense, the court may order the defendant to reimburse the victim for lost income or other expenses, other than attorney's fees, incurred as a result of the offense.

(e) If conduct that constitutes an offense under this section also constitutes an offense under any other law, the actor may be prosecuted under this section or the other law.

UTAH [UTAH CODE AN. §§ 76-6-1101; 76-6-1102]

76-6-1101. Identity fraud.

This part is known as the "Identity Fraud Act."

76-6-1102. Identity fraud crime.

(1) For purposes of this part, "personal identifying information" may include:

(a) name;

(b) address;

(c) telephone number;

(d) driver's license number;

(e) Social Security number;

(f) place of employment;

(g) employee identification numbers or other personal identification numbers;

(h) mother's maiden name;

(i) electronic identification numbers;

(j) digital signatures or a private key; or

(k) any other numbers or information that can be used to access a person's financial resources or medical information in the name of another person without the consent of that person except for numbers or information that can be prosecuted as financial transaction card offenses under Sections 76-6-506 through 76-6-506.4.

(2) A person is guilty of identity fraud when that person knowingly or intentionally:

(a) obtains personal identifying information of another person without the authorization of that person; and

(b) uses, or attempts to use, that information with fraudulent intent, including to obtain, or attempt to obtain, credit, goods, services, any other thing of value, or medical information in the name of another person without the consent of that person.

(3) Identity fraud is:

(a) a class B misdemeanor if the value of the credit, goods, services, or any other thing of value is less than $300;

(b) a class A misdemeanor if:

(i) a value cannot be determined and the personal identifying information has been used without the consent of that person to obtain medical information or to obtain employment; or

(ii) the value of the credit, goods, services, or any other thing of value is or exceeds $300 but is less than $1,000;

(c) a third degree felony if the value of the credit, goods, services, or any other thing of value is or exceeds $1,000 but is less than $5,000; or

(d) a second degree felony if the value of the credit, goods, services, or any other thing of value is or exceeds $5,000.

(4) Multiple violations within a 90-day period may be aggregated into a single offense, and the degree of the offense is determined by the total value of all credit, goods, services, or any other thing of value used, or attempted to be used, through the multiple violations.

VIRGINIA [VA. CODE AN. § 18-2-186.3]

Identity fraud; penalty; victim assistance.

A. It shall be unlawful for any person, without the authorization or permission of the person who is the subject of the identifying information, with the intent to defraud, for his own use or the use of a third person, to:

1. Obtain, record or access identifying information which is not available to the general public that would assist in accessing financial resources, obtaining identification documents, or obtaining benefits of such other person; or

2. Obtain goods or services through the use of identifying information of such other person; or

3. Obtain identification documents in such other person's name.

B. It shall be unlawful for any person to use identification documents or identifying information of another to avoid summons, arrest, prosecution, or to impede a criminal investigation.

C. As used in this section, "identifying information" shall include but not be limited to: (i) name; (ii) date of birth; (iii) social security number; (iv) driver's license number; (v) bank account numbers; (vi) credit or debit card numbers; (vii) personal identification numbers (PIN); (viii) electronic identification codes; (ix) automated or electronic signatures; (x) biometric data; (xi) fingerprints; (xii) passwords; or (xiii) any other numbers or information that can be used to access a person's financial resources, obtain identification, act as identification, or obtain goods or services.

D. Violations of this section shall be punishable as a Class 1 misdemeanor. Any violation resulting in financial loss of greater than $200 shall be punishable as a Class 6 felony. Any second or subsequent conviction shall be punishable as a Class 6 felony. Any violation resulting in the arrest and detention of the person whose identification documents or identifying information were used to avoid summons, arrest, prosecution, or to impede a criminal investigation shall be punishable as a Class 6 felony. In any proceeding brought pursuant to this section, the crime shall be considered to have been committed in any locality where the person whose identifying information was appropriated resides, or in which any part of the offense took place, regardless of whether the defendant was ever actually in such locality.

E. Upon conviction, in addition to any other punishment, a person found guilty of this offense shall be ordered by the court to make restitution as the court deems appropriate to any person whose identifying information was appropriated. Such restitution may include the person's actual expenses associated with correcting inaccuracies or errors in his credit report or other identifying information.

F. Upon the request of a person whose identifying information was appropriated, the Attorney General may provide assistance to the victim in obtaining information necessary to correct inaccuracies or errors in his credit report or other identifying information; however, no legal representation shall be afforded such person.

WASHINGTON [WASH. REV. CODE § 9.35.020]

Identity theft.

(1) No person may knowingly obtain, possess, use, or transfer a means of identification or financial information of another person, living or dead, with the intent to commit, or to aid or abet, any crime.

(2)(a) Violation of this section when the accused or an accomplice uses the victim's means of identification or financial information and obtains an aggregate total of credit, money, goods, services, or anything else of value in excess of one thousand five hundred dollars in value shall constitute identity theft in the first degree. Identity theft in the first degree is a class B felony.

(2)(b) Violation of this section when the accused or an accomplice uses the victim's means of identification or financial information and obtains an aggregate total of credit, money, goods, services, or anything else of value that is less than one thousand five hundred dollars in value, or when no credit, money, goods, services, or anything of value is obtained shall constitute identity theft in the second degree. Identity theft in the second degree is a class C felony.

(3) A person who violates this section is liable for civil damages of five hundred dollars or actual damages, whichever is greater, including costs to repair the victim's credit record, and reasonable attorneys' fees as determined by the court.

(4) In a proceeding under this section, the crime will be considered to have been committed in any locality where the person whose means of identification or financial information was appropriated resides, or in which any part of the offense took place, regardless of whether the defendant was ever actually in that locality.

(5) The provisions of this section do not apply to any person who obtains another person's driver's license or other form of identification for the sole purpose of misrepresenting his or her age.

(6) In a proceeding under this section in which a person's means of identification or financial information was used without that person's authorization, and when there has been a conviction, the sentencing court may issue such orders as are necessary to correct a public record that contains false information resulting from a violation of this section.

WEST VIRGINIA [W. VA. CODE § 61-3-54]

Taking identity of another person; penalty.

Any person who knowingly takes the name, birth date, social security number or other identifying information of another person, without the consent of that other person, with the intent to fraudulently represent that he or she is the other person for the purpose of making financial or credit transactions in the other person's name, is guilty of a felony, and upon conviction, shall be punished by confinement in the penitentiary not more than five years, or fined not more than one thousand dollars, or both: Provided, That the provisions of this section do not apply to any person who obtains another person's drivers license or other form of identification for the sole purpose of misrepresenting his or her age.

WISCONSIN [WIS. STAT. § 943.201]

Misappropriation of personal identifying information or personal identification documents.

(1) In this section:

(a) "Personal identification document" means a birth certificate or a financial transaction card, as defined in s. 943.41 (1) (em).

(b) "Personal identifying information" means any of the following information:

1. An individual's name.

2. An individual's address.

3. An individual's telephone number.

4. The unique identifying driver number assigned to the individual by the department of transportation under s. 343.17 (3) (a) 4.

5. An individual's social security number.

6. An individual's employer or place of employment.

7. An identification number assigned to an individual by his or her employer.

8. The maiden name of an individual's mother.

9. The identifying number of a depository account, as defined in s. 815.18 (2) (e), of an individual.

(2) Whoever intentionally uses or attempts to use any personal identifying information or personal identification document of an individual to obtain credit, money, goods, services or anything else of value without the authorization or consent of the individual and by representing that he or she is the individual or is acting with the authorization or consent of the individual is guilty of a Class D felony.

WYOMING [WYOMING STATUTES 6-3-901]

Unauthorized use of personal identifying information; penalties; restitution

(a) Every person who willfully obtains personal identifying information of another person, and uses that information for any unlawful purpose, including to obtain, or attempt to obtain, credit, goods, services or medical information in the name of the other person without the consent of that person is guilty of theft of identity.

(b) As used in this section "personal identifying information," means the name, address, telephone number, driver's license number, social security number, place of employment, employee identification number, tribal identification card number, mother's maiden name, demand deposit account number, savings account number, or credit card number of an individual person.

(c) Theft of identity is:

(i) A misdemeanor punishable by imprisonment for not more than six (6) months, a fine of not more than seven hundred fifty dollars ($750.00), or both, if no economic benefit was gained or was attempted to be gained, or if an economic benefit of less than one thousand dollars ($1,000.00) was gained or was attempted to be gained by the defendant; or

(ii) A felony punishable by imprisonment for not more than ten (10) years, a fine of not more than ten thousand dollars ($10,000.00), or both, if an economic benefit of one thousand dollars ($1,000.00) or more was gained or was attempted to be gained by the defendant.

(d) If a restitution plan is ordered pursuant to W.S. 7-9-101 through 7-9-115, the court may include, as part of its determination of amount owed pursuant to W.S. 7-9-103, payment for any costs incurred by the victim, including attorney fees, any costs incurred in clearing the credit history or credit rating of the victim or in connection with any civil or administrative proceeding to satisfy any debt, lien or other obligation of the victim arising as a result of the actions of the defendant.

(e) In any case in which a person willfully obtains personal identifying information of another person, and without the authorization of that person uses that information to commit a crime in addition to a violation of subsection (a) of this section, and is convicted of that crime, the court records shall reflect that the person whose identity was falsely used to commit the crime did not commit the crime.

APPENDIX 16:
DIRECTORY OF STATE CONSUMER
PROTECTION AGENCIES

STATE	ADDRESS	TELEPHONE NUMBER
Alabama	Consumer Protection Division Office of the Attorney Genera 11 S. Union Street Montgomery, AL 36130	205-261-7334
Alaska	Consumer Protection Section Office of the Attorney General 1031 W. 4th Avenue Suite 110-B Anchorage, AK 99501	907-279-0428
Arizona	Financial Fraud Division Office of the Attorney General 1275 W. Washington St. Phoenix, AZ 85007	602-542-3702
Arkansas	Consumer Protection Division Office of the Attorney General 200 Tower Building 4th & Center Streets Little Rock, AR 72201	501-682-2007
California	Public Inquiry Unit Office of the Attorney General 1515 K Street, Suite 511 Sacramento, CA 94244-2550	916-322-3360
California	Consumer Protection Division Los Angeles City Attorney's Office 200 N. Main Street 1600 City Hall East Los Angeles, CA 90012	213-485-4515

Colorado	Consumer Protection Unit Office of the Attorney General 1525 Sherman Street 3rd Floor Denver, CO 80203	303-866-5167
Connecticut	Department of Consumer Protection 165 Capitol Avenue Hartford, CT 06106	203-566-4999
Delaware	Division of Consumer Affairs Department of Community Affairs 820 N. French Street 4th Floor Wilmington, DE 19801	302-571-3250
District of Columbia	Department of Consumer & Regulatory Affairs 614 H Street NW Washington, DC 20001	202-737-7000
Florida	Division of Consumer Services 218 Mayo Building Tallahassee, FL 32399	904-488-2226
Georgia	Governor's Office of Consumer Affairs 2 Martin Luther King Jr. Drive SE Plaza Level E Tower, Atlanta, GA 30334	404-656-7000
Hawaii	Office of Consumer Protection 828 Fort St. Mall Honolulu, HI 96812-3767	808-548-2560
Idaho	None Listed	
Illinois	Consumer Protection Division Office of the Attorney General 100 W. Randolph Street 12th Floor Chicago, IL 60601	312-917-3580
Indiana	Consumer Protection Division Office of the Attorney General 219 State House Indianapolis, IN 46204	317-232-6330
Iowa	Consumer Protection Division Office of the Attorney General 1300 E. Walnut Street 2nd Floor Des Moines, IA 50319	515-281-5926
Kansas	Consumer Protection Division Office of the Attorney General Kansas Judicial Center 2nd Floor Topeka, KS 66612	913-296-3761

Kentucky	Consumer Protection Division Office of the Attorney General 209 St. Clair Street Frankfort, KY 40601	502-564-2200
Louisiana	Consumer Protection Section Office of the Attorney General State Capitol Building P.O. Box 94005 Baton Rouge, LA 70804	504-342-7013
Maine	Consumer and Antitrust Division Office of the Attorney General State House Station #6 Augusta, ME 04333	207-289-3716
Maryland	Consumer Protection Division Office of the Attorney General 7 N. Calvert Street 3rd Floor Baltimore, MD 21202	301-528-8662
Massachusetts	Consumer Protection Division Office of the Attorney General One Ashburton Place, Room 1411 Boston, MA 02108	617-727-7780
Michigan	Consumer Protection Division Office of the Attorney General 670 Law Building Lansing, MI 48913	517-373-1140
Minnesota	Office of Consumer Services Office of the Attorney General 117 University Avenue St. Paul, MN 55155	612-296-2331
Mississippi	Consumer Protection Division Office of the Attorney General P.O. Box 220 Jackson, MS 39205	601-359-3680
Missouri	Trade Offense Division Office of the Attorney General P.O. Box 899 Jefferson City, MO 65102	314-751-2616
Montana	Consumer Affairs Unit Department of Commerce 1424 9th Avenue Helena, MT 59620	406-444-4312
Nebraska	Consumer Protection Division Department of Justice 2115 State Capitol P.O. Box 98920 Lincoln, NE 68509	402-471-4723

Nevada	Department of Commerce State Mail Room Complex Las Vegas, NV 89158	702-486-4150
New Hampshire	Consumer Protection and Antitrust Division Office of the Attorney General State House Annex Concord, NH 03301	603-271-3641
New Jersey	Division of Consumer Affairs 1100 Raymond Boulevard Room 504 Newark, NJ 07102	201-648-4010
New Mexico	Consumer and Economic Crime Division Office of the Attorney General P.O. Box Drawer 1508 Santa Fe, NM 87504	505-872-6910
New York	Consumer Protection Board 99 Washington Avenue Albany, NY 12210	518-474-8583
New York	Consumer Protection Board 250 Broadway 17th Floor New York, NY 10007-2593	212-587-4908
North Carolina	Consumer Protection Section Office of the Attorney General P.O. Box 629 Raleigh, NC 27602	919-733-7741
North Dakota	Consumer Fraud Division Office of the Attorney General State Capitol Building Bismarck, ND 58505	701-224-2210
Ohio	Consumer Frauds and Crimes Section Office of the Attorney General 30 E. Broad Street 25th Floor Columbus, OH 43266-0410	614-466-4986
Oklahoma	Consumer Affairs Office of the Attorney General 112 State Capitol Building Oklahoma City, OK 73105	405-521-3921
Oregon	Financial Fraud Section Office of the Attorney General Justice Building Salem, OR 97310	503-378-4320

Pennsylvania	Bureau of Consumer Protection Office of the Attorney General Strawberry Square 14th Floor Harrisburg, PA 17120	717-787-9707
Rhode Island	Consumer Protection Division Office of the Attorney General 72 Pine Street Providence, RI 02903	401-277-2104
South Carolina	Department of Consumer Affairs P.O. Box 5757 Columbia, SC 29250	803-734-9452
South Dakota	Division of Consumer Affairs Office of the Attorney General State Capitol Building Pierre, SD 57501	605-773-4400
Tennessee	Division of Consumer Affairs Department of Commerce & Insurance 500 James Robertson Parkway 5th Floor Nashville, TN 37219	615-741-4737
Texas	Consumer Protection Division Office of the Attorney General Box 12548 Capitol Station Austin, TX 78711	512-463-2070
Utah	Division of Consumer Protection Department of Business Regulation 160 E. Third South P.O. Box 45802 Salt Lake City, UT 84145	801-530-6601
Vermont	Public Protection Division Office of the Attorney General 109 State Street Montpelier, VT 05602	802-828-3171
Virginia	Division of Consumer Counsel Office of the Attorney General Supreme Court Building 101 N. 8th Street Richmond, VA 23219	804-786-2116
Washington	Consumer and Business Fair Practices Division 710 2nd Avenue Suite 1300 Seattle, WA 98104	206-464-7744

West Virginia	Consumer Protection Division Office of the Attorney General 812 Quarrier Street 6th Floor Charleston, WV 25301	304-348-8986
Wisconsin	Office of Consumer Protection Department of Justice P.O. Box 7856 Madison, WI 53707	608-266-1852
Wyoming	Office of the Attorney General 123 State Capitol Building Cheyenne, WY 82002	307-777-6286

APPENDIX 17:
ANNUAL CREDIT REPORT REQUEST FORM

EQUIFAX·   **experían**   **TransUnion.**

Annual Credit Report Request Form

You have the right to get a free copy of your credit file disclosure, commonly called a credit report, once every 12 months, from each of the nationwide consumer credit reporting companies - Equifax, Experian and TransUnion.

For instant access to your free credit report, visit www.annualcreditreport.com.

For more information on obtaining your free credit report, visit www.annualcreditreport.com or call 877-322-8228.

Use this form if you prefer to write to request your credit report from any, or all, of the nationwide consumer credit reporting companies. The following information is required to process your request. **Omission of any information may delay your request.**

Once complete, fold (do not staple or tape), place into a #10 envelope, affix required postage and mail to:
Annual Credit Report Request Service P.O. Box 105281 Atlanta, GA 30348-5281.

Please use a Black or Blue Pen and write your responses in PRINTED CAPITAL LETTERS without touching the sides of the boxes like the examples listed below:

A B C D E F G H I J K L M N O P Q R S T U V W X Y Z   0 1 2 3 4 5 6 7 8 9

Social Security Number:

Date of Birth:

Month   Day   Year

Fold Here   Fold Here

First Name   M.I.

Last Name   JR, SR, III, etc.

Current Mailing Address:

House Number   Street Name

Apartment Number / Private Mailbox   For Puerto Rico Only: Print Urbanization Name

City   State   ZipCode

Previous Mailing Address (complete only if at current mailing address for less than two years):

House Number   Street Name

Fold Here   Fold Here

Apartment Number / Private Mailbox   For Puerto Rico Only: Print Urbanization Name

City   State   ZipCode

Shade Circle Like This → ●

Not Like This → ☒ ∅

I want a credit report from (shade each that you would like to receive):
○ Equifax
○ Experian
○ TransUnion

○ Shade here if, for security reasons, you want your credit report to include no more than the last four digits of your Social Security Number.

If additional information is needed to process your request, the consumer credit reporting company will contact you by mail.

Your request will be processed within 15 days of receipt and then mailed to you.

Copyright 2004, Central Source LLC

31238

APPENDIX 13:
SAMPLE NOTIFICATION LETTER TO A
CREDIT REPORTING AGENCY

Date: _____

Name of Credit Reporting Agency

Address

City, State, Zip Code

Attn: Fraud Adjustment

Dear Sir/Madam:

I am writing to advise you that I have been the victim of identity theft. While reviewing my credit report, I found several credit card accounts that were opened in my name using my stolen identity. I have enclosed a copy of my credit report from your company and, after reviewing my report, I found that these fraudulent credit card accounts now appear on my credit report as follows:

[Identify items you claim are fraudulent accounts]

I have also circled these items on the attached copy of my credit report.

I am requesting that the above-listed item(s) and any related inquiry information be removed immediately and that a fraud alert be placed in my file advising creditors that I have been the victim of identity theft and that no new accounts should be opened in my name without first contacting me directly and obtaining my authorization.

I have also enclosed copies of the following supporting documentation:

[Identify documents which support your position, e.g., police reports or other complaints to government agencies]

Please investigate this matter as soon as possible and make the necessary corrections. I would appreciate it if you would send me a copy of my corrected report upon completion of your investigation.

Sincerely yours,

_____

APPENDIX 18:
SAMPLE NOTIFICATION LETTER TO
CREDIT REPORTING AGENCY

Date

Name of Credit Reporting Agency

Address

City, State, Zip Code

Attn: Fraud Department

Dear Sir/Madam:

I am writing to advise you that I am the victim of identity theft. In connection with this crime, it appears that certain credit card accounts were opened in my name using my stolen identity. I obtained a copy of my credit report from your Company and, after reviewing my report, I found that these fraudulent credit card accounts now appear on my credit report, as follows:

[Identify item(s) you claim are fraudulent accounts].

I have also circled these items on the attached copy of my credit report.

I am requesting that the above-listed item(s) and any related derogatory information be removed immediately and that a fraud alert be placed in my file advising creditors that I have been the victim of identity theft and that no new accounts should be opened in my name without contacting me directly and obtaining my authorization.

I have also enclosed copies of the following supporting documentation:

[Identify documents which support your position, e.g., police reports or other complaints to government agencies].

Please investigate this matter as soon as possible and make the necessary corrections. I would appreciate if you would send me a copy of the corrected report upon completion of your investigation.

Very truly yours,

[Signature Line]

Enclosures:
[list all attachments]

APPENDIX 19:
SAMPLE NOTIFICATION LETTER TO A
CREDIT CARD ISSUER

Date

Name of Creditor

Address

City, State, Zip Code

Attn: Fraud Department

Dear Sir or Madam:

It has recently come to my attention that I have become a victim of identity theft. My personal information has been used without my knowledge or consent as follows:

[Explain how personal information was misused, e.g., to obtain a fraudulent account, etc.]

[If applicable] I have reason to believe that the following person is responsible for the above-referenced action:

[Insert identification information of person suspected, e.g., name, address, telephone number and relationship (if applicable), etc.]

I have made an official complaint to the following law enforcement agency:

[Insert complaint date and file number and the name, address, and telephone number of the law enforcement agency with whom your complaint was filed]

Please correct your records as follows:

[Describe relief requested as applicable, e.g., close unauthorized account/delete tunauthorized charges, credit any finance and/or other charges related to the fraudulent charge/have any negative information reported to credit reporting agency removed, etc.]

Please investigate this matter and make the necessary corrections as soon as possible. I would appreciate if you would send me a revised statement as soon as your investigation is completed.

If you have any questions or concerns please contact me. Thank you.

Very truly yours,

[Signature Line]

Enclosures:

[list all attachments]

APPENDIX 20:
U.S. POSTAL SERVICE MAIL THEFT AND
VANDALISM COMPLAINT FORM

UNITED STATES POSTAL SERVICE™	**Mail Theft and Vandalism Complaint**	1. Post Office *(Including Station or Unit and ZIP + 6)*

2. Name of Complainant

Street Address		Apt. No.	Home Telephone *(Include Area Code)*
City, State, and ZIP + 4			Work Telephone *(Include Area Code)*

3. Nature of Complaint

☐ Theft of Mail ☐ Damage to Mailbox ☐ Mail Tampering ☐ Mail Rifling ☐ False Change of Address

☐ Fire in Mailbox ☐ Other *(Describe)*

Occurrence Date and Hour

4. Contents of Mail Stolen

☐ Correspondence ☐ Currency ☐ Check ☐ Bank Statement ☐ Credit Card ☐ ATP *(Food stamps card)*

☐ Credit Card Statement ☐ Other *(Describe)*

5. Type of Delivery

☐ Apt. House; No. of Families_____ ☐ Private Home ☐ P.O. Box ☐ Rooming House ☐ Office Building ☐ Rural or HCR

☐ Hotel/Hospital ☐ Other *(Describe)*

6. Type of Receptacle

☐ Door Slot ☐ NDCBU ☐ Approved Apartment Panel ☐ Collection ☐ Residence **Locked?** ☐ Yes

☐ Desk Service ☐ Rural Type ☐ Combination ☐ No

7. Particulars of Stolen Check

☐ 01) Personal ☐ 02) Commercial ☐ 03) Local ☐ 04) State ☐ 05) Federal ☐ 06) Money Order ☐ 07) ATP

Sender's Name and Address

Payee *(If different from complainant)*

Amount $	Check No.	Date	Symbol No. *(If U.S. Treasury)*
Maker of Check		Bank on Which Drawn	

8. Purpose for Which Check Issued

9. If Check or Money Order Was Cashed, Obtain Particulars *(Date, place, person accepting it, etc.)*

10. Suspects *(Name, address, physical description, car description and license no.)*

11. Were Police Notified?

☐ Yes *(If "Yes," give Police Report No.:_____)* ☐ No *(If "No," instruct complainant to do so.)*

12. Remarks *(Continue on reverse, if necessary)*

13. Date of Complaint	14. Complaint Received by *(Signature)*

PS Form **2016**, March 1994

APPENDIX 21:
FCC COMPLAINT FORM

Approved by OMB
3060-0874
Estimated time per response: 30 minutes

Federal Communications Commission
Washington, DC 20554

FCC Form 475 – General Communications Related Issues

This form can only be used for complaints related to: 1) wireless and wireline telecommunication services; 2) non-programming related cable, broadcasting and satellite services; and 3) communications accessibility issues. For example, use Form 475 for general telephone complaints such as billing disputes, <u>cramming</u>, telephone company advertising practices, paging services, <u>unsolicited telephone marketing calls</u> and <u>unwanted faxes</u>, and accessibility by persons with disabilities to telecommunications equipment and services. If you are complaining that your telephone company was changed to another telephone company without your permission (<u>SLAMMING</u>), you must use <u>Form 501</u> to file the complaint. If you are complaining about the allegedly obscene, profane, or indecent content of a radio or television program, you must use <u>Form 475B</u>.

Required Information

1. <u>Consumer's Information</u>:

   a. *First Name: _____

   b. Middle Initial: _____

   c. *Last Name: _____

   d. Your Company Name: _____
   (Complete only if you are filing this complaint on behalf of a company or an organization.)

   e. Post Office Box Number: _____

   f. Street Address: _____

   _____

   *Either Street Address OR Post Office Box Number is Required

   g. *City: _____

   h.*State: _____

   i. *Zip Code: _____

   j. Your E-Mail Address: _____

Revised November 2005

2

k. *Your Telephone Number (Residential or Business): _____

l. Your Daytime Contact Telephone Number: _____

m. The Best Time to Contact You: _____

2. Complaint Information:

a. *Name of carrier(s) or company(ies) involved in your complaint: _____

_____

b. Telephone number for the carrier(s) or company(ies) involved with your complaint, including area code: _____

c. Which type of service is involved with your complaint:
__Your Home (Residential) Telephone Service __Your Business (Commercial) Telephone Service

d. List the Telephone Numbers (Maximum of 2), with which you are experiencing a problem – including Area Codes:

     1. *Telephone Number One: (_____) _____
     2. *Telephone Number Two: (_____) _____

e. Complete the following if you are disputing charges listed on a telephone bill:

     1. Have you paid any of the disputed charges? _____Yes _____No

     2. Did the billing company adjust or refund the disputed charges? ___Yes ___No

     3. If yes, what was the amount of the adjustment or refund? _____

f. *Briefly describe your complaint and include the following information in your statement, if applicable:

     • account number(s) involved with your complaint if that number is different than your telephone number;

     • date(s) of the telephone bill involved with your complaint;

     • the resolution you are seeking:

_____

_____

_____

_____

_____

_____

_____

Revised November 2005

g. For Telephone Consumer Protection Act violations such as an unsolicited telephone call in violation of your do-not-call preference; a pre-recorded message; or an unsolicited advertisement sent to your fax machine, please provide:

    1. the telephone number of the individual or company who called or faxed you: _____

    *2. your telephone number(s) on which the call or fax was received: _____

    *3. a description of the telemarketing call, pre-recorded message, or unsolicited fax, including an identification of the company whose products or services were being advertised, and any phone numbers that were included in the call or fax:: _____
    _____

    *4. the opt-out number(s) provided in the call(s) or, on the fax(es): (List number(s) given in the calls(s) or fax(es) for you to contact if you do not want to receive any additional calls or faxes.) _____
    _____

    *5. Have you: (a) purchased anything from the company being advertised in the call or fax; (b) made an inquiry or application to that company; or (c) given consent to the company to send you the call or fax? If so, please describe and state when you had such contact with the company. _____
    _____

Revised November 2005

FCC NOTICE REQUIRED BY THE PRIVACY ACT AND PAPERWORK REDUCTION ACT

The Federal Communications Commission is authorized under the Communications Act of 1934, as amended, to collect the personal information that we request in this form. This form is used for informal complaints between consumers and telecommunications carriers. If we believe there maybe a violation or potential violation of a statute, FCC regulation, rule or order, your complaint may be referred to the Federal, state, or local agency responsible for investigating, prosecuting, enforcing or implementing the statute, rule, regulation, or order.

The public reporting for this collection of information is estimated to average 30 minutes per response, including the time for reviewing instructions, searching existing data sources, gathering and maintaining the required data, and completing and reviewing the collection of information. If you have any comments on this burden estimate, or how we can improve the collection and reduce the burden it causes you, please write to the Federal Communications Commission, AMD-PERM, Paperwork Reduction Project (3060-0874), Washington, DC 20554. We will also accept your comments regarding the Paperwork Reduction Act aspects of this collection via the Internet if you send them to Leslie.Smith@fcc.gov. PLEASE DO NOT SEND YOUR COMPLETED FORMS TO THIS ADDRESS.

Remember - You are not required to respond to a collection of information sponsored by the Federal government, and the government may not conduct or sponsor this collection, unless it displays a currently valid OMB control number or if we fail to provide you with this notice. This collection has been assigned an OMB control number of 3060-0874.

THE FOREGOING NOTICE IS REQUIRED BY THE PRIVACY ACT OF 1974, PUBLIC LAW 93-579, DECEMBER 31, 1974, 5 U.S.C. SECTION 552a(e)(3) AND THE PAPERWORK REDUCTION ACT OF 1995, PUBLIC LAW 104-13, OCTOBER 1, 1995, 44 U.S.C. SECTION 3507.

Revised November 2005

APPENDIX 22:
U.S. FEDERAL AGENCY AND OFFICE
MEMBERS OF CONSUMER SENTINEL

Amtrak Inspector General
Commodity Futures Trading Commission
Consumer Product Safety Commission
Department of Housing and Urban Development, Compliance Division
Department of Justice, Fraud Section, Criminal Division
Department of Justice, Office of Consumer Litigation, Civil Division
Federal Bureau of Investigation
Federal Communications Commission, Enforcement Bureau
Federal Deposit Insurance Corporation, Inspector General
Federal Reserve Board, Inspector General
Federal Trade Commission
Internal Revenue Service, Criminal Investigations
Nuclear Regulatory Commission
Office of the Comptroller of the Currency
Postal Inspection Service
Secret Service
Securities and Exchange Commission
Small Business Administration-Office of Inspector General
Social Security Administration, Office of Inspector General
Treasury Inspector General for Tax Administration
U.S. Air Force, Judge Advocate General, Office of Special Investigations
U.S. Army, Judge Advocate General
U.S. Attorney's Office
    Southern District of Alabama
    District of Arizona
    Central District of California
    Eastern District of California
    Southern District of California
    District of Colorado

District of Columbia
Northern District of Florida
Middle District of Florida
Southern District of Florida
Southern District of Illinois
Northern District of Indiana, Fort Wayne Division
Northern District of Iowa
Southern District of Iowa
Eastern District of Kentucky
Middle District of Louisiana
Western District of Louisiana
Eastern District of Michigan
Western District of Michigan
District of Minnesota
Southern District of Mississippi
Western District of Missouri
District of Montana
District of New Hampshire
District of New Jersey
Eastern District of New York
Western District of New York
Southern District of New York
Eastern District of North Carolina
Middle District of North Carolina
District of Oregon
Eastern District of Pennsylvania
Western District of Pennsylvania
District of South Dakota
Eastern District of Tennessee
Eastern District of Texas
District of the Virgin Islands
Eastern District of Virginia
Western District of Virginia
Eastern District of Washington
Western District of Washington
Southern District of West Virginia
U.S. Coast Guard
U.S. Customs Service
U.S. Department of Commerce Inspector General
U.S. Department of Defense Criminal Investigative Service
U.S. Department of Education Inspector General

U.S. Department of Veterans Affairs Inspector General

U.S. Federal Election Commission, Division of Enforcement

U.S. Food and Drug Administration

U.S. General Services Administration Inspector General

U.S. Immigration and Customs Enforcement

U.S. Library of Congress Police Department

U.S. Marine Corps., Office of Legal Assistance

U.S. Marshals Service, Investigative Services Division

U.S. Navy, Judge Advocate General

U.S. Park Police

U.S. Probation Office
    Northern District of Georgia
    Northern District of Massachusetts
    Western District of Missouri
    Western District of Washington
    Eastern District of New York

U.S. State Department, Bureau of Diplomatic Security, Criminal Investigations Divisions

U.S. Trustees, Executive Office

Source: Consumer Sentinel

APPENDIX 23:
FTC ID THEFT AFFIDAVIT AND INSTRUCTIONS

Instructions for
Completing the ID Theft Affidavit

To make certain that you do not become responsible for any debts incurred by an identity thief, you must prove to each of the companies where accounts were opened or used in your name that you didn't create the debt.

A group of credit grantors, consumer advocates, and attorneys at the Federal Trade Commission (FTC) developed an ID Theft Affidavit to make it easier for fraud victims to report information. While many companies accept this affidavit, others require that you submit more or different forms. Before you send the affidavit, contact each company to find out if they accept it.

It will be necessary to provide the information in this affidavit anywhere a **new** account was opened in your name. The information will enable the companies to investigate the fraud and decide the outcome of your claim. If someone made unauthorized charges to an **existing** account, call the company for instructions.

This affidavit has two parts:
- **Part One** — the ID Theft Affidavit — is where you report general information about yourself and the theft.
- **Part Two** — the Fraudulent Account Statement — is where you describe the fraudulent account(s) opened in your name. Use a separate Fraudulent Account Statement for each company you need to write to.

When you send the affidavit to the companies, attach copies (NOT originals) of any supporting documents (for example, driver's license or police report). Before submitting your affidavit, review the disputed account(s) with family members or friends who may have information about the account(s) or access to them.

Complete this affidavit as soon as possible. Many creditors ask that you send it within two weeks. Delays on your part could slow the investigation.

Be as accurate and complete as possible. You may choose not to provide some of the information requested. However, incorrect or incomplete information will slow the process of investigating your claim and absolving the debt. Print clearly.

When you have finished completing the affidavit, mail a copy to each creditor, bank, or company that provided the thief with the unauthorized credit, goods, or services you describe. Attach a copy of the Fraudulent Account Statement with information only on accounts opened at the institution to which you are sending the packet, as well as any other supporting documentation you are able to provide.

Send the appropriate documents to each company by certified mail, return receipt requested, so you can prove that it was received. The companies will review your claim and send you a written response telling you the outcome of their investigation. Keep a copy of everything you submit.

If you are unable to complete the affidavit, a legal guardian or someone with power of attorney may complete it for you. Except as noted, the information you provide will be used only by the company to process your affidavit, investigate the events you report, and help stop further fraud. If this affidavit is requested in a lawsuit, the company might have to provide it to the requesting party. Completing this affidavit does not guarantee that the identity thief will be prosecuted or that the debt will be cleared.

DO NOT SEND AFFIDAVIT TO THE FTC OR ANY OTHER
GOVERNMENT AGENCY

If you haven't already done so, report the fraud to the following organizations:

1. Any one of the nationwide consumer reporting companies to place a fraud alert on your credit report. Fraud alerts can help prevent an identity thief from opening any more accounts in your name. The company you call is required to contact the other two, which will place an alert on their versions of your report, too.

   - **Equifax:** 1-800-525-6285; www.equifax.com

   - **Experian:** 1-888-EXPERIAN (397-3742); www.experian.com

   - **TransUnion:** 1-800-680-7289; www.transunion.com

In addition to placing the fraud alert, the three consumer reporting companies will send you free copies of your credit reports, and, if you ask, they will display only the last four digits of your Social Security number on your credit reports.

2. The security or fraud department of each company where you know, or believe, accounts have been tampered with or opened fraudulently. Close the accounts. Follow up in writing, and include copies (NOT originals) of supporting documents. *It's important to notify credit card companies and banks in writing.* Send your letters by certified mail, return receipt requested, so you can document what the company received and when. Keep a file of your correspondence and enclosures.

When you open new accounts, use new Personal Identification Numbers (PINs) and

passwords. Avoid using easily available information like your mother's maiden name, your birth date, the last four digits of your Social Security number or your phone number, or a series of consecutive numbers.

3. Your local police or the police in the community where the identity theft took place to file a report. Get a copy of the police report or, at the very least, the number of the report. It can help you deal with creditors who need proof of the crime. If the police are reluctant to take your report, ask to file a "Miscellaneous Incidents" report, or try another jurisdiction, like your state police. You also can check with your state Attorney General's office to find out if state law requires the police to take reports for identity theft. Check the Blue Pages of your telephone directory for the phone number or check www.naag.org for a list of state Attorneys General.

4. The Federal Trade Commission. By sharing your identity theft complaint with the FTC, you will provide important information that can help law enforcement officials across the nation track down identity thieves and stop them. The FTC also can refer victims' complaints to other government agencies and companies for further action, as well as investigate companies for violations of laws that the FTC enforces.

You can file a complaint online at **www.consumer.gov/idtheft**. If you don't have Internet access, call the FTC's Identity Theft Hotline, toll-free: 1-877-IDTHEFT (438-4338); TTY: 1-866-653-4261; or write: Identity Theft Clearinghouse, Federal Trade Commission, 600 Pennsylvania Avenue, NW, Washington, DC 20580.

DO NOT SEND AFFIDAVIT TO THE FTC OR ANY OTHER GOVERNMENT AGENCY

Name _____ Phone number _____ Page 1

ID Theft Affidavit

Victim Information

(1) My full legal name is _____
                                (First)   (Middle)   (Last)   (Jr., Sr., III)

(2) (If different from above) When the events described in this affidavit took place, I was known as

     _____
     (First)   (Middle)   (Last)   (Jr., Sr., III)

(3) My date of birth is _____
                          (day/month/year)

(4) My Social Security number is_____

(5) My driver's license or identification card state and number are_____

(6) My current address is _____

     City _____ State _____ Zip Code _____

(7) I have lived at this address since _____
                                    (month/year)

(8) (If different from above) When the events described in this affidavit took place, my address was

     _____

     City _____ State _____ Zip Code _____

(9) I lived at the address in Item 8 from _____ until _____
                                    (month/year) (month/year)

(10) My daytime telephone number is (____)_____

      My evening telephone number is (____)_____

DO NOT SEND AFFIDAVIT TO THE FTC OR ANY OTHER GOVERNMENT AGENCY

Name _____ Phone number _____ Page 2

How the Fraud Occurred

Check all that apply for items 11 - 17:

(11) ❑ I did not authorize anyone to use my name or personal information to seek the money, credit, loans, goods or services described in this report.

(12) ❑ I did not receive any benefit, money, goods or services as a result of the events described in this report.

(13) ❑ My identification documents (for example, credit cards; birth certificate; driver's license; Social Security card; etc.) were ❑ stolen ❑ lost on or about _____.
(day/month/year)

(14) ❑ To the best of my knowledge and belief, the following person(s) used my information (for example, my name, address, date of birth, existing account numbers, Social Security number, mother's maiden name, etc.) or identification documents to get money, credit, loans, goods or services without my knowledge or authorization:

Name (if known)	Name (if known)
Address (if known)	Address (if known)
Phone number(s) (if known)	Phone number(s) (if known)
Additional information (if known)	Additional information (if known)

(15) ❑ I do NOT know who used my information or identification documents to get money, credit, loans, goods or services without my knowledge or authorization.

(16) ❑ Additional comments: (For example, description of the fraud, which documents or information were used or how the identity thief gained access to your information.)

_____

_____

_____

_____

(Attach additional pages as necessary.)

DO NOT SEND AFFIDAVIT TO THE FTC OR ANY OTHER GOVERNMENT AGENCY

Identity Theft and How to Protect Yourself

Name _____ Phone number _____ Page 3

(17) (check one) I ☐ am ☐ am not   willing to assist in the prosecution of the person(s) who committed this fraud.

(18) (check one) I ☐ am ☐ am not   authorizing the release of this information to law enforcement for the purpose of assisting them in the investigation and prosecution of the person(s) who committed this fraud.

(19) (check all that apply) I ☐ have ☐ have not   reported the events described in this affidavit to the police or other law enforcement agency. The police ☐ did ☐ did not   write a report. In the event you have contacted the police or other law enforcement agency, please complete the following:

(Agency #1)	(Officer/Agency personnel taking report)
(Date of report)	(Report number, if any)
(Phone number)	(email address, if any)
(Agency #2)	(Officer/Agency personnel taking report)
(Date of report)	(Report number, if any)
(Phone number)	(email address, if any)

Please indicate the supporting documentation you are able to provide to the companies you plan to notify. Attach copies (NOT originals) to the affidavit before sending it to the companies.

(20) ☐ A copy of a valid government-issued photo-identification card (for example, your driver's license, state-issued ID card or your passport). If you are under 16 and don't have a photo-ID, you may submit a copy of your birth certificate or a copy of your official school records showing your enrollment and place of residence.

(21) ☐ Proof of residency during the time the disputed bill occurred, the loan was made or the other event took place (for example, a rental/lease agreement in your name, a copy of a utility bill or a copy of an insurance bill).

DO NOT SEND AFFIDAVIT TO THE FTC OR ANY OTHER GOVERNMENT AGENCY

Name _____ Phone number _____ *Page 4*

(22) ❏ A copy of the report you filed with the police or sheriff's department. If you are unable to obtain a report or report number from the police, please indicate that in Item 19. Some companies only need the report number, not a copy of the report. You may want to check with each company.

Signature

I certify that, to the best of my knowledge and belief, all the information on and attached to this affidavit is true, correct, and complete and made in good faith. I also understand that is affidavit or the information it contains may be made available to federal, state, and/or local law enforcement agencies for such action within their jurisdiction as they deem appropriate. I understand that knowingly making any false or fraudulent statement or representation to the government may constitute a violation of 18 U.S.C. §1001 or other federal, state, or local criminal statutes, and may result in imposition of a fine or imprisonment or both.

_____   _____
(signature)   (date signed)

_____
(Notary)

[Check with each company. Creditors sometimes require notarization. If they do not, please have one witness (non-relative) sign below that you completed and signed this affidavit.]

Witness:

_____   _____
(signature)   (printed name)

_____   _____
(date)   (telephone number)

DO NOT SEND AFFIDAVIT TO THE FTC OR ANY OTHER GOVERNMENT AGENCY

APPENDIX 24:
ORGANIZATIONS THAT ENDORSE THE
IDENTITY THEFT AFFIDAVIT

ACA International
Altoona Postal Employees Credit Union
Amcrin Corporation
American Bankers Association
American Contracting Exchange
America's Community Bankers
Arkansas Federal Credit Union
AT&T
Atlantic Credit Union
Bank of Alameda
Bank of America
Bankers Trust Company, N.A.
Call for Action
Capital One
Chase Manhattan Bank
Coastal Federal Credit Union
Computer Sciences Corporation
Corporate America Family Credit Union
Council of Better Business Bureaus
Credit Bureau of East Tennessee Inc.
Direct Marketing Association
Equifax
Experian
Federal Reserve Board
Fifth Third Bank
First National Bank Omaha
FleetBoston Financial
GE Capital
GetThere LP

Gold Quest Realty, LTD. CO.
Identity Theft Resource Center
Investors Savings Bank
Iowa Independent Bankers
Key Federal Credit Union
Kimberly Clark Credit Union
Merrill Lynch
Nexity Bank
Nissan Motor Acceptance Corporation
Oregon Telco Community Credit Union
Privacy Guard
Privacy Rights Clearinghouse
Provident Credit Union
Providian
SBC Service
Sears
The California Office of Privacy Protection
The Simpson Organization, Inc.
TransUnion
Tri-County Debt Management of CWO, Inc.
U.S. Bank
U.S. Postal Inspection Service
VW Credit
Western Capital
Western Funding.com

APPENDIX 25:
LETTER FROM IDENTITY THIEF ACCEPTING RESPONSIBILITY FOR FRAUDULENT ACCOUNT

Date

Name of Creditor
Address
City, State, Zip Code
Attn: Fraud Department

Dear Sir/Madam:

I am writing to advise you that I [describe fraudulent activity committed, e.g., opened an account, made additional charges to an existing account, etc. and identify account] without the knowledge or consent of [insert victim's name].

I have agreed to assume financial responsibility for all charges made by me in connection with this account. Please remove any negative information that may have erroneously been reported in the name of [insert victim's name] to any credit reporting agency and send written confirmation to [insert victim's name] that they have been relieved of responsibility for this account.

Please contact me as soon as possible to arrange for repayment of this debt. Thank you.

Signature Line

Printed Name of Identity Thief

Social Security Number/Date of Birth

Address

Telephone Number

APPENDIX 26:
NOTIFICATION OF DATA BREACH

Dear _____:

We are contacting you about a potential problem involving identity theft. [Describe the information compromise and how you are responding to it.]

We recommend that you place a fraud alert on your credit file. A fraud alert tells creditors to contact you before they open any new accounts or change your existing accounts. Call any one of the three major credit bureaus.

Equifax—800-525-6285

Experian—888-397-3742

TransUnionCorp—800-680-7289

As soon as one credit bureau confirms your fraud alert, the others are notified to place fraud alerts. All three credit reports will be sent to you, free of charge, for your review.

Even if you do not find any suspicious activity on your initial credit reports, the Federal Trade Commission (FTC) recommends that you check your credit reports periodically. Victim information sometimes is held for use or shared among a group of thieves at different times. Checking your credit reports periodically can help you spot problems and address them quickly.

If you find suspicious activity on your credit reports or have reason to believe your information is being misused, call [insert contact information for law enforcement] and file a police report. Get a copy of the report; many creditors want the information it contains to absolve you of the fraudulent debts.

You also should file a complaint with the FTC at www.consumer.gov/idtheft or at 1-877-ID-THEFT (438-4338). Your complaint will be added to the FTC's Identity Theft Data Clearinghouse, where it will be accessible to law enforcers for their investigations.

We have enclosed a copy of ID Theft: When Bad Things Happen to Your Good Name, a comprehensive guide from the FTC to help you guard against and deal with identity theft.

[Insert closing]

Your Name

Source: Federal Trade Commission

GLOSSARY

Ad Blocker—Software placed on a user's personal computer that prevents advertisements from being displayed on the Web.

Ad Network—Companies that purchase and place banner advertisements on behalf of their clients.

Anonymizer—A service that prevents Web sites from seeing a user's Internet Protocol (IP) address. The service operates as an intermediary to protect the user's identity.

Bankrupt—Bankrupt refers to the state or condition of one who is unable to pay his debts as they are, or become, due.

Bankruptcy—Bankruptcy is the legal process under federal law intended to insure fairness and equality among creditors of a bankrupt person, also known as a debtor, and to enable the debtor to start fresh by retaining certain property exempt from liabilities and unhampered by preexisting debts.

Banner Ad—Advertisement for a product or company that is placed on a Web page in order to sell site visitors a good or service. Clicking on a banner will take the visitor to a site to learn more about that product or service.

Bookmark—A bookmark is an online function that lets the user access their favorite web sites quickly.

Browser—A browser is special software that allows the user to navigate several areas of the Internet and view a website.

Bulletin Board—A bulletin board is a place to leave an electronic message or share news to which anyone can read and reply.

Chat Room—A chat room is a place for people to converse online by typing messages to each other.

Chatting—Chatting is a way for a group of people to converse online in real-time by typing messages to each other; also known as a Clear Gif.

Common Law—Common law is the system of jurisprudence which originated in England and was later applied in the United States. The common law is based on judicial precedent rather than statutory law.

Compensatory Damages—Compensatory damages are those damages directly referable to the breach or tortious act and which can be readily proven to have been sustained and for which the injured party should be compensated as a matter of right. Also referred to as actual or general damages.

Consequential Damages—Consequential damages are those damages which are caused by an injury but which are not a necessary result of the injury and must be specially pleaded and proven in order to be awarded.

Cookie—When the user visits a site, a notation may be fed to a file known as a "cookie" in their computer for future reference. If the user revisits the site, the "cookie" file allows the web site to identify the user as a "return" guest and offers the user products tailored to their interests or tastes.

Cookie Buster—Software that is designed to block the placement of cookies by ad networks and Web sites thus preventing companies from tracking a user's activity.

Credit—Credit is that which is extended to the buyer or borrower on the seller or lender's belief that that which is given will be repaid.

Credit Report—A credit report refers to the document from a credit reporting agency setting forth a credit rating and pertinent financial data concerning a person or a company, which is used by banks, lenders, merchants, and suppliers in evaluating a credit risk.

Criminal Impersonation—As it pertains to identity theft, means to knowingly assume a false or fictitious identity or capacity, and in that identity or capacity, doing any act with intent to unlawfully gain a benefit or injure or defraud another.

Cyberspace—Cyberspace is another name for the Internet.

Damages—In general, damages refers to monetary compensation which the law awards to one who has been injured by the actions of another, such as in the case of tortious conduct or breach of contractual obligations.

Data Spill—The result of a poorly designed form on a Web site which may cause an information leak to Web servers of other companies, such as an ad network or advertising agency.

Digital Signature—A digital signature is a digital certification or stamp that uses encryption technology to authenticate an individual's signature is legitimate.

Disclosure—Disclosure is the act of disclosing or revealing that which is secret or not fully understood. The Truth in Lending Act provides that there be disclosure to the consumer of certain information deemed basic to an intelligent assessment of a credit transaction.

Download—A download is the transfer of files or software from a remote computer to the user's computer.

Dynamic IP Address—An IP address that changes every time a user logs on, or dials-up, to a computer.

Encryption Software—Often used as a security measure, encryption software scrambles data so that it is unreadable to interceptors without the appropriate information to read the data.

E-Mail—E-mail is computer-to-computer messages between one or more individuals via the Internet.

Federal Trade Commission—The Federal Trade Commission is an agency of the federal government created in 1914 for the purpose of promoting free and fair competition in interstate commerce through the prevention of general trade restraints such as price-fixing agreements, false advertising, boycotts, illegal combinations of competitors and other unfair methods of competition.

Filter—Filter is software the user can buy that lets the user block access to websites and content that they may find unsuitable.

Finance Charge—A finance charge is any charge assessed for an extension of credit, including interest.

Financial Information—Refers to information identifiable to an individual that concerns the amount and conditions of an individual's assets, liabilities, or credit, including (a) Account numbers and balances; (b) Transactional information concerning an account; and (c) Codes, passwords, social security numbers, tax identification numbers, driver's license or permit numbers, state identification numbers and other information held for the purpose of account access or transaction initiation.

Financial Information Repository—Refers to a person engaged in the business of providing services to customers who have a credit, deposit, trust, stock, or other financial account or relationship with the person.

Firewall—A hardware or software device that controls access to computers on a Local Area Network (LAN). It examines all traffic routed between the two networks – inbound and outbound – to see if it meets certain criteria. If it does it is routed between the networks, otherwise it is stopped. It can also manage public access to private networked resources such as host applications.

Fraud—Fraud is a false representation of a matter of fact, whether by words or by conduct, by false or misleading allegations, or by concealment of that which should have been disclosed, which deceives and is intended to deceive another so that he shall act upon it to his legal injury.

General Damages—General damages are those damages directly referable to the breach or tortious act and which can be readily proven to have been sustained and for which the injured party should be compensated as a matter of right. Also referred to as actual or compensatory damages.

Grace Period—The grace period is the period beyond the due date set forth in the contract during which time payment may be made without incurring a penalty.

GUID—Acronym for Globally Unique Identifier, a unique code used to identify a computer, user, file, etc., for tracking purposes.

Host Name—Each computer is given a name which typically includes the user name and the organizational owner of the computer.

Impossibility—Impossibility is a defense to breach of contract and arises when performance is impossible due to the destruction of the subject matter of the contract or the death of a person necessary for performance.

Indemnification Clause—An indemnification clause in a contract refers to the agreement by one party to secure the other party against loss or damage which may occur in the future in connection with performance of the contract.

Installment Contract—An installment contract is one in which the obligation, such as the payment of money, is divided into a series of successive performances over a period of time.

Interest—Interest is the compensation paid for the use of money loaned.

Internet—The Internet is the universal network that allows computers to talk to other computers in words, text, graphics, and sound, anywhere in the world.

IP—Refers to "Internet Protocol"—the standards by which computers talk to each other over the Internet.

IP Address—A number or series of numbers that identify a computer linked to the Internet and which is generally written as four numbers separated by periods, e.g. 12.24.36.48.

ISP—Refers to "Internet Service Provider"—a service that allows the user to connect to the Internet.

Joint and Several—Joint and several refers to the sharing of rights and liabilities among a group of people collectively and individually.

Judgment—A judgment is a final determination by a court of law concerning the rights of the parties to a lawsuit.

Junk E-mail—Junk e-mail is unsolicited commercial e-mail also known as "spam."

Keyword—A keyword is a word the user enters into a search engine to begin the search for specific information or websites.

Liability—Liability refers to one's obligation to do or refrain from doing something, such as the payment of a debt.

Links—Links are highlighted words on a website that allow the user to connect to other parts of the same website or to other websites.

Listserve—Listserve is an online mailing list that allows individuals or organizations to send email to groups of people at one time.

Local Area Network (LAN)—A computer network limited to the immediate area, usually the same building or floor of a building.

Means of Identification—As it pertains to identity theft, refers to any name or number that may be used, alone or in conjunction with any other information, to identify a specific individual, including a current or former name of the person, telephone number, an electronic address, or identifier of the individual or a member of his or her family, including the ancestor of the person; information relating to a change in name, address, telephone number, or electronic address or identifier of the individual or his or her family; a social security, driver's license, or tax identification number of the individual or a member of his or her family; and other information that could be used to identify the person, including unique biometric data.

Modem—a modem is an internal or external device that connects the computer to a phone line and, if the user wishes, to a company that can link the user to the Internet.

Online Service—An online service is an ISP with added information, entertainment and shopping features.

Opt-In—Refers to when a user gives explicit permission for a company to use personal information for marketing purposes.

Opt-Out—Refers to when a user prohibits a company from using personal information for marketing purposes.

P3P—Acronym for Platform for Privacy Preferences Project—a proposed browser feature that would analyze privacy policies and allow a user to control what personal information is revealed to a particular site.

Password—A password is a personal code that the user selects to access their account with their ISP.

Personal Information—As it relates to identity theft, refers to information associated with an actual person or a fictitious person that is a name, an address, a telephone number, an electronic mail address, a driver's license number, a social security number, an employer, a place of employment, information related to employment, an employee identification number, a mother's maiden name, an identifying number of a depository account, a bank account number, a password used for accessing information, or any other name, number, or code that is used, alone or in conjunction with other information, to confirm the identity of an actual or a fictitious person.

PII—Acronym for Personally Identifiable Information—refers to information such as name, mailing address, phone number or email address.

Pose—As it relates to identity theft, means to falsely represent oneself, directly or indirectly, as another person or persons.

Privacy Policy—A privacy policy is a statement on a website describing what information about the user is collected by the site and how it is used; also known as a privacy statement or privacy notice.

Privacy Seal Program—A program that certifies a site's compliance with the standards of privacy protection. Only those sites that comply with the standards are able to note certification.

Remedy—The remedy is the means by which a right is enforced or a violation of a right is compensated.

Restitution—Restitution refers to the act of restoring a party to a contract to their status quo, i.e., the position the party would have been in if no contract had been made.

Screen Name—A screen name is the name the user selects to be known by when the user communicates online.

Search Engine—A search engine is a function that lets the user search for information and websites. Search engines or search functions may be found on many web sites.

Secure Anonymous Remailer—Web sites that will strip a consumer's identifying information so they can surf other Web sites and send email anonymously.

Spam—Email from a company or charity that is unsolicited and sent to many people at one time, usually for advertising purposes; also known as junk email.

Third Party Cookie—A cookie that is placed by a party other than the user or the Web site being viewed, such as advertising or marketing groups who are trying to gather data on general consumer use third party cookies.

Tracker GIF—Electronic images, usually not visible to site visitors, that allow a Web site to count those who have visited that page or to access certain cookies; also known as a "Clear GIF".

URL (Uniform Resource Locator)— A URL is the address that lets the user locate a particular site. For example, http://www.ftc.gov is the URL for the Federal Trade Commission. Government URLs end in .gov and non-profit organizations and trade associations end in .org. Commercial companies generally end in .com, although additional suffixes or domains may be used as the number of Internet businesses grows.

Victim—As it relates to identity theft, refers to any person who has suffered financial loss or any entity that provided money, credit, goods, services or anything of value and has suffered financial loss as a direct result of the commission or attempted commission of a violation of this section.

Virus—A virus is a file maliciously planted in the user's computer that can damage files and disrupt their system.

Waiver—Waiver refers to an intentional and voluntary surrender of a known right.

Website—A website is an Internet destination where the user can look at and retrieve data. All the web sites in the world, linked together, make up the World Wide Web or the "Web."

BIBLIOGRAPHY

Black's Law Dictionary, Fifth Edition. St. Paul, MN: West Publishing Company, 1979.

Consumer Information Center (Date Visited: March 2006) <http://www.pueblo.gsa.gov>.

Consumer Sentinel (Date Visited: March 2006) <http://www.consumer.gov/ sentinel>.

Direct Marketing Association (Date Visited: March 2006) <http://www.the-dma.org>.

Federal Bureau of Investigation Internet Fraud Complaint Center (Date Visited: March 2006) <http://www.ifccfbi.gov>.

Federal Deposit Insurance Corporation (Date Visited: March 2006) <http://www.fdic.gov>.

Federal Trade Commission (Date Visited: March 2006) <http://www.ftc.gov>.

Identity Theft Resource Center (Date Visited: March 2006) <http://www.idtheftcenter.org>.

National Consumer's League (Date Visited: March 2006) <http://natlconsumersleague.org>.

Privacy Rights Clearinghouse (Date Visited: March 2006) <http://www.privacyrights.org>.

United States Department of Justice (Date Visited: March 2006) <http://www. usdoj.gov/criminal/fraud/idtheft.html>.

United States General Accounting Office (Date Visited: March 2006) <http://www.gao.gov>.

United States Secret Service (Date Visited: March 2006) <http://www.treas.gov/usss>.

United States Social Security Administration (Date Visited: March 2006) <http://www.ssa.gov>.